DATE DUE

DEMCO 38-296

ECONOMIES OF CHANGE

Economies of Change

Form and Transformation
in the Nineteenth-Century Novel

MICHAL PELED GINSBURG

STANFORD UNIVERSITY PRESS

Stanford, California

1996

Stanford University Press
Stanford, California

© 1996 by the Board of Trustees of the
Leland Stanford Junior University

Printed in the United States of America

CIP data are at the end of the book

Stanford University Press publications are
distributed exclusively by Stanford University Press
within the United States, Canada, Mexico, and Central America; they
are distributed exclusively by Cambridge University Press
throughout the rest of the world.

For Daniela and Raphael,

who have asked for it

~

Acknowledgments

It gives me great pleasure to thank friends and colleagues who read parts of this manuscript at various stages of its elaboration and from whose comments and suggestions I greatly benefited: Marshall Brown, Lucien Dällenbach, Peter Fenves, Hannan Hever, Jules Law, Gerald Mead, and Moshe Ron. My special thanks go to Wallace Martin for a stimulating critique; to John Brenkman for his sound advice and true friendship; and to Helen Tartar for her unfailing support.

An earlier version of Chapter 7 appeared in *ELH*, 59 (1992), 175–95; I thank the Johns Hopkins University Press for permission to reprint. A French version of Chapter 3 appeared in *Poétique*, 83 (Sept. 1990), 343–60.

M.P. G.

Contents

A Note to the Reader

The following editions are cited (in order of discussion):

Balzac
La Peau de chagrin, ed. Pierre Citron (Paris: Garnier-Flammarion, 1971); *The Wild Ass's Skin*, tr. Herbert J. Hunt (New York: Penguin Classics, 1986)

Le Lys dans la vallée, ed. Nicole Mozet (Paris: Garnier-Flammarion, 1972); *The Lily of the Valley*, tr. Lucienne Hill (New York: Carroll & Graf, 1989)

Stendhal
Preface to *Chroniques italiennes* and *L'Abbesse de Castro*, in *Romans et nouvelles*, Vol. 2 (Paris: Bibliothèque de la Pléiade, 1952); *The Abbess of Castro and Other Tales*, tr. K. Scott-Montcrieff (New York: Boni-Liveright, 1926). The Preface translations are my own.

La Chartreuse de Parme, ed. Henri Martineau (Paris: Classiques Garnier, 1961); *The Charterhouse of Parma*, tr. Margaret R. B. Shaw (New York: Penguin Classics, 1983)

Austen
Mansfield Park, ed. Reuben A. Brower (Boston: Houghton Mifflin, 1965)

Emma, ed. Lionel Trilling (Boston: Houghton Mifflin, 1957)

Dickens
Our Mutual Friend, ed. Stephen Gill (New York: Penguin Books, 1971)

Bleak House, ed. Morton Zabel (Boston: Houghton Mifflin, 1956)

James
The Princess Casamassima, ed. Derek Brewer (New York: Penguin Classics, 1987)

The Awkward Age (New York: Penguin Classics, 1985)

A word on the conventions used. In the parenthetical references to the French novels, the page citations for the English translations are routinely italicized. I have made some slight emendments in the translations where the discussion required a more literal reading. Typographical errors in the Penguin edition of *The Awkward Age* have been silently corrected with reference to the New York Edition. In both the French and English quotes, I have capitalized or not as the syntax required. All emphasis in these quotes and others is in the original unless otherwise noted.

ECONOMIES OF CHANGE

Introduction

Studies of narrative in the last twenty years have been marked in one way or another by the legacy of structuralist analysis, of what became known as narratology. The hope that energized the narratologist project was to create a "science" of literature, but disenchantment very quickly set in. As Roland Barthes put it on the first page of *S/Z*:

> There are said to be certain Buddhists whose ascetic practices enable them to see a whole landscape in a bean. Precisely what the first analysts of narrative were attempting: to see all the world's stories (and there have been ever so many) within a single structure: we shall, they thought, extract from each tale its model, then out of these models we shall make a great narrative structure, which we shall reapply (for verification) to any one narrative: a task as exhausting (ninety-nine percent perspiration, as the saying goes) as it is ultimately undesirable for the text thereby loses its difference.[1]

Most post-narratological critics would join Barthes in rejecting the "scientific" impulse behind narratology and for much the same reason: the emphasis on a structure that underlies all narratives obscures the historical and cultural particularities of each narrative. Correlatively, by privileging paradigmatic, "static" structures, narratology fails to take into account what Peter Brooks calls "the temporal dynamics" of narrative. Taking his distance from the structuralist project, Brooks writes:

> My interest in the dynamics of narrative, and in plotting as human activity, entails an attempt to move beyond strict allegiance to the various formalisms that have dominated the study of narrative in recent decades, including the substantial body of structuralist work on narrative. . . . For my purposes, narratological models are excessively static and limiting. Whatever its larger ambi-

tions, narratology has in practice been too exclusively concerned with the identification of minimal narrative units and paradigmatic structures; it has too much neglected the temporal dynamics that shape narratives in our reading of them, the play of desire in time that makes us turn the pages and strive toward narrative ends.[2]

Brooks's move away from this "formalism" toward a more historical understanding of narrative is manifested not only in his attention to the temporal and contingent dimension of particular texts—"plotting as human activity," "the play of desire in time"—but also in his limiting his object of study to a historically specific set of texts: "nineteenth-century novels and . . . those twentieth-century narratives that . . . maintain a vital relation to it."[3]

The starting point for this study is the concern I share with Barthes and Brooks about the "difference" of particular texts and the "dynamic" aspect of narrative. But though I join them both in their critique of narratology I would like also, and more importantly, to argue against the widespread tendency of literary studies today to take the critique of formalism as license to disregard form altogether. Though this disregard is often motivated by an interest in the ideological role of literature, I would like to argue that such an interest is not well served by erasing the difference between literature and other cultural phenomena. Such an erasure occurs, it seems to me, when literature is treated strictly thematically or when its relation to other discourses and practices is seen as analogous and parallel (rather than, say, as intersecting and diverging).

In the more restricted area of studies of narrative, I would like to emphasize that the desire to go "beyond narratology" (which is common to many critics) does not in itself produce readings more attentive either to a text's specificity or to its properly narrative, "dynamic" aspect. Indeed, it often serves merely to reproduce narratology's own assumptions and shortcomings in a displaced form. Brooks's *Reading for the Plot* is a case in point. Brooks identifies within the traditional novel a "masterplot," which he articulates as a specific relation between beginnings, middles, and ends: "If in the beginning stands desire, and this shows itself ultimately to be desire for the end, between beginning and end stands a middle which we feel to be necessary (plots, Aristotle tells us, must be of 'a certain length')." This middle he defines as "the 'dilatory space' of postponement and error."[4] Yet powerful as Brooks's model of plot (or, more precisely, of reading) undoubtedly is, there is no reason to assume—as he does—that it is a "masterplot," a model that can account for all narratives, even within the specific tradition he discusses. Moreover, Brooks's move away from the ahistorical formalism of the narratologists is complemented by an ahistorical formalism of his own—the claim that a single structure underlies all specific instances of desire, that desire is *always* a desire for the end, moving from "arousal" through some necessary delay to "significant discharge."[5] Not only is this claim ahistorical in the sense of ideological (taking one, culturally determined form of desire—"male" desire—as the natural, as indeed the only form of desire); it is also "ahistorical" in the sense that it leads Brooks to see the middle, what lies between arousal and fulfillment, the realm of transformation in time, as the purely negative realm of "postponement and error." Acknowledging that desire may not always be desire for the possession/annihilation of an object, that it may have other structures—Ross Chambers, for example, sees desire as "the force that can change things"[6]—would allow us to see plots differently (or to see different plots, a difference within plots).

Where the narratologists would construct as their object of study a structure that (presumably) transcends specific cultural determinations, Marxist literary critics would not only emphasize the historical determination of cultural products but often link the historical context specifically to literary form. A recent exemplar of this line of criticism is Franco Moretti's "sociology of literary forms."[7] The "form" Moretti speaks about is not that of a particular literary text but rather that of a genre, understood as a "symbolic form." Moretti's focus on genres should be seen in terms of his attempt to write a literary history that would be neither purely literary (a history of influence, imitation, misreading, innovation, etc.) nor simply a "reflection" of history. In Moretti's scheme, historical context intervenes in the literary scene by "selecting" a certain preexisting form as "symbolic form," suitable for performing certain functions within the culture.[8] The advantage of such a view is that it allows him to avoid a mechanistic notion of literary form as the inevitable, automatic product of a certain sociopolitical reality. Moretti's argument has its logical point of departure not in a historical account of the genesis of form but rather in the descriptive account of a certain state of affairs—the dominance of a certain form in a specific cultural context. He then shows how this specific form, though not absolutely inevitable, becomes meaningful in—and thus is explicable in terms of—this particular sociopolitical reality.

But by shifting emphasis to the selection of symbolic form, Moretti is left without a historical explanation for the production of particular forms—for novelistic practice. Thus in tracing the history of the novel, Moretti identifies a first stage in which "rhetorical variations are generated." But since historical necessity intervenes only later (in "selection"), this variety looks like "a field of random, unoriented, co-existing possibilities." On the other hand, after historical necessity has intervened, what we find is a more or less mechanical reproduction. Once the novel is selected, says Moretti, "it starts behaving like a genre in the strong sense—reproducing itself with abundance, regularity and without too many variations."[9] Avoiding a mechanistic view of the genesis of "symbolic forms," Moretti is led to posit the production of particular forms as the result of either pure chance or a more or less automatic reproduction. In contrast, I would like to emphasize the way in which each particular novel functions as an instance of narrative practice within a specific context.

The shift in emphasis from the historicity of particular texts to that of a broader category receives a somewhat different inflection in Moretti's rich and stimulating book *The Way of the World: The Bildungsroman in European Culture*, which I will discuss in some detail in my chapter on Dickens. Here Moretti takes a formal argument—narrative texts are generated by the opposing principles of transformation and classification—and historicizes it: he shows how the tension between "dynamism and limit" that characterizes the Bildungsroman obeys a sociohistorical necessity (modernity's need to come to terms with its self-contradictory nature) rather than an abstract, logical one.

But such a historicization of the formal model leads, ultimately, to a certain distortion or simplification. This simplification occurs when Moretti recasts the tension between transformation and classification as an opposition between two traditions: between the truly modern continental tradition, with its valorizing of transformation, and the tradition in England—"perhaps the only European nation for which 1789 did not seem like year one of modernity"[10]—which valorizes classification. The emphasis on transformation in the continental tradition is itself, for Moretti, subject to transformation: "Picking up *The Red and the Black* after finishing *Wilhelm Meister*," he writes, "one is struck by how much the structure of the Bildungsroman has changed in a little more than thirty years." Conversely, since the English tradition devalues transformation in favor of classification, it is seen as static: looking at the English Bildungsroman from Fielding to Dickens, says Moretti, "we are struck by the stability of narrative conventions and basic cultural assumptions."[11] To parody Tolstoy, we can say that, according to Moretti, all nonmodern novels are nonmodern in the same way, whereas each truly modern novel is modern in its own way.

This view of the English tradition is the product (or manifestation) of various assumptions that remain unexamined. At its most basic level, it indicates a tendency to view the culture of "others," the "other" culture (here, pre- or nonmodern culture) as monolithically uniform, and one's own as varied and made of significantly different strands and elements. At the same time, it betrays the assumption that "conservative" novelists, who are not promoting change, merely reproduce each other in the process of reproducing the status quo (and that reproduction does not entail a transformation, hence does not have a history).

But Moretti's view of the English Bildungsroman may also be the result of his overall argument that it is on the level of "symbolic forms" in general, rather than of particular texts, that historical "necessity" manifests itself. The difference between his analysis and that of formalist critics thus becomes the following. When Iurii Lotman spoke of classification and transformation as two elements that are in tension in every narrative text, it was clear that every text would articulate this tension in a somewhat different way. When a narratologist such as A. J. Greimas developed the "actantial model," it was similarly clear that this model, as a purely formal construct, would not have the same existential status as the texts from which it is abstracted, so that each would constitute a somewhat different articulation of the model. In the analogy often made between narratology and linguistics, the model as a "langue" does not have its own existence; it can be found only in the partial and always different manifestations of "paroles." When abstract, formal models or categories become "historicized," as they do in Moretti's treatment of the Bildungsroman, they acquire a certain material density: we attribute to the model itself a reality that is appropriate only to particular texts and, as a result, the differences among the particular texts from which the model is derived recede from our horizon. It is this "reification" of the model that ends up bringing us back close to the formalist approach, where the specificity of each text as a particular articulation of a particular cultural context is lost.

It may be, however, that it is Moretti's dependence on a formal, binary model that generated this distortion. This point will become clearer if we look for a moment at the question of "closure." In the "history" of the debates about "closure," we can see how oppositions such as open/closed form (but also writerly/readerly, dialogic/monologic texts) generate, or are generated by, a particular view of history.[12] The study of closure begins with the observation that not all texts end in the same way. This variety is channeled into an opposition between "closed" texts (where the end transforms what precedes it into a totalized whole) and "open" texts (texts that merely end but do not reach totalization). This distinction is never neutral but carries with it a relative valorization of the two terms, usually the superiority of the "open" form: open narrative is celebrated as radical and liberating, whereas closed narrative is seen as authoritative, repressive, conservative. This valorization produces, or is produced by, a narrative of progress (that is, surprisingly, a "closed" narrative), where open form is seen as particularly modern, a demystification of the ideological bias of the closed form, or at least a step ahead in the representation of experience in all its complexity. (The "minority view" that prefers closed form produces the symmetrical reversal of this—a narrative of degeneration.) The resemblance between this configuration and Moretti's suggests that the formal, binary model, rather than being historicized, has a certain "built-in" historical scheme, and that in moving from abstract categories to semantic-historical ones, we have merely given "material support" for the (ideological) value judgments that subtend this opposition.

My own discussion of specific novels would show some similarities between texts (for example, between Stendhal's view of history in *La Chartreuse de Parme* and James's in *The Awkward Age*) that undermine any simple opposition between closed and open form, premodern and modern, or English and French tradition. But my point in drawing attention to such similarities is not to prove the untenability of translating a formal opposition into a historical periodization (the argument that we can find "open" form prior to the modern period has long been made). Nor is it my purpose to try to efface the opposition between open and closed form by dwelling on the excesses and lacks that undermine closure and the pressures that inevitably produce it. My point, rather, is to dislodge the underlying assumption that a certain form has an inherent ideological content to it—that closed form, for example, is inherently conservative, and open form inherently radical or subversive. I would argue that no form is inherently "conservative" or "radical"—every form can be put to various uses. Novels can reach closure or remain open in different ways and this too makes a difference.

The Marxist way of looking at the relation between literary texts and their broader historical context has been eclipsed in recent years by the Foucauldian approach. In studies of the nineteenth-century European novel, it is D. A. Miller who articulates most clearly and forcefully the difference between his Foucauldian approach and the Marxist tradition, and precisely on the question of form. I will be discussing his *Novel and the Police* in some detail in my chapter on Stendhal's *Abbesse de Castro*; for the moment, let me just raise one issue. Miller explicitly argues in this book against a view that sees literature qua artistic form as in some sense outside ideology—"beyond social tensions or, what comes to the same, invariably on the right side of the struggle."[13] Rather than seeing artistic form as performing the task of undermining ideology (revealing its gaps and inner contradictions), he sees the whole array of possible formal elements as so many strategies of the "policing function," the means by which the novel reinvents in its form the policing power whose goal it is to shape our identity. Admittedly dealing with the limited corpus of the Victorian novel (rather than "narrative"), Miller argues that as a practice the novel's function is always the same: "to confirm the novel reader in his identity as 'liberal subject.' "[14] But what makes such a claim possible is a view of Form as independent not only of content but also of "forms" (no matter what the novel's form is, as Form it always performs one thing only). I would argue that although no specific ideological baggage is inherent in a particular formal feature of the novel, it does not at all follow that the Novel-Form, always and independent of its variety, is merely an instrument of perpetuating power. Novels, it seems to me, do many different things, negotiate between different demands and come up with different solutions. In arguing for a recognition of this diversity, I am not invoking the "richness" of reality, the plurality of the things of the world; nor am I relying on the myth of the author-genius, producing in each case a unique work of art. Rather, I would like to call attention to the way narrative practice, negotiating among different imperatives and needs, uses certain formal possibilities active within the culture, and in so doing, combines them in different ways, producing different articulations. This "relative autonomy" of form does not deny it historical particularity but also does not reduce it to the mere expression of one ideology or to a practice that can perform only one function.

In the chapters that follow, I will analyze ten novels by five novelists. My choice to read two novels by each novelist (rather than give a broad account of the author's entire production or read one single novel) should be seen as a token of my commitment to produce a theoretically informed criticism that is attentive to the specificity of each author's—indeed, each novel's—own project. My use of concepts and methods of reading drawn from various theoretical projects of the last decades is an indication of my belief that theory should be a tool that sharpens our view and understanding of particular issues, problems, and modes of dealing with them (rather than a grid that produces its own meaning). This, of course, does not mean that we can (or should) do away with generalizing explanatory models; such models constitute the basis of theory (implicit or explicit) as a set of general assumptions about what a text, narrative, literature, or language is. The reading of particular literary texts is always done against the background of such assumptions, though literary texts themselves, I would claim, always modify these assumptions by the very fact that they give them a particular, historically contingent articulation. My reading will attempt to capture this interplay.

My insistence on the "relative autonomy" of particular narrative texts can also be put in somewhat different terms. I would be using at certain points in my argument Jacques Lacan's distinction between the "symbolic" and the "real" in order to articulate a specific way of looking at the relation between representations and what they ostensibly represent. What I would like to

emphasize about the relation between the symbolic and the real is the following paradox: since the symbolic cannot be understood except as the symbolization of the real, it is seen as determined by the real and thus telling us
something about it; but since the real does not include in it the mode of its
symbolization-representation, the symbolic is always also arbitrary, the result
of an ungrounded act of positing.[15] The symbolic as a representation is thus
both grounded and arbitrary, both a truthful representation and a sham. To
see representation as both determined and ungrounded allows us to see novelistic texts as, on the one hand, related to certain cultural contexts while, on
the other hand, creating or positing symbolizations by the manipulation of
formal possibilities. The double nature of representation will come up in
various guises in the pages that follow (most explicitly in the chapters on *Le
Lys dans la vallée* and *The Princess Casamassima*). Since some of the novels
(notably *Mansfield Park*) regard "action" as representation (as what makes
characters visible), my discussion of the concept of action in these novels will
also contribute to an understanding of the notion of representation.

In my analysis of each novel, my main concern will be the notion of
transformation, by which I mean the notion or "economy" of change that
informs the text and/or our understanding of it. In some cases, my focus will
be on transformations that occur on the level of "plot"; in others, I will focus
on the process that underlies the production of meaning or knowledge; in still
others, the focus will be on the particular transformation that constitutes the
text as representation. In each case I will use notions of transformation present in the text itself or in common readings of it to foreground a different
notion of transformation, a different economy of change. This does not mean
that I see the particular texts I have chosen as "subversive" texts or as deviating
from a norm; my point, rather, is to argue that the "norm" is a certain field of
possibilities that every particular text handles in a particular way. I will argue
that the author of each text, in his or her practice of writing, deals with
certain cultural issues, social values, or ideological purposes by or through the
manipulation of these possibilities.

Before we proceed to a full discussion of these purposes and possibilities,
let me sketch out some widely accepted understandings of narrative transformation that would be at the background of my discussion. Every theory of
narrative has to account for transformation, since it is transformation that
gives narrative its specificity as a literary form. At the same time, we very
often think of "meaning" as what "we try to wrest from human temporality",[16] as what lies on the other side of time-as-change, hence beyond change,
fixed. Interpreting narrative, then, takes the somewhat paradoxical form of
"overcoming" narrative, of transforming transformation into something that

is fixed and unchanging.[17] Such a view of meaning is particularly conspicuous among structuralists who contend that the precondition for knowledge and understanding is the transformation of a temporal sequence into a synchronic structure.[18] The "paradigmatic" example of this view is Lévi-Strauss's analysis of the Oedipus myth, where elements of the narrative are ordered on a time-line but all functions and meanings belong to—or can be reassembled as—a spatial grid. To *understand* the myth, one must read the spatial grid, not the temporal narrative.[19]

This view of interpretation as a "translation" of a sequence into a para-digm depends on the assumption that the sequence itself is but a projection or deployment of a paradigm.[20] It presupposes, then, a commensurability be-tween sequence and paradigm (at the same time that it valorizes the paradigm as the meaning—origin and goal—of the sequence). Very few critics today would claim that interpretation recovers the original meaning of a text, in a process of translation that leaves no residue. But a "weaker" version of this assumption remains, it seems to me, whenever we think of a "plot" as ex-pressing "themes" and of "themes" being the meaning of the "plot." Though a narrative text may be thought of in terms of plot and themes, it is not necessary to see these two aspects as commensurate. In some texts this as-sumption of commensurability and translatability is undermined; different texts may have different ways of relating temporality to systems of meaning (or to meaning as a system). The narrative text, I will argue, may be both sequence and structure, but the one may have a different meaning from the other, creating a self-contradictory text.

In Lévi-Strauss's example, the meaning of the myth lies in the grid rather than in the sequence. I am arguing that the view of "meaning" as in some sense outside of time, beyond the realm of narrative transformations, is not unique to structuralist thought, that it underlies other readings, for example thematic readings, of narrative.[21] Characters also often interpret their life experience in this way, transforming a temporal sequence into a "spatial form" (a picture, a structure) that fixes and thus abolishes it.[22] We will see an example of this in the first chapter, on Balzac's *Peau de chagrin*, where in trans-forming his entire life into a "picture," the protagonist grasps the meaning of his life in a moment of understanding and by the same stroke draws out of his particular experience a "general truth." Thus the transformation of temporal, contingent experience into an aesthetic object ("picture"), or into general, fixed knowledge, "redeems" it. Leo Bersani, in his *Culture of Redemption*, has pointed out the prevalence of this view in our culture and the way in which it casts experience as flawed, and reduces art, which redeems it, to "a kind of superior patching function."[23] But Bersani's major interest within this "culture of redemption" is in the relation between sexuality and art, the way in which art is seen as both deriving from and transcending (infantile, repressed) sexuality. What he seeks to tease out of psychoanalytical theory and literary texts is a view of art as produced by "sexual energies detached from sexual desires."[24] I am quite indebted to Bersani's study, but my own interest lies primarily with the epistemological aspect of the "redemptive assumption."

The transformation of experience into knowledge (whose agent can be the author, character, or reader) implies a certain kind of economy: a loss on one level allows (and necessitates) a gain on another, presumably higher level. Knowledge is gained at the expense of experience, but the loss of experience, the experience of loss, is recuperated through knowledge of this experience (and of this loss). Not only do many traditional novels narrate the process by which characters, at the end, gain knowledge of their by now lost and gone experience; we, in our reading of these novels, also transform their "lost time" into an understanding that "regains" it. One can understand much of Henry James's literary production as an attempt to come to terms with what he has perceived to be the immorality of such an economy. I would like to argue that though this economy prevails in many narrative texts and many interpretations, it is not the only one. More specifically, as I hope to show in the two chapters on Balzac, not all texts are concerned with the production of knowledge, nor do they all see knowledge (only) as what lies on the other side of experience, or as general laws that we "draw" out of contingent experience.

The negative valuation of "experience" often has as its correlative the negative valuation of the "middle"—the realm of transformation in time, of the "narratable," what lies, in Brooks's terms, between arousal and fulfill-ment—as a realm of postponement or error. If the view of the middle as postponement echoes not only the Russian Formalists' idea of "retardation," but also Aristotle's claim that plots have to be "of a certain length," the idea of the middle as error produces a view of narrative transformation as a process of "becoming." The characters go through the negativity of the middle and emerge on its other side—better, morally superior to their former selves, with greater understanding, more "socialized." The tendency to equate narrative transformation with a process of becoming results in the judgment (often negative) of narratives that do not conform to this scheme as static—as de-valuing transformation and thus manifesting a negative attitude to change in time. I will argue that novels that in some way resist the idea of "becoming"— as do, for example, *Mansfield Park* and *The Princess Casamassima*—do not lack transformation or ideologically refuse change, being in time, or history. They simply have different concepts of transformation, different ideas of history.

This idea was recognized long ago by those critics who sought to dislodge the teleological model of narrative and history that underlies the idea of
"becoming." The proponents of "open" form were right in arguing that not
all narratives abide by a teleological view of transformation (where middles
are always geared toward ends that are there potentially from the very beginning). But by celebrating "open" texts as "liberating" the middle from the
"tyranny" of the end, critics too quickly equated the nonteleological with the
subversive. Such an equation, I will argue, is unwarranted; my discussion of
Austen's *Emma* will specifically address this issue. Moreover, I will argue, if
the end in texts that resist retrospective totalization (that lack "closure") is an
arbitrary limit, it does not follow that the limit has no function. It is important
to determine, in that event, what, in each particular case, its function may be.
The question of the limit will come up, in different ways, in my discussion of
Le Lys dans la vallée, L'Abbesse de Castro, and *The Princess Casamassima.*

I am arguing, in short, for a reading that foregrounds the specificity of
each narrative project. This specificity relates to the particular issues the
author as practitioner faces—issues that are, in their turn, related to a broadly
defined cultural context. But by insisting on the notion of transformation, I
would also like to suggest, among other things, that by dealing with certain
cultural issues through the manipulation of formal possibilities, an author
produces new articulations—produces a specific configuration that is not
entirely determined by context.

A word about the order of chapters. For reasons that should become
obvious, a reading of Balzac's *Peau de chagrin* seemed to me the best place to
start my discussion of "economies of change." This meant that I could not
order my readings of the five novelists chronologically. The resulting order—
Balzac, followed by Stendhal, followed by Austen, Dickens, and James—is
not intended to oppose a French tradition to an English one; indeed, as I have
already indicated, some of my arguments undermine such an opposition.

CHAPTER I

Reading Temporality in
'La Peau de chagrin'

∾

I have suggested in the Introduction that the structuralist move of "translating a narrative sequence into a paradigm that is its "meaning" merely makes explicit what is implicit in most thematic readings.[1] Looking at the development of narratology (for example, the move from Vladimir Propp's analysis of a tale as a sequence of functions to A. J. Greimas's atemporal matrix[2]), we can see what motivates this process: the desire to find an explanatory model of maximum applicability—which will be, at the limit, universal—dictates the reduction, or simplification, of the "inventory" presented by a particular text or corpus. Thus the more general the model's applicability, the simpler, barer, and more stripped of detail it is, so that ultimately all narratives can be explained by the simplest model of all, that of pure binary opposition (say, nature/culture). Viewed this way, the narratologist technique of reading is but a latter-day formulation of the basic "philosopheme" that the gain of knowledge (abstract, universal) is produced by the negation of experience (contingent, individual).

Balzac is a particularly suitable author for exemplifying the workings of this procedure and testing its limit. His predilection for binary thinking makes him a structuralist *avant la lettre*. Thinking in binary oppositions is related in Balzac to the desire to create a totality. This totality is logical, not empirical. It is generated not by including all the particulars and contingencies of reality but rather by an a priori act of classification, through binary oppositions that structure this reality and allow for its saturation. Thus even though Balzac rightly insists on the irreducible cultural specificity of his representations—on the first pages of *Père Goriot* he doubts whether the story would be understood outside of Paris—he would also have to insist that the telling of the particular, contingent story of particular individuals produces a knowledge that is far broader, and that this gain in applicability makes up for the loss or sacrifice of particularity.

In the following pages I propose to read *La Peau de chagrin* (1831) as an allegory of these procedures of sense production. In the first part of the chapter, I will show how *La Peau*, in its structure, as well as in the theories and practice of some of its characters, presents narrative as a representation whose principle is the transformation of temporality (of life) into a spatial pattern or a picture. Concomitantly, knowledge will be defined as the sacrifice (or negation, or reduction) of the particular, the contingent, the material, counterbalanced by the gain in applicability. My argument, however, is that though these views are present and important in the text, they cannot account for its central emblem—the object that gives the text its hyperbolic specificity as "fantastic"—the skin. In the rest of the chapter, I will show how and why the skin, as a representation of Raphaël's life, resists interpretation as the transformation of material contingency to generalizable knowledge. Such a division of the text against itself can be seen as an indication of Balzac's attempt to think through the value (or cognitive yield) of his own representations.

I

La Peau de chagrin is a novel that in different ways and on different levels dramatizes the urge to transform a temporal sequence into a spatial configuration in order to produce "meaning" or "knowledge." On the one hand, the passage of time is the very subject of the novel and receives in it the most palpable representation of the deterioration of a body from health to disease and death;[3] on the other hand, everything on the structural and formal level seems to negate temporality, to freeze or spatialize it. Let me briefly indicate some of the elements in the structure of the novel that produce this effect.

The novel is divided into three parts: the first and the third are narrated by an anonymous, third-person narrative voice; the middle part is Raphaël's retrospective narration of his past life. The first and third sections are structured as a series of scenes or "tableaux," where the temporal relation between scenes—be it sequential or causal—is deemphasized in favor of paradigmatic relations of similarity and opposition.[4] An obvious example of such structuring is the explicit opposition between the gambling house where the novel begins and the ensuing scene in the antique shop. Though the relation between the two scenes is chronological as well as causal (Raphaël visits the shop after his visit to the gambling house and as a result of a chain of events that starts with the loss of money he suffered there), what is emphasized in the text is the "thematic" opposition between the bareness of the gambling house (which expresses its "essence" as the locus of loss) and the opulence of the store (the locus of riches and of a "gift").[5] What is true of the relation between tableaux is also true of the elements within each of them. Thus, for example, in the third part of the novel, the scene in the theater brings together all the characters in Raphaël's life; but whereas in Raphaël's narrative they appear in sequential order, here they are grouped in a "pattern" or a "design," rich in meaning.

This difference in the ordering of characters may suggest that Raphaël's retrospective narration resists the paradigmatic or thematic ordering we find elsewhere in the novel. But this is only seemingly the case, since the personal narrative shows the same tendency to subsume the temporal within spatial configurations. One can argue, in fact, that the "motivation" for having a first-person narration within the novel (despite its glaring incongruity) is precisely its structural tendency to effect such a subsumption. Clearly no other motivation is given for the personal narration. The gratuitousness is conveyed by the clichéd nature of the reason given for it: "Ah! si tu connaissais ma vie [says Raphaël]. Ah! s'écria Emile, je ne te croyais pas si vulgaire, la phrase est usée" (" 'Ah! If you knew the life I have led!' 'Ah!' Emile exclaimed. 'I didn't know you were so commonplace. It's an outworn phrase' "; 125; *89*).[6] Not only is the act of narration unmotivated; it also lacks verisimilitude, since we are to assume that the long, elaborate, and rhetorically crafted narrative is pronounced by a very drunk Raphaël to his equally drunk friend Emile in the midst of an orgy.[7]

The lack of narrative motivation and verisimilitude calls attention to the form of the narrative; it suggests that though a first-person retrospective narration is here both unlikely and gratuitous, there is some other reason why the story of Raphaël's life must be told in this way. The motivation for the form of narration is compositional: its retrospection deprives the story of temporal openness to an unknown future, and its being in the first person guarantees that the narrative will return at its end to its point of beginning, thus embedding the lived experience (ten years in the life of Raphaël) within the much shorter and spatially contained temporality of its narration (the time it took Raphaël to narrate this life to Emile during the orgy at Taillefer's).[8] And indeed, at the end of Raphaël's narrative, we are back at the point where he started: on the level of "discourse" (or narration) we are still at Taillefer's; on the level of "story," Raphaël's last words, "Enfin, je me trouvai seul avec une pièce de vingt francs" ("In the end I found myself with a twenty-franc piece"; 214; *184*), bring us back to the very first page of the novel, where we have seen the same Raphaël with the same coin of twenty francs entering the gambling house.

Though Raphaël does not repeat at the end of his narrative the last episodes of his story—how having been left with just one coin, he entered the gambling house, lost his coin, decided first to commit suicide and then to postpone his death till evening, wandered around in the streets, entered the antique shop, met its enigmatic owner, and was given the skin—he does relate this segment of his story at the very beginning of his narrative, thus again weakening, through repetition and through the reversal of beginning and end, the temporal aspect of his story.[9] Moreover, in narrating to Emile that part of the story (which we have already read), Raphaël makes a strange reversal:

> Il faudrait t'avouer que vous m'avez arrêté sur le quai Voltaire, au moment où j'allais me jeter dans la Seine. . . . Par un hasard presque fabuleux, les ruines les plus poétiques du monde matériel venaient alors de se résumer à mes yeux par une traduction symbolique de la sagesse humaine; tandis qu'en ce moment les débris de tous les trésors intellectuels que nous avons saccagés à table aboutissent à ces deux femmes. (123)

> (I ought to confess that you stopped me on the Quai Voltaire at the moment when I was about to throw myself into the Seine. . . . Thanks to an almost fabulous stroke of chance, the most poetic ruins of the material world have just then been summed up before my gaze in a symbolic representation of human wisdom; whereas at this present moment the debris of all the intellectual riches that we ransacked at table are summed up in these two women; *88*.)

By reversing the order of the meeting with Emile and the visit to the shop (a change producing a sequence that does not quite make sense), Raphaël shifts from a temporal, sequential, causal explanation (I wanted to commit suicide, I went to the shop, as a result I didn't commit suicide and met you) to a paradigmatic, thematic statement of the equivalence between the scene at the shop and the scene of the orgy: similarity ("ruines" = "débris") and opposition ("monde matériel" vs. "trésors intellectuels").

We see, then, that *La Peau*, in its structure or form, resists temporality by freezing "stories" into "tableaux," by subordinating or even transforming sequentiality into spatial relations. As an "étude philosophique," *La Peau* produces meaning through the transformation of time into space, of a syntagmatic chain into paradigmatic structure, and this transformation involves a movement of concentration or abbreviation. Having summarized the entire first part of the novel in twelve lines, Raphaël concludes by saying that they amount to "deux systèmes d'existence . . . diametralement opposés" ("two diametrically opposed systems of existence"). Emile calls this rather short speech "bavardage" and chides Raphaël: "Tes deux systèmes peuvent entrer dans *une seule phrase* et se réduisent à *une pensée*. . . . En *un mot* . . . " ("The two systems you mention can be put in a single sentence and reduced to a single thought. . . . In one word . . . "). Raphaël reciprocates in kind: telling Emile, "Continue à t'abréger toi-même ainsi, tu feras des volumes" ("If you go on abridging yourself like this, you'll run into volumes"), he proposes his own abbreviation: "Aussi, le grand abstracteur de quintessence a-t-il jadis exprimé ces deux systèmes en *deux mots*" ("Did not the great abstractor of quintessence once express these two systems in two words"). Standing his ground, Emile responds that Rabelais "a résolu cette philosophie par *un mot plus bref*" ("summed up this philosophy in a still briefer formula") and finally states that "ces derniers mots de la science morale" can be expressed by "l'*exclamation* de Purrhon restant entre le bien et le mal" ("these two ultimate words of moral science are scarcely different from the exclamation of Pyrrho, half way between good and evil"; 124; *88–89*; emphasis mine). In this exchange, a sequential-causal narrative is transformed into a short statement that draws out of the narrative its essence, its meaning; and from then on, it is as if the summarizing process keeps going on out of some kind of inner force: from a long description, to two systems, to one sentence, one thought, two words, one word, an exclamation.

This "shrinking" of experience is called knowledge ("philosophie," "science morale"). Narrative, from this perspective, is no different from philosophy, since it too participates in this process of contraction. Raphaël opens his retrospective, sequential narrative by repeating the gesture of spatializing time: "[une] espèce de lucidité . . . me permet d'embrasser en cet instant toute ma vie comme un même tableau" ("a kind of lucidity . . . enables me at this instant to take in my whole life as one single picture"). Then, in the next breath, he gives its correlative, the summary: "Vue à distance, ma vie est comme rétrécie par un phénomène moral. Cette longue et lente douleur qui a duré dix ans peut aujourd'hui se reproduire par quelques phrases dans lesquelles la douleur ne sera plus qu'une pensée, et le plaisir une réflexion philosophique" ("Seen from a distance, my life is as it were contracted by some moral phenomena. The protracted misery which has dragged on for ten years can be rendered today in a few sentences in which suffering will be no more than an idea and pleasure a philosophical reflection"; 127; *91*). Critics have noticed the similarity between the opening of Raphaël's narration and the description that the antique dealer gives of his "reading" of his life.[10] The act of "seeing"—the philosophical act par excellence ("Voir, n'est-ce pas savoir?"; *89*)—is common to both and is the means by which temporal experience is transformed into a spatial representation, thus drawing out of expe-

rience its meaning. What Raphaël and the shopowner make explicit is a
rather common understanding of narrative: that is, that the activity we
call reading or narrating (and their similarity makes them interchangeable),
whereby a reader interprets the "meaning" of a narrative, or whereby a
narrator relates a story in order to draw from it "its lesson," is precisely an act
of "shrinking" a temporal sequence into "a thought," "a philosophical reflection" (expressed most often, explicitly or implicitly, by a paradigmatic structure of opposition and similarity).

It is the antique dealer who spells out in the most explicit form the
economy of this shrinking as a stripping off of the contingent and superfluous
so that the essential can manifest itself, a production of a "gain" of knowledge
through an act of negation (a loss).[11] The sequence of the two scenes—
Raphaël's walk through the curiosity shop and his meeting with its owner—
casts the narrative production of knowledge as the dialectical overcoming of
death (that is, of time as sheer sequentiality, without meaning).

The store "represents" human history and human civilization through
synecdoche or "échantillons" (72)—a part taken for the whole. These "parts"
combine along the axis of temporal succession (Egypt, then Greece, Rome,
Christianity, etc.; 73) but more often along the axis of spatial or paradigmatic
opposition: ancient and modern, death and life, east and west, religious and
secular, and so on:

> Un tournebroche était posé sur un ostensoir, un sabre républicain sur une
> hacquebute du Moyen Age. . . . Les instruments de mort, poignards, pistolets
> curieux, armes à secret, étaient jetés pêle-mêle avec des instruments de vie:
> soupière en porcelaine, assiettes de Saxe. (72)

> (A roasting-jack was on a monstrance, a Republican sabre on a medieval arque-
> bus. . . . Instruments of death, poniards, quaint pistols, weapons with secret
> springs were hobnobbing with instruments of life: porcelain soup-tureens,
> Dresden china plates; *34*.)[12]

Both the choice of a part for the whole, of representative objects that
capture the spirit of a period or of a culture, and the juxtaposing of these
objects not along the temporal axis (which would insist on their participation
in a temporal process) but rather according to a principle of similarity and
opposition that allows their "meaning" to dominate their material, historical
existence are aspects of thematic interpretation and narration as production of
meaning: the arrangement of the store is an act of narration of human history
just as its perception, the walk that Raphaël takes through the galleries, is an
act of reading, insisting on the thematic meaning of the sequence and on
"knowledge." And yet the store, with all its ability to represent a totality
("Tous les pays de la terre"; 72; "toutes les joies . . . toutes les douleurs . . .

toutes les formules d'existence"; 75; "toutes ces pensées humaines"; 77),
remains the site of confusion, disgust, and death; rather than being a site of
knowledge it is a "fumier philosophique" ("philosophical dunghill"; 72; *35*).
Only at one moment does Raphaël as a reader react with something other
than disgust or a sense of futility: when he, through his imagination, vicariously experiences the lives that he sees represented (75; *37–38*). At that
moment he anticipates the doctrine of the antiquarian.

The antiquarian bears a certain resemblance to his store: "Les moeurs de
toutes les nations du globe et leurs sagesses se résumaient sur sa face froide,
comme les productions du monde entier se trouvaient accumulées dans ses
magasins poudreux" ("The morality of every nation on the globe, their wisdom too, were summed up on his chilly countenance, just as the products of
the entire world were piled up in his dusty showrooms"; 81; *44*). But the act
of "summary" that produces the antiquarian's knowledge cannot be simply
equated with the synecdochal representation of human history in his store.
The antiquarian's kind of summary involves not only selection but also transformation, a transformation whose basis is negation. The transformation is
obviously from the material to the spiritual or mental, from the contingent,
finite, and imperfect to the essential, eternal, and perfect, from the outside to
the inside:

> Que reste-t-il d'une possession matérielle? une idée. Jugez alors combien doit
> être belle la vie d'un homme qui, pouvant empreindre toutes les réalités dans sa
> pensée, transporte en son âme les sources du bonheur, en extrait mille voluptés
> idéales dépouillées des souillures terrestres. (89–90)
>
> (What remains of a material possession? Only an idea. So then, judge now how
> magnificent must be the life of a man who, being able to imprint his mind with
> every reality, transports into his soul the sources of happiness and extracts from
> them a thousand ideal ecstasies free of all earthly defilement; *53*.)

What takes place in this process of internalization is not mere selection
but the act of "extracting" or of "stripping" ("dépouiller"). And this stripping
means a negation, a sacrifice of something for the sake of knowledge, now
defined as the dialectical regaining or recuperation of everything that has
been negated or sacrificed: "j'ai tout obtenu, parce que j'ai tout su dé-
daigner"; "j'ai un sérail imaginaire où je possède toutes les femmes que je n'ai
pas eues" ("I have had everything I wanted because I have learnt to dispense
with everything"; "I have an imaginary seraglio in which I possess all the
women I have never had"; 89, 90; *52, 53*).

Thus, though knowledge was initially defined as the opposite of desire
and power, it is in fact the regaining of desire and power through negation:
"Ma seule ambition a été de voir. Voir, n'est-ce pas savoir?...Oh! savoir,

jeune homme, n'est-ce pas jouir intuitivement? n'est-ce pas découvrir la substance même du fait et s'en emparer essentiellement?" ("My sole ambition has been to see. To see, is that not to know? Oh! to know, is that not to enjoy intuitively? Is it not to discover the very substance of fact and take possession of its very essence?" 89; *52–53*). Certainly, what is recuperated through negation is not identical to what has been negated: material, sensual desire is replaced by "jouir intuitivement," and gross, crude power is replaced by "s'emparer essentiellement" (just as in the "progress" from the store to its owner, the dusty material products of civilization are transformed into their meaning, a "morality" that sums them up). But the very way in which the terms are valorized indicates that what is recuperated is superior to what has been negated, so that—and this is of course the most important point—every loss is actually a gain (or every abbreviation, summing up, shrinking, is an increase).[13]

The hyperbolic character of the store and its owner suggests that their function as representations is to produce a totality (the store represents the totality of human history, as its owner's face summarizes its wisdom and morality). The representation of the totality is achieved not through the minute inclusion of manifold details, of limitless empirical variety, but rather through the selection of "representative" elements and their reordering in an idealized temporal sequence and in paradigms. These paradigms express a "general truth," whose explanatory power is in proportion to how much particularity was "stripped off." Raphaël himself produces such a representation when he draws from his material, contingent experience its "essence." That he tells the story of his life after he has decided to commit suicide suggests how much this operation involves the "sacrifice" of life, though the gain of knowledge is apparently more than enough to redeem this loss—hence the philosophical serenity with which he tells it.

II

But *La Peau* does not simply represent, *en abîme*, the process by which it, as a narrative, produces its meaning and the process by which critics will interpret it. It also contains a representation of the literal—and hence trivial— way in which narrative involves the spatializing and shrinking of temporality: the fact that narrating an experience, a life, literally involves its spatialization/ reduction, with so many lines or so many pages in the book "standing for" so many hours or so many years in life. What is curious about *La Peau* is that it represents this trivial fact about narrating and reading through an object cast as supernatural—the skin.

The skin is a representation of Raphaël's life, but it is not a representation of the content or of the meaning ("lesson," or "essence") of this life; it is a (negative) representation of life as a certain amount of time to be lived.[14] It represents this sheer temporality through a spatial form: so many millimeters of the skin equal so many days or months in the life of Raphaël. This is analogous to having so many phrases (now in the sense not of philosophical statements of meaning but of material sentences, of words and lines on the page) in Raphaël's narrative represent so many days of his life. When Raphaël sees the skin gradually shrinking, he is not much different from us, the readers, when we notice the decrease in the number of pages we are left with as we read on, a decrease that tells us, as the shrinking of the skin tells Raphaël, that the end, death, is approaching. Thus the skin represents the spatializing/shrinking of time inherent in writing and reading a narrative; but writing and reading are now understood in their most mechanical and literal sense and not as metaphors for the production of meaning.[15]

The reading of the skin as a literal representation of his life is for Raphaël a terrifying experience. The terror cannot be simply the result of being both inside and outside the story, reader and character at the same time. Certainly, this is a common position, especially for characters who tell their own life story. Thus when Raphaël, at the beginning of his narrative, sees "toute [sa] vie comme un même tableau," he sees/reads his life, is a reader and a character, is inside and outside the story. But Raphaël's attitude to his predicament as a reader/narrator who can see his own life from the outside—that is, from the perspective of a dead man (remember that he has just decided to commit suicide, and that acquiring the skin both brought him back to life and, in the eyes of the antiquarian, accomplished his suicide)—is that of serene melancholy, very different from the anguished frenzy he experiences when he literally sees the skin/his life shrinking, when he "reads" on and on, to the end, the book of his life.

The reason for this difference is clear. When Raphaël, talking to Emile, sees his life from "outre tombe," he has both died (to experience) and survived his death as the subject who knows, who has drawn from life its meaning—a few phrases that summarize it. But as the reader of the skin, his own book of life, he has not died to experience: in spite of himself, he continues to desire. Indeed, he cannot *not* desire. Nor can he survive death, the approach of which he reads in the skin's shrinking, as a knowing subject who understands and thus regains his past experience. Since the reading of the skin is a literal one—not outside and above material experience but continuous with it—when all phrases are read and the "book" is finished, there are no phrases "gained" to recuperate the loss. The skin, then, in representing *en abîme* a literal understanding of narrating and reading, forces the character to see his life as simply flowing on, with no possibility of stepping outside of life to gain a vantage point from which it can be viewed as an object of knowledge, thus transforming the loss of life into a gain of knowledge. The skin undermines the understanding of narrating and reading as the dialectical overcoming of material experience, hence of death, by and through the acquisition of knowledge, of an understanding of this experience, of its generalized applicability.

From the moment Raphaël gets the skin, the literal reading of his life becomes inevitable—he cannot not read the skin, he cannot not read in the skin the approach of a death that nothing can overcome. From the "literal" perspective the skin introduces, stepping outside of experience, regaining it through knowledge, are merely metaphors; they function only on a figurative level, and no metaphor can really and literally allow him to overcome his death. Alongside the shrinking that produces knowledge, meaning as a summary or essence of experience, is a shrinking that is just shrinking, the literality of death and of the passage of time.[16]

If my reading up to now suggests that *La Peau* is "about" the way meaning relates to individual experience, the skin itself, paradoxically, resists this "aboutness," resists the transformation of narrative, its reduction/expansion into a meaning with a certain scope of generality. The skin, rather, represents a kind of reading that stubbornly resists the production of meaning. And it is by this resistance to meaning that it can represent sheer temporality—sheer waste, sheer loss, a movement toward death that cannot be dialectically recuperated. As such, the skin is a representation of Raphaël's life in its irreducible particularity—its being subject to complete destruction. We can measure the "strangeness" of such a perspective for Balzac, committed as he is to a certain narrative project (representation of the totality, an "étude philosophique"), by reminding ourselves that it required a "supernatural" object to make that perspective apparent. The skin is "strange" or "supernatural" because it presents a perspective that cannot be integrated into this project and yet cannot be gotten rid of (remember Raphaël's failed attempt to "forget" the skin). It is only by insisting on this aspect of the skin that we can understand the difference it makes in Raphaël's life.

III

The difference the skin makes in Raphaël's experience is precisely what has to be explained. After all, the shopowner does not think that possessing the skin will make such a great difference for a man who has decided to commit suicide: "Après tout, vous vouliez mourir? hé! bien, votre suicide n'est que retardé" ("After all, you were bent on dying: well, your suicide is merely postponed"; 92; 55). If acquiring the skin meant simply a "suicide retardé," it would not, indeed, make much of a difference, since Rastignac's "dissipational system," to which Raphaël has been introduced before he acquires the skin, is precisely such a "long suicide" (203–4; 173).

Dissipation can be seen as the opposite of the life advocated by the shopowner (and of the life Raphaël attempts to live after the death of his father and before his meeting with Rastignac). Meaning literally a scattering, a dispersal, dissipation is opposed to the process of gathering and extracting that produces knowledge. Related to excess, to extravagance, luxury, purchase of superfluous items, it is opposed to the bareness and nudity that characterize not only Raphaël's life-style at the time he was seeking knowledge, but also the very process of producing knowledge. Dissipation refuses to subscribe to the wisdom of accepting dying as one thing in order to be reborn as another, or to the practicality of accepting death for a while now in order to live later on. It refuses both sublimation and postponement, since it is the realization of material desires right here and now.

The specific relation the "dissipational system" establishes between life and death is already indicated by the fact that it is elaborated twice in the novel (before and after the encounter with Foedora), once as a way of living and once as a way of dying. As a "long suicide," a death with duration, dissipation abolishes the difference between life and death. This abolition of difference is manifested by a constant possibility of exchanging "life" for "death." Having adopted the dissipational system in order to die, Raphaël becomes "un *viveur*" (207; 176). At another point he describes the dissipater as a man who "a troqué sa mort contre toutes les jouissances de la vie" ("bartered his death for all the pleasures of life") similar to those who sell their soul to the devil to gain power (209; 179); but one could say with equal justice that the dissipater is a man who bartered his life, rather than his death (especially since the analogy with those who sell their soul to the devil suggests an equation of soul with life).[17] This exchange between death and life is not at all like the dialectical exchange between life and death that is possible only because life and death *are* seen as opposites (an opposition that can be then canceled out). Here life and death are seen as identical, as undifferentiated either temporally (you die now in order to live later on) or qualitatively (you die as one thing in order to live as another).

Raphaël can be seen as oscillating between a life of dissipation and life as a search for knowledge, the two extremes represented by Rastignac and the antiquarian, respectively. During his father's lifetime, Raphaël is eager—

though unable—to live a life of dissipation, of spending, of excess ("J'avais vingt ans, je souhaitais passer une journée entière plongé dans les crimes de mon âge"; "I was twenty and would have liked to spend a whole day sowing the wild oats appropriate to my years"; 130; *93–94*); but when the father dies, Raphael internalizes the Law of the Father in the hope of recuperating through denial all that he is forced to sacrifice: "Comme les chrysalides, je me bâtissais une tombe pour renaître brillant et glorieux. J'allais risquer de mourir pour vivre" ("Like a chrysalis, I was building a tomb around me in order to be reborn in brilliance and glory. I was going to risk dying so as to live"; 141; *105*).[18] But Raphaël's mistake (and his difference from the anti-quarian) is that he thinks he can regain the same things he gives up rather than a sublimated—spiritual, internal—version of them; he accepts postponement but not transformation. Hence, rather than reaching a synthesis, he remains torn between two irreconcilable impulses:

> Amant efféminé de la paresse orientale, amoureux de mes rêves, sensuel, j'ai toujours travaillé, me refusant à goûter les jouissances de la vie parisienne. Gourmand, j'ai été sobre; aimant et la marche et les voyages maritimes, désirant visiter plusieurs pays, trouvant encore du plaisir à faire, comme un enfant, ricocher des cailloux sur l'eau, je suis resté constamment assis, une plume à la main; bavard, j'allais écouter en silence les professeurs aux Cours publics de la Bibliothèque et du Muséum; j'ai dormi sur mon grabat solitaire comme un religieux de l'ordre de Saint Benoît, et la femme était cependant ma seule chimère, une chimère que je caressais et qui me fuyait toujours! Enfin, ma vie a été une cruelle antithèse, un perpétuel mensonge. (147)

> (Effeminate in my love of oriental indolence, enamored of my dreams, a sensual-ist, I nevertheless went on working and refusing myself the pleasures which life in Paris could offer. I was fond of good cheer, but lived like an ascetic. I loved walking and the idea of sea voyages, wanted to visit various countries, and still enjoyed the childish pastime of making stones skim across the water, but I stayed constantly at my desk, pen in hand. I was talkative by nature but went to listen in silence to the professors who gave public lectures at the Bibliothèque Nationale and the Museum. I slept on my lonely pallet like a Benedictine monk and yet woman was my sole chimaera, a chimaera that I fondled but which constantly eluded me. In short, my life was one cruel antithesis, a perpetual falsehood; *111–12*.)

The similarity and difference between this passage and passages where the antiquarian speaks about his life are accurate measures of the extent to which Raphaël's experience is that of a failed dialectics, of his inability to fully negate and hence to recuperate; what he denies himself is not really negated, and thus his desires, rather than being sublimated, come back to torment him and expose his denial as a lie.

It should be clear from the preceding analysis that the antiquarian and Rastignac define two different views of the relation between temporality and knowledge: for the antiquarian, time lost is always dialectically regained as knowledge; for Rastignac, time is sheer loss and waste, a movement toward death, and dissipation is not knowledge but merely a technique.[19] Raphaël can be seen as wavering between these two extremes, wanting both, unable to subscribe fully to either. Thus with the antiquarian, Rastignac, and Raphaël, the text of *La Peau* covers the totality of possible articulations of its thematic content; any other articulation would be subsumed in one or another of these three attitudes. The question, then, is: what about the skin itself? If the skin too can be subsumed within this totalizing system, how can we account for the need for it in the plot of the novel or the difference that it makes in Raphaël's life?

At first it seems as if the skin indeed merely repeats already stated positions; it would then be a symbolic object that, complex and even contradictory as it may be, does not disrupt the totalizing system erected by the text (and for which it is, precisely, a symbol). On the one hand, as a physical object, it shows sheer shrinking, a sheer loss or waste of time and life without any gain or recuperation, and is thus compatible with the materiality of dissipation. On the other hand, the skin is also a text, an inscription that can be read and understood.[20] As such, the skin is not simply a material object but also a source of knowledge; reading it would show precisely how the loss (inherent in its material aspect) can be recuperated through an act of understanding (Balzac's theory of energy, a theory of desire, a theory of narrative) that transforms it. Most readings of *La Peau de chagrin* are informed by some such notion of what the skin, as a symbolic object, means or represents. When critics claim, for example, that the skin represents human desire—represents the fact that desire moves toward its own death, that its accomplishment is the death of the subject inasmuch as that subject is a desiring subject[21]—their reading of the text confirms the antiquarian's dialectical model of reading: we recuperate the death of the desiring subject by its rebirth as a knowing subject, as the subject who knows that its desire is its death. Just like the antiquarian, we "sacrifice" desire in order to "gain" knowledge.

This act of interpreting the skin, endowing it with meaning, occurs also within the novel. When Raphaël is presented with the skin and sees its inscription, he immediately engages in an act of interpretation, translating the Sanskrit text into French.[22] Through this process of interpretation the text gains meaning and at the same time acquires a new shape—the inverted cone—which reflects its meaning, thus, incidentally, emphasizing the complete compatibility between "content" and "form" that underlies a thematic reading of the text.

And yet the peculiarity of the skin manifests itself precisely at this moment through the existence of a certain residue, a certain heterogeneity: if the writing in French stands for meaningful interpretation and its formal reflection in a design, it is still not clear precisely what it is an interpretation of. For Raphaël, it is presumably an interpretation of a text in Sanskrit. Yet this Sanskrit text for some reason is not given in the novel; what is given instead is a text in Arabic, a text that though present on the page for the reader, has no place within the world of the novel.[23] This seems at first nothing more than a curious case of disjunction between character and reader. Whereas for Raphaël the empirical-physical text is the one in Sanskrit, and he does not "see" the Arabic text, the opposite is true for the reader; the Arabic text will then be the equivalent for the reader of what the Sanskrit text is for the character. The problem with such an explanation, however, is that the representation in the novel of the act of interpretation—the translation of a material text into a meaningful one—is carried out precisely in such a way as not to allow for this kind of disjunction between reader and character. The scene deliberately creates a rhetorical effect of immediacy, that is, of a complete convergence of reader and character: the "translation" of the text is undertaken simultaneously by the reader and by Raphaël, as if both were reading the same text together. This collapse of reader and character is fundamental to the novel: while Raphaël is reading "la peau," we are reading *La Peau*, and the *mise en abîme* blurs the distinction between reader in the text and reader of the text, between skin and novel.

The disjunction we find in this scene, accordingly, is not between reader and character or between material object and a meaningful text, but rather between the empirical or phenomenal—which always gets transformed into the meaningful—and a nonrepresentable materiality that is not open to such transformations. Though this disjunction is "represented" in the text, its two terms are not entirely differentiated: we cannot say which one is represented by the Sanskrit text and which by the Arabic text (if we could, then the nonrepresented materiality would have ended up being subsumed within the phenomenal and thus subject to intelligible transformations). We are presented, in other words, with a text, a certain materiality, that is neither the phenomenal nor the intelligible, and that can be presented only as the difference between two possible phenomenal-intelligible objects. The "presence" of such nonrepresented textuality within the skin accounts for its resistance to interpretation (in the sense of "translation," the "sacrifice" of material text for the "gain" of meaning), and it is this resistance that explains the difference the skin makes in Raphaël's life.

IV

It is easy to see how the magical skin abolishes the possibility both of the antiquarian's dialectical sublimation and of Raphaël's attempt at postponement. With the skin, every desire of Raphaël's is fulfilled, literally and immediately.[24] Since dissipation has also been understood as the fulfillment of material desires right here and now, there is no difference, in this respect, between living under the spell of the skin and living/dying the life of dissipation. Therefore, if the skin makes a difference in the life of Raphaël, it is not because it fulfills all his desires but because it forces him to read his desires in a particular way.

The skin cannot *not* fulfill Raphaël's desires, and this automatic, mechanical fulfillment of desire is paralleled by a certain automatism in Raphaël himself: he himself cannot *not* desire. This must have been true of Raphaël even before he acquired the skin (the skin does not change him), but it has become manifest only with the skin. The skin makes visible Raphaël's desire, and when made manifest, his desire is revealed as nonvolitional, hence not really a desire, but rather a compulsion, an automatism. Raphaël is subject to, rather than the subject of, his desires. Though his desires cannot be perceived or made sense of except as "his" desires, they have a certain existence that is independent of him and over which he has no control. At the moment in which the skin accomplishes Raphaël's desires and by so doing makes them visible, it also makes apparent that a series of events, anterior and exterior to Raphaël's act of desiring, would have brought about the same results, thus again questioning the relation between Raphaël and "his" desires. With the skin, in other words, what becomes visible is that Raphaël's desires are neither "his" nor, properly speaking, "desires."

If desire is a certain impersonal automatism, it is not, properly speaking, desire at all; the same process that makes desire visible—hence a possible object of knowledge—also makes it other than itself. At the same time, this impersonal automatism called desire can never be perceived "in itself" but only through or as the desire of concrete persons. The skin, then, demystifies a certain understanding of desire but does not let us see, or know, desire itself, or desire "as it really is."

Now if indeed the appearance of desire were *always* an illusion, there would still be a certain kind of knowledge gained: the knowledge that desire cannot be known as it really is, that appearances are always a certain deformation of an essence (or a mechanism, a law, a structure) that cannot be grasped except through a misleading medium. Though this knowledge may not be as exhilarating as the omniscience claimed by the antiquarian, it would be knowledge nonetheless. But if this were the case, the skin, as a "strange" perspective, would lose its strangeness: the idea that all we can know of desire is its appearance is merely one "theme" among others, one explanatory model extracted from the contingent story of an individual as a lesson that transcends it. I have been arguing, however, that if Balzac introduced the skin as a supernatural object, it is because it stands for a perspective that is radically different from the official, philosophical project of his text.

The strange perspective introduced with the skin displaces emphasis from the "philosophical" question—what general, conceptual knowledge can be extracted from contingent, particular reality—to a "literary" question: what is the relation between a sign, or a material vehicle, and the meaning or reality this vehicle makes manifest. We can say that this shift of perspective is effected by the skin, since with it, Raphaël is no longer simply an individual whose life can teach us some general truth; he is also, as I have indicated above, a material vehicle—a means of making visible—a reality that is independent of him (the chain of events leading to the fulfilling of "his desires"). But before I elaborate on this point, I would like to briefly show another way in which this question is addressed in the novel—through the representation of feminine figures.

We should note, first, that for Raphaël woman has no existence except as the exteriorization, or representation, of his own desires. Early on in his narrative Raphaël says: "Toutes les femmes se résumaient par une seule, et cette femme je croyais la rencontrer dans la première qui s'offrait à mes regards" ("All women were summed up in one single one, and I believed I had found this woman in the first my eye fell upon"; 139; *104*). The phantasmatic figure of "woman" is pure exteriority, pure form, or else pure matter. Either as form or as matter, woman for Raphaël is in herself devoid of all meaning; in her emptiness (form) or lack of meaning (matter) she can become a vehicle for representing his interiority, his desire, the meaning of his life. Thus all the feminine figures in the novel are presented as first and foremost representations of Raphaël's life. When Rastignac first mentions Fœdora to Raphaël, Raphaël immediately sees her as the external, material representation of an internal meaning ("le symbole de tous mes désirs") and as the summary or the essence of his life ("le thème de ma vie"; 154; *120*). He similarly calls Pauline "belle image de ma vie" (310; *282*) and says about Euphrasie and Aquilina that they are his "histoire personnifiée, une image de [sa] vie" (210; *180*). Meaning needs a material vehicle, or a form, to make it visible, and in *La Peau* woman functions as this vehicle.

But the four women do not only represent Raphaël's desire or the meaning of his life; they also relate to one another in a relation of outside/inside, that is, a relation of representation (Pauline is the inside, the "soul" whereas Fœdora is the outside, "riches"; Aquilina is "l'âme du vice," whereas Euphrasie is "le vice sans âme"). Moreover, each of them is double, made of an inside and an outside, and thus offers a different model for articulating the relation of representation, the relation between a material vehicle (or a form) that represents and an intelligible meaning that is represented. What are these four models?

Aquilina is presented as a transparent image of pleasure, dissipation, and vice. She embodies the simplest case of all, that of complete accord between inside and outside, between meaning and expression, which allows for full transparency, for the direct access to a meaning, to an essence—she is "l'âme du vice." Aquilina is totally readable in the sense that we do not really have to read or interpret her for her meaning to become accessible.

By contrast, Euphrasie's external appearance of innocence is deceiving, and Emile and Raphaël are both "trompés d'abord par les célestes promesses écrites dans les suaves attraits de cette jeune fille" ("misled at first by the celestial promise contained in this girl's sweetness and charm"; 119; *83–84*). If Aquilina does not require any reading, the reading triggered by Euphrasie's face is the reading of demystification: with Euphrasie the outside is a screen, a veil that has to be removed if the corrupt inside is to appear. We can say that Aquilina's "meaning" is literal, whereas Euphrasie's is "figurative" or more precisely ironic (she appears the opposite of what she is). But for all this opacity, the inside is still accessible and when reached causes a "transfiguration" of the outside (of the lovely face), so that through the work of interpretation, the outside ends up corresponding to the inside. The outside is initially deceiving, but it is precisely the task of interpretation to remove this deception, this veil, and thus transform the outside, make it appear as what it really is—a deception. The discrepancy between the outside and the inside is itself subject to interpretation; it receives a meaning, a name: monstrosity, or a "lack." It is because Euphrasie's outside deceives that she is seen as a monster and is called a demon without heart.

Pauline stands for a very different model of meaning production: that of meaning independent of an external sign. Pauline's outside neither reveals nor hides her inside; her soul is neither hidden under her poor clothes nor revealed by her rich clothes (or vice versa), since in her case clothes are indeed what is "least womanly in a woman," a mere exterior that does not enable or impede meaning. This exterior is necessary since, as the text insists, every idea, every meaning, needs some material vehicle to make it visible; but in Pauline's case precisely what this means of expression is does not really matter. Pauline's beauty, riches, and general desirability at the end of the novel are merely a conventional sign for all the qualities that make her, independent of this sign and before this sign, totally desirable. As meaning prior to and independent of any means of expression, she can have the most conventional means of expression.

If Fœdora is indeed the opposite of Pauline, she has to be seen as an instance of complete opacity. (This opacity, however, is not a lack which, as we have seen, is merely the name given to the recuperable discrepancy between outside and inside.) Foedora is a sign independent of meaning, a material vehicle (or a form) whose meaning is indeterminate. She cannot be read in any of the three ways the other women were. In calling Fœdora "a woman without a heart," Raphaël fails to understand (misreads) her—he confuses nonmeaning with a lack of meaning. His attempt to explain Fœdora as a monster—as the woman without desire, without heart, without sex, with some horrible defect or sickness—fails when, spying on her from behind the curtains, he faces the totally impenetrable perfection of her body. The complete perfection of her body (or, alternatively, her complete narcissism) does not give Raphaël any point of entry, any access to her inside, to her meaning; Fœdora resists Raphaël's attempt to read her as an enigma (which needs to be solved), a lack (which may be filled).

We are thus brought to the conclusion that meaning can be either literal (Aquilina) or figurative (Euphrasie). Though in itself figurative meaning is recuperable (Euphrasie can be read), what is not easily determined is how we know whether to read literally or figuratively. Indeed, the scene in Fœdora's bedroom prior to her undressing dramatizes this difficulty. Here Fœdora takes an ironic praise of Raphaël literally, but when she responds by attacking him "sans pitié," he reads the attack figuratively, as a disguised expression of affection (192; *159–60*). If a praise can be read as its opposite, an attack, and an attack can be read either as an attack or as its opposite, a dissimulation of love, words do not have stable meaning. The only way to get to meaning, then, is by some direct access to the inside, not dependent on words (Pauline). It is this possibility that the perfect, impenetrable body of Fœdora forecloses. Or, put differently, the impenetrability of Fœdora, her total inaccessibility to interpretation, is what puts in motion the entire system of interpretation with its various modes.

V

Seeing Fœdora as resistant to interpretation would make her similar to the skin and would thus explain why she is eclipsed with its advent. Once Raphaël has the skin, he "forgets" Fœdora since in some sense it takes her place. But the skin is not a redundunt object (it is a strange object), and the effect it has on Raphaël's life is not quite the same as Fœdora's.

What is most disquieting about the skin is that it does not fulfill Raphaël's desires in any magical or supernatural way; rather, they seem to be fulfilled in the most natural fashion.[25] The skin is not a magical object, an Aladdin's lamp. It does not supernaturally intervene in the world, to make the impossible possible. Nor does it intervene in Raphaël's life, making him, magically, different. As we have seen, the skin merely makes visible the constant desiring that was there all along, and the life Raphaël leads after he has acquired the skin shows the same oscillation between excess and deprivation, dissipation and asceticism, that characterized his life before.

What is uncanny about life under the spell of the skin is that it shows repeatedly how Raphaël's "desire" intersects with a chain of events totally independent of him. As the two first examples of the functioning of the skin demonstrate, the fullfilling of his desires is not the result of his wishing, but the result of events that occurred long before he pronounces his wishes.[26] In fact, these two examples show that the chains of events that led to Raphaël's participation in the orgy and to his inheritance had started long before he had even seen the skin.[27] What takes place with the skin, then, is not that a wish gets magically fulfilled but rather that a chain of events, which is independent of the individual's desire, is made visible, or is represented, as the answer to this individual's desire. The concept of representation implicit in the functioning of the skin is, then, the traditional one, whereby representation makes accessible a world that is totally independent of it, anterior and exterior to it. But this anodyne notion of representation has all of a sudden become strange, since what the skin points out is the totally unaccountable "miracle" of the intersection of a chain of events with the means of making them visible.

So understood, what the text emphasizes, then, is not the individual's lack of control over the *means* of representation but rather the individual's lack of control over *what* he or she represents or renders visible. This is why it is important to insist that the chains of events that become visible as fulfillments of Raphaël's desires start long before he expresses his desires and even before he sees the skin. It demonstrates that Raphaël himself does not determine which events may, eventually, be seen as responding (or corresponding) to his desires.

This point is made particularly clear with Pauline's transformation into a rich heiress. This change occurs through a chain of events independent of Raphaël's act of desiring. The function of the scene in which Pauline's mother "sees" the future return of the lost father who will eventually bring about his daughter's change of fortune is precisely to highlight the independence of Pauline's transformation from Raphaël's act of desiring and from the skin. To say that this chain fulfills Raphaël's desire is not quite exact, because it is only when "fulfilled" that Raphaël's desire for Pauline becomes visible to him: she has become his desire. That Pauline's transformation into a desirable woman is not related to the skin may, of course, be read ironically, as a comment on Raphaël's misguided life: not only does the skin, "fulfilling his desires," leave him dissatisfied; had he never acquired it, he might have both fulfilled his true desire for a rich and desirable Pauline and been satisfied. The problem with such a reading (which is probably that of Raphaël himself) is that it depends on understanding the skin as a magic object—that is, an intervention that changes the subject or the world around him. We have seen, however, that this is not the case, and the fact that Pauline's transformation does not depend on the skin makes precisely this point. Since all of Raphaël's desires are fulfilled not through his wishing them, but through a process that starts long before and independently of his wishing, there is no reason to see the transformation of Pauline as in some important way different from, say, the transformation of Raphaël himself into a rich heir.[28]

It seems that with this formulation we have denied the skin any function; but this is not the case. If indeed Raphaël's desires, rather than depending on him, befall him, what is it that limits the scope of "his desires"? The answer is, of course, the skin; but the skin not as a magical object whose "power" wears out through usage but as a representation of life. The representation of reality, its being made visible through an individual's "desires," is limited by that individual's life. When that life is over, the book is closed, the curtain falls on this particular "representation." The skin is a representation not of the meaning of Raphaël's life, but of the limit (the outward envelope so to speak) within which a certain number of chains of events are made visible as the fulfillment of the desires of "a subject."

As we see, then, *La Peau* is divided between two views of narrative representation. One is the "philosophical" view, according to which the contingent life story of an individual is but a material that can be transformed into knowledge, generalizable and applicable to others (at the limit—to all); sacrificing or negating the contingent particularity of particular individuals or objects, extracting from them their "essence," allows ultimately for the representation of reality as a totality. The other is the "literary" view, opened up by the skin, according to which a totality may be "out there" (a multiplicity of chains of events) but is accessible to us, is articulated, only through a specific material vehicle—a subject—and is thus limited by the scope of this subject's life. Since the "piece of reality" made manifest is coterminous with the material existence of the subject-vehicle who articulates it, it is nongeneralizable—it is irreducibly specific.

I have discussed up to now the tension in the novel in terms of an opposition between philosophical and literary projects—understandable in a text that in its first appearance was called a "roman philosophique." But we can see it equally as a tension within the literary project itself, and even more specifically within the project of "realism." I hinted at the beginning of the chapter at one way of understanding this tension: the commitment of realism to the representation of particular experience may lead to its unintelligibility ("Will it be understood outside of Paris? One may doubt it.") But the preceding analysis allows us to see the idea of particularity itself in a somewhat different way. The particularity Balzac attempts to capture in his novels is not the particularity of an individual, product of a specific milieu (such particularity can always be subsumed within a universal), but rather the irreducible particularity of a historical reality, of a specific historical moment that cannot be "seen" except through the life of individuals. It is a certain idea of the irreducible specificity of a historical moment that the skin pushes to the extreme and thus makes strange.[29]

CHAPTER 2

Escaping Death: The Gendered Economy
of 'Le Lys dans la vallée'

∼

We have seen that the antiquarian in *La Peau de chagrin* sees knowledge as gained through the negation (sacrifice or loss) of experience. The same view informs most autobiographical writing, where the narrating-I finds compensation for the failures (emotional, epistemological, moral) in his experience in the knowledge that he has acquired and that gives him the authority to tell his life story. The paradigmatic example of such an endeavor is Proust's *Recherche* where, through the autobiographical work of art, "lost time" of experience (or wasted life) is "regained," recuperated and transformed.

This would seem at first to also be the goal in Balzac's *Le Lys dans la vallée* (1836), a first-person narrative in which Félix de Vandenesse tells his mistress, Natalie, the story of his life. Beginning his long letter—a letter that is as intimate in its confession as it is elaborate in its rhetoric and style—Félix evokes the figure of the poet who would tell his life story:

> A quel talent nourri de larmes devrons-nous un jour la plus émouvante élégie, la peinture des tourments subis en silence par les âmes dont les racines tendres encore ne rencontrent que de durs cailloux dans le sol domestique, dont les premières frondaisons sont déchirées par des mains haineuses, dont les fleurs sont atteintes par la gelée au moment où elles s'ouvrent? Quel poète nous dira les douleurs de l'enfant dont les lèvres sucent un sein amer, et dont les sourires sont réprimés par le feu dévorant d'un œil sévère? (45)

> (What unknown talent, nourished with tears, will some day give us the most moving elegy; the portrayal of torments undergone in silence by souls whose still tender roots meet nothing but hard pebbles in the soil of home; whose first green shoots are torn by hate-filled hands, whose flowers are nipped by frost just as they open? What poet will sing the heartaches of the child whose lips have sucked a bitter breast, whose smiles are driven back by the consuming fire of a stern eye?; *1–2*.)

The distinction between the poet who tells the story and the child whose story it is is quickly undone (Félix will shift into the first person after the next sentence), since the two share the same lot: if the poet is "nourished with tears," the child sucks at a "bitter breast." This convergence of the poet-narrator who creates a rhetorically powerful work of art (a "moving elegy") with the child who is the subject matter of the elegy is by no means coincidental. The tears that are the sign of deprivation, of the lack of maternal love, end up being a nourishment, and they nourish a "talent," a poet who produces a work of art. A "talent nourished with tears" articulates in as concise a manner as possible the paradox of a lack or loss (in experience) being turned into a gain (in and through a work of art). A lack of nourishment is repeatedly presented in the novel as a sign of a lack of love (as when at school, the lack of love shown by his family and the hostile attitude of his schoolmates are crystallized around his "panier peu fourni," his "meagre lunch basket"; 47; 4); but this lack of nourishment, or bad nourishment, ends up being the opposite: food for a budding talent. The bad mother, whose eyes burn and whose touch is like frost, is not a bad mother after all. Her parsimony, her miserliness, her reluctance to give (because she has nothing to give?), turns into giving. She cannot *not* give, she cannot *not* nourish, and the lack of nourishment itself turns into nourishment. I will come back to this paradox of the bad/good mother, to the fact that her icy touch, rather than killing the child-plant, preserves its life. For the moment, I would like simply to insist on the way in which *Le Lys* starts out by affirming a dialectical relation between art and experience, in which art is what turns a lack or privation (in experience) into a gain. The work of art is both the means and the product of this transformation.

This work of art, this moving elegy, however, is also a first-person auto-biographical narration, that is, a representation of the poet's experience. It is not only that the poet is nourished by the lack in his experience; he also uses his talent to tell the story of this experience. The unhappy childhood to which he refers in the opening sentences is at once the source of his talent and the object to which that talent will be applied. The question then arises of whether his narration is a mastering of experience, that is, the drawing out of a flawed experience of the "gain" of knowledge and self-understanding, or the compulsive repetition of experience, the acting out in art of the same experience as that of the child he was.

The first possibility would put Félix in the position of the typical first-person narrator, the one "who knows," and would make of the novel, his narration, a re-presentation of a previous experience from which he, as a narrator, is in some sense detached. On this formulation, Félix (like Raphaël at the beginning of *La Peau de chagrin*) would be looking back at his experi-

ence with an understanding he did not have before, and will tell his story with
the "difference" of knowledge. As the example of Raphaël in *La Peau* re-
minds us, this vantage point of knowledge is that of (metaphorical) death:
Raphaël tells his life story to Emile after he has made up his mind to commit
suicide and was brought back to life by the "gift" of the skin. This vantage
point is in some sense a point outside or beyond experience; it is a point of
"rest," to use Saint Augustine's word, that is, beyond the change in time that
life (and learning) entail. Autobiographical narration often presents itself as
from "outre tombe," though autobiographers, real and fictive, from Rousseau
to Butor, have questioned the possibility or demonstrated the impossibility of
this kind of writing. In short, the position of the authoritative narrator who
re-presents his experience with the difference of complete understanding is
the position of someone who has died (to experience) and survives only as
knowledge of that experience.

As we shall see shortly, Félix the narrator does not assume such a vantage
point. The particularity of *Le Lys* is that against the background of autobiographical narration, Balzac places a narrator-character who has not gained
self-understanding, who, indeed, would not have become a narrator *had* he
gained self-understanding. Through the figure of Félix the narrator, then,
Balzac raises the possibility that narrative representation may not be predicated on knowledge. To the extent that this narrative representation is a
powerful work of art, "a moving elegy," its capacity to produce certain effects
would be independent of cognitive value.

The possibility Balzac here raises has implications beyond the particular
case of first-person narrative as a transformation of past experience into the
knowledge that redeems it. The cornerstone of Balzacian narrative is the
assumption that the narrator is an observer who interprets the signs of reality,
reads the hieroglyphs of the past, and produces a discourse of knowledge,
which the events of the narrative in some sense merely corroborate. I would
like to suggest that through the figure of Félix another possibility (which, one
may argue, lurks in all of Balzac's texts) comes to the forefront: that of a
narrator who is far from omniscient (in fact, lacks knowledge) but who
produces nevertheless a powerful discourse, a persuasive representation that
empowers him, that places him in advantageous relation to others. This
advantageous relation will be thematized in the novel as "escaping death."

I

Le Lys dans la vallée takes the form of a long letter in which Félix ostensibly tells Natalie, the young woman he loves, his past life: his unhappy child-

hood, his unconsummated love for Henriette de Mortsauf, his seduction by Lady Arabelle Dudley, the death of Mme. de Mortsauf. Many critics have pointed out that this instance of first-person retrospective narration violates most of the assumptions on which this form is predicated.[1] For our purposes, the point to be kept in mind is that, whereas a first-person retrospective narration normally assumes an ironic distance between the narrated-I (the youthful hero) and the narrating-I (the somewhat older and wiser narrator), in *Le Lys* we have a first-person narrator telling the story of his youth but claiming, "Chez moi l'enfant ignore, et l'homme ne sait rien" ("In my case the child has no inkling and the man knows nothing"; 45; 2). If the statement is ironic—Félix does not "know" the extent of his ignorance—this irony is not the controlled one by which a mature narrator critically distances himself from his early version, the illusioned or naive hero. Félix is notorious for his lack of self-irony, and the sentimental attitude that he manifests toward his past (and that he cultivates in his reader) is the result of his attempt to protect himself (qua narrator) against understanding the meaning of his narrative. Unlike the typical first-person narrator who, having reached the position of knowledge and understanding, can interpret his experience, Félix refuses to have his experience interpreted or reshaped in or through his narration.

We can read this refusal in the text of *Le Lys* because Félix's letter incorporates interpretations of his experience, such as the letter of confession Mme. de Mortsauf gives him on her deathbed. Such interpretations remain external to Félix, contained within the letters of Henriette or, later on, of Natalie, which he merely quotes; he never makes these letters his own, either formally—by telling them "in his own words"—or substantively—by letting them modify his understanding and hence his narration. Whereas knowledge creates self-irony, its refusal generates an ironic gap between reader and narrator, a gap that marks precisely the ignorance of the latter. Thus Félix, in his detailed letter of confession to the young Natalie de Manerville, quotes Mme. de Mortsauf's letter, including a long harangue against young women and a warning against talking about oneself at any length: "Une des règles les plus importantes de la science des manières est un silence presque absolu sur vous-même" ("One of the most important rules in the science of good manners is an almost total silence about oneself"; 161; 118). That Félix simply quotes this sentence in his letter to Natalie shows his inability to read Henriette's letter, his active resistance to knowledge.

Le Lys, then, cannot be understood on the model of a typical autobiographical narration. Even if the lack in experience was transformed into a gain of talent, this talent is not used to master experience through knowledge and understanding. On the contrary, knowledge is resisted or refused, and the purpose of the narration, despite what the initial letter to Natalie seems to indicate, is not to *tell* "how I became the person I am now"—through my experience and through my subsequent understanding of it. Rather, it is to *show* "how I remained the person I have always been"—in spite of all that has happened to me. Félix, in other words, does not "tell," or interpret, his experience; he merely "shows," or repeats, it.

The difference between what I have called "telling" and "showing" (I am *not* using these terms in their Jamesian sense) is that between two views of representation as a "repetition" of life or experience: one would have representation as repetition with the difference of knowledge; the other would have representation as repetition through displacement, the reenactment of experience by other means (in "art"). This difference will become clearer if we look for a moment at Félix's other "artistic" creation—the bouquets he makes for Mme. de Mortsauf. As others have pointed out, the composing of the bouquets cannot be reduced to a mode of communication;[2] rather, the bouquets accomplish an act. Moreover, this act is not simply the seduction of Mme. de Mortsauf, to be followed by a "real" consummation later on; composing the bouquets is an act of seduction, and their acceptance is an act of succumbing to seduction: "Cependant à l'aspect de ces bouquets, j'ai souvent surpris Henriette les bras pendants, abîmée en ces rêveries orageuses pendant lesquelles les pensées gonflent le sein, animent le front, viennent par vagues, jaillissent écumeuses, menacent et laissent une lassitude énervante" ("I have often come upon Henriette before these bouquets, her arms hanging loosely by her side, sunk in those stormy daydreams during which thoughts swell the breast, animate the brow, come in waves, gush out foaming, loom threateningly and leave behind them an enervating lassitude"; 131; *87*). The bouquets, rather than telling of a desire for an erotic relation, are the instrument through which an erotic relation takes place; they allow desire to be satisfied in a displaced fashion.

If we further insist on the lack of referential (botanical and physical) verisimilitude of these bouquets, on their sheerly textual existence as "fleurs de l'écritoire" (127; *83*)[3] possessing a certain power to produce a certain effect, we will see how they can serve as a *mise en abîme* for what the text of *Le Lys* in general does. Just as the bouquets are botanically implausible (if not impossible), the novel's status as a letter is blatantly lacking in verisimilitude. (Félix's text cannot "really" be a letter: apart from its excessive length and ornate style, it is formally divided into titled chapters, explicitly addresses a general, public readership, and so on.) And just as the bouquets perform an act rather than communicate a desire, the novel does not interpret experience and communicate the knowledge gained as a result; rather it performs an act—it does something or makes something happen.[4] In this sense, there can be no "A ce soir" (45; *1*)—a night of love to follow the narration—since the text is not a means for a further act but the act itself. The displacement of erotic desire and its enactment in a displaced form prevent the "real" consummation of desire, so that Félix's refusal of knowledge (the knowledge that would have allowed him to "tell" a story) is joined by his refusal of consummation (a refusal that enables him to perform this consummation repeatedly in a displaced form). The performative aspect of the text thus joins the refusal of knowledge displayed by its narrator. Both indicate that the text is not strictly speaking mimetic: rather than being separated from experience (the gap of knowledge, of mastery), it is continuous with it; it is a displacement of experience. The narrative, the "moving elegy" evoked in the opening paragraph, is thus rhetorical in both senses of the word: in its use of those "fleurs de l'écritoire" where the substitution of one sign for another creates a figurative meaning, and in its power to do something and make something happen through these substitutions.

II

If rhetoric allows us to understand the substitution of signs as a means of producing certain effects, psychoanalysis specifies that substitution or displacement is a means of bringing about the fulfillment of desire. But in Félix's case, things are a bit more complicated, since for him the displacement of desire onto new objects entails a repetition of an experience of frustration. Félix's life strings out in a chain of substitutions, where love is displaced from one object to another. His childhood love for his mother meets with cold indifference, so that when he meets the maternal and sympathetic Henriette de Mortsauf, he transfers onto her this unused love. But Mme. de Mortsauf's insistence that she remain his "mother" leaves his desire unfulfilled, so he transfers his love to the willing Lady Arabelle. Having conquered his loyalty to Mme. de Mortsauf, Arabelle rejects him at the same time that Mme. de Mortsauf herself dies as a result of his betrayal. Abandoned again, Félix displaces his love for Henriette onto her daughter (following Henriette's own plan). But Madeleine turns her angry back on him, and he returns to Paris to seek comfort in the arms of the young Natalie. What motivates substitution and displacement is failure or rejection. But what guarantees the continuation of the chain (presumably even beyond Natalie's cutting letter) is Félix's inability to understand what has caused this failure. Having failed, and having failed to understand why he has failed, he will try again, for the same reason fail again, and will then start again, endlessly. Thus the continuation of experience (including the act of narration) depends on the repetition of frustration in spite of (or through) displacement and substitution.

Thus frustration remains constant through all possible displacements. As a child Félix displaces his frustrated love for his mother onto a love for a star; later on, the displacement takes on other shapes: a love of books, "gourmandise," the desire for a prostitute. But displacement here does not prevent frustration (lack of fulfillment) or compensate for it; rather, it ensures its repetition. Initially, the lack of fulfillment of desire in one place does not only motivate displacement; it is also seen as permitting satisfaction elsewhere: the child, rejected by mother and siblings, counts on their indifference so he can stay in the garden gazing lovingly at his star, just as the young man counts on the indifference of his aunt to allow him make his escape to Port Royal. But his communion with the star is brutally interrupted by the governess, his desire to go to dinner and to the theater is frustrated by the discovery of his debts, his plan to escape to the prostitutes of Port Royal is interrupted by the arrival of his parents in Paris, and so on. This is Félix's "destiny": the logic of substitution and displacement, put in place in order to find fulfillment elsewhere, is counterbalanced by a logic of fixation—fixation on the frustration of desire. Félix presents himself as the passive victim of these misfortunes, but this, we can argue, is simply the result of his lack of self-understanding or of his refusal to see the active role he plays in bringing this "fate" about. And once we start suspecting that Félix may be in some sense responsible for his malignant fate, we can ask what its payoff may be. This can be summarized as follows: the frustration of desire brings about the postponement of fulfillment, and its repetition guarantees that this postponement will be without term. Félix's fixation on the experience of frustration is a refusal to move toward an end (consummation); like the refusal of knowledge, it is a refusal of change, of a movement toward death. Thus, the logic of narration joins the logic of desire, both directed at an escape from death, doubly signified as the consummation of desire and the achievement of knowledge.

This combination of displacement and fixation is possible because in Félix's history (his life or the narration thereof) a star, food, books, women, do not function as objects that, different from one another, cannot "serve" the same purpose (that have, if you will, different "use value"). Rather, they function as signs in a system of representation. Within that system, they stand or are exchanged for something else, and this gives them a certain amount of freedom from their empirical fixity. Indeed, we should go even further and say that the signs in this system function rhetorically rather than referentially, since Félix's frustrated desire can be displaced onto, and hence signified by, many different objects-signs.

If, up to now, I have been using what is, broadly speaking, a psychoanalytical vocabulary (compulsion to repeat, fixation, displacement, etc.), it is not because I wish to "diagnose" Félix's particular neurosis but, rather, because I believe that psychoanalysis, as a theory of signification, can help us see something important about the way *Le Lys* produces its meaning. More precisely, the psychoanalytical theory that character and life story can be understood in terms of an interplay between fixation and displacement can help us understand the way rhetorical systems of signification operate.[5] Generalizing from the preceding analysis of Félix, the question to be posed is the following: if desire can be displaced onto any number of vastly different objects, if excitation can cathect any number of zones or activities, and these zones and activities can be invested with different kinds of excitation, how can we read or interpret these objects or activities? The "emptiness" of the signs—their availability to a multiplicity of heterogeneous investments—should make them totally opaque and unreadable. And yet psychoanalysis does produce readings—of dreams, of literary texts, character traits, symptoms—because the unlimited displacement (of affect, of meaning) is grounded in a fixation that, as the origin of displacement and investment, is what all the signs ultimately refer to, what gives them their meaning. But Freud's insistent and repeated problematization of the notion of origin in all its forms should warn us against understanding fixation as determining the signs in the manner of cause and effect. "Fixation" should be understood, rather, in terms of its hermeneutically enabling function: in a system that is purely rhetorical, meaning can be guaranteed (or saved, so that it is not lost or wasted) only by *limiting* the system; the origin, signified, or referent—what is "fixed" and "fixes"—is precisely that which limits the rhetorically undecidable play of the system.[6] We shall see how this question of the "limit" appears in *Le Lys* in various guises.

III

I have been arguing that in *Le Lys* it is the repetition of rejection and failure, grounded in and sustained by a lack of understanding, that assures the continuation of the story (the "experience" of the main character, Félix) and explains the act of narration that repeats this experience and makes it accessible to us. Though Félix toward the end of the text presents himself as an "omniscient narrator," as the only person who knows everything about Henriette and so can serve as her historian and the historian of many other women who resemble her, his narration to Natalie cannot be grounded in such knowledge (though of course the fact that he is the one who lives to tell the tale is crucial). Rather, that narration is grounded in his lack of knowledge of himself: had he understood himself he would never have told the story to Natalie and hence to us. The continuation of life and/in narration depends on an ignorance that generates the repetition of frustration.[7]

This is why the lack of fulfillment can figure in the novel as the preservation of life. To take just one example. Describing his life at school, Félix presents it as a repetition of his experience at home: "Là, comme à la maison, je me repliai sur moi-même. Une seconde tombée de neige retarda la floraison des germes semés en mon âme" ("There, as at home, I turned in upon myself. A second snowfall delayed the flowering of the seeds sown in my soul"; 49; 5). His rejection by his schoolmates resembles or repeats his rejection by his mother; it is a second snowfall retarding the blooming of the seed sown in his soul. But this snowfall does not kill the seed; on the contrary, by retarding or delaying its blooming, it preserves it. Should this delay not occur, the seed would bloom and then die. By contrast, under repeated snowfalls the seed of love is preserved, and Félix can speak of "l'or vierge de mes désirs, tout un coeur brûlant conservé sous les glaces de ces Alpes entassées par un continuel hiver" ("the virgin gold of my desires, a whole burning heart preserved beneath the alpine ice piled high by a perpetual winter"; 100; 58). The displacement of desire is not an attempt to escape rejection but rather a manifestation of a fixation on frustration (on snowfalls), a frustration that is now to be understood as the guarantee of preservation, of immortality.

Felix can thus represent his compulsion to repeat as the victory of innate nature over experience. This is the way he explains why the harsh treatment to which he was subjected did not turn him into a weak, vicious monster: "Déjà déshérité de toute affection, je ne pouvais rien aimer, et la nature m'a fait aimant! . . . Si dans quelques âmes les sentiments méconnus tournent en haine, dans la mienne ils se concentrèrent et s'y creusèrent un lit d'où, plus tard, ils jaillirent sur ma vie" ("Already dispossessed of all affection, there was nothing I could love, and nature had made me loving! . . . If in some souls slighted feelings turn to hate, in mine they drew in upon themselves and hollowed out a bed whence, later on, they gushed forth onto my life"; 46; 2). In other words, deprivation is not in itself sufficient for the creation of a genius; tears do not always turn into talent. For this economy to function, for the lack to turn into gain, it has to be supplemented by a gift of nature (the seeds sown in his soul, his loving nature), something that, as "nature," can be neither lost nor changed. It is the positing of a gift of nature, of innate character traits, that does the work of explaining and justifying why Félix does not change, resists experience, does not acquire knowledge. Arrested development (the adult Félix looks like a child) becomes the sign of the preservation of innate qualities that are kept intact by never becoming actual (part of experience, which will waste them), by remaining pure potentiality. Though Félix in this passage speaks the language of postponement—the love that for the moment remains without object is kept (is even strengthened through keeping) and will become manifest "later on"—the novel as a whole shows how, through the repetition of frustration and rejection, this "later on" never comes, how postponement is, in fact, without term.

Thus the resistance to experience—arrested development and the refusal to learn—and the compulsion to repeat an experience of frustration and rejection are both presented in Félix's narrative as the keeping intact of the gift of nature, as what prevents waste and loss. What Félix tries to protect himself against is a complete loss of self, annihilation, the encounter with "l'inutilité du néant," where, according to him, with neither sympathy nor antagonism to absorb affect, "notre puissance s'échappe tout entière sans aliment, comme le sang par une blessure inconnue. La sensibilité coule à torrents, il en résulte d'horribles affaiblissements" ("our entire strength leaks away without nourishment, like blood from an unknown wound. Feeling flows in torrents, resulting in dreadful fits of weakness"; 92; *49*). What saves the soul from this hemorrhaging is "nourishment" ("aliment"), and this nourishment can be either love or hostility, since, with the gift of nature, rejection (lack of nourishment) preserves the self, *is* nourishment. The gift of nature is what allows a lack of nourishment to "turn" into nourishment. As we shall see later on, Henriette is in complete agreement with Félix about the need to "bind" affect—"feed" the soul—in order to prevent loss and waste; but her death shows that she is not as successful in this project as Félix is, that in her case things did not "turn" quite the same way. This suggests that Félix's discourse about the soul is not a discourse of knowledge, expressing certain generalized truths about human nature—"notre puissance"—but rather a rhetorically powerful discourse by means of which his own "nature" as powerful is both posited and proved (the gift of nature that saves him from loss and waste, from disempowerment, turns him into a poet whose discourse has power over others, specifically, over Henriette).

Thus we can make sense of Félix's appearance, experience, and narrative stance by showing, first, how it is strategically directed toward a certain goal (preservation) and, second, how achieving this goal depends on positing something like "inherent nature." But we still need to ask whether and to what extent Balzac shares Félix's "theory." The answer, as I have suggested, is that Balzac, through the figure of Félix, questions the status of narrative discourse as "theory," as a discourse of knowledge. But his stance here is not ironical. To be sure, by the end of the novel Félix is entirely ironized: Henriette's posthumous confession shows that he failed to understand her, and Natalie's letter shows how his own confession produced her rejection. But then Félix never wished to understand, and rejection, as we have seen, is what keeps him going. Irony, clearly, is irrelevant here. Balzac neither demystifies nor endorses Félix's hypothesis of "given nature"; rather, he shows (like Félix or *as* Félix) how it works: what calls for this hypothesis and what its function may be.

IV

The narrative logic and the logic of desire I have described up to now depend on (or produce) a specific view of the mother figure. Félix's life has the form of a series of repetitions, and what is repeated is the "original" relation to the mother. But the mother cannot be the point of origin, since she is divided: the source of life and love, she also threatens life and has no love to give. This division or contradiction is represented as a doubling of the mother: the parsimonious mother who does not give anything, or who gives only grudgingly, is supplemented by a generous mother nature who gave him his sensibility, his own ability to love. But the opposition is not a stable one: the bad mother is in fact a good mother, since she preserves the gift of the good mother, which, without her, would have ended up being spent and lost.

It is this contradictory character of the mother figure that shapes the series of substitutions. Each woman in the series wants, or is supposed, to give what the other (or the mother) has refused; but since the mother is "double," displacing or supplementing her results in repetition.[8] Thus Henriette, wanting to fill up the lack caused by the deficiency of the mother, merely repeats that deficiency: "Qu'ai-je voulu dans votre coeur? la place laissée vide par Mme de Vandenesse. Oh! oui, vous vous êtes toujours plaint de ma froideur! Oui, je ne suis bien que votre mère" ("What did I want in your heart? Simply the place left unfilled by Madame de Vandenesse. Oh, yes! You have always complained of my coldness. I am indeed no more than your mother"; 240; *199*). One hence "reads" the name of the good mother—"le lys"—in the name of the bad one: Listomère ("Lys ta mère").

Supplanting or supplementing, making up, does not create closure, does not "fill up," but rather calls for further supplementing, more repetition. Moving away means staying in one place, since this one place is not an undivided origin, which can originate a sequence, but a divided "origin," which can only generate the repetition of the contradiction. Staying a child forever (abstaining from/frustrating sexual consummation) means either enjoying the protection of a loving mother or preserving the innate good qualities from the chilling atmosphere of the mother and all those who model their behavior on hers (or both). The world has the power to frustrate desire because it is not motherly (the world of the family, school, etc.) and/or because it is motherly (Henriette).

Both the love and the rejection of the mother prevent the series of displacements from effecting a real displacement, a going elsewhere, a change. Félix remains a child both by the rejection of his mother and by the love of Henriette. But this blocking of change and growth is not death; on the contrary, it is a preservation of potentiality and a gain of life. It is the doubleness of the mother that ultimately allows Félix to survive.

V

We can say that Félix, both as a hero and as a narrator, does not try to fulfill desire or achieve understanding (both of which he avoids); his goal, rather, is to escape death, and in this he is doubly successful. Like the Comte's ancestor who gave the family its name, and like the Comte himself, Félix is someone who is "Mort-sauf," someone who escapes death.

It is indeed remarkable that the weak and sickly male characters of this novel escape death, whereas the main female character, who radiates strength and health, ends up dead.[9] This raises the question of whether the libidinal-narrative logic I have described up to now, where knowledge and consummation are resisted in order to escape death, is the only logic in the novel. Is Félix simply wrong when he thinks that Henriette, like him, is motivated by the logic of postponement? If she is governed by another logic, is it because she is a woman? And what is the relation of this other logic, and of Félix's logic, to her actual death? Does she die because Félix misunderstood her to be like him, or does she die because her own logic, her own strategy for survival, backfires and kills her?

Félix and Henriette are twin souls, and the most salient point of similarity between them is their childhood experience. The title of the first part of the novel—"Les Deux enfances"—draws attention to this similarity between the two childhoods, similarities that account for the affinity and love between Félix and Henriette. It is possible, however, to interpret this title also as referring to *Félix's* two childhoods: his real childhood and his second, metaphorical childhood, with Henriette playing the role of (repeating) the mother. The first interpretation implies that Félix and Henriette, having had the same kind of childhood experience, have grown to be the same kind of people; the second implies that Félix is arrested in his development (repeating childhood figuratively rather than moving from childhood to adulthood), whereas Henriette has moved from her childhood relation to her own mother to a relation where she herself is the mother. Taking these two interpretations together, we can say that the similarity highlights a difference: starting from the same childhood experience, Félix resists change and growth (and thus escapes death), whereas Henriette is subject to change in time; her real childhood, rather than being repeated by a metaphorical one, is followed by a real adulthood (and then a real death). If we turn back for a minute to *La Peau de chagrin*, we can say that though Félix and Raphaël resemble each other in their resistance (willed or not) to an economy whereby knowledge is produced at the cost of experience, Félix (unlike Raphaël) grasps the "symbolic dimension" of lived reality, where rhetorical displacement and supplementation are not "mere words" but have power and effects in the real.

At any rate, both Félix and Henriette have a similar childhood experience of deprivation, of a lack of maternal love. We have seen how in Félix's case this lack turns into a gain, and the question is whether Henriette is subject to the same economy. We have also seen how in Félix's case this "turn" (or "trope") was made possible by a doubling of the mother, by a supplementary act—the gift of nature. In Henriette's case, too, the bad mother is doubled by a good one, her aunt, who gives her not one gift but two—a name, Henriette (as opposed to Blanche) and a domain, Clochegourde. But whereas Félix can keep the gift of nature intact, as pure potentiality that is never lost or wasted, Henriette does not or cannot keep these gifts to herself. She gives her name to Félix ("Une seule personne au monde, celle que j'ai le plus aimée, mon adorable tante, me nommait Henriette. Je redeviendrai donc Henriette pour vous" ["One person in the world, the one I loved the most, my adored aunt, called me Henriette. So I shall be Henriette again for you"; 107; *66*]), just as she gives Clochegourde to the Comte. Though this act of giving is carried out with true generosity, without calculation, there is no reason to idealize it and see it as an "absolute surrender." Indeed, Henriette's giving is predicated on the assumption that such selflessness, such acts of generosity, are always reciprocated. But this is precisely what does not happen:

> En se mariant, elle possédait ses épargnes, ce peu d'or qui représente les heures joyeuses, les mille désirs du jeune âge; en un jour de détresse, elle l'avait généreusement donné [à son mari] sans dire que c'était des souvenirs et non des pièces d'or; jamais son mari ne lui en avait tenu compte, il ne se savait pas son débiteur! En échange de ce trésor englouti dans les eaux dormantes de l'oubli, elle n'avait pas obtenu ce regard mouillé qui solde tout, qui pour les âmes généreuses est comme un éternel joyau dont les feux brillent aux jours difficiles.
> (101–2)

(When she married, she had her savings, that little store of gold which represents the happy hours, the hundred and one whims of youth. On one needy day, she had generously parted with it, without mentioning that they were memories and not gold coins. Her husband never so much as mentioned it again; he did not even realize that he was in her debt. In exchange for this treasure, sunk in the still waters of oblivion, she was never given that soft look which cancels every debt and which is, for generous souls, the eternal gem whose fires shine on difficult days; *59–60*.)

Henriette's "logic," as I will show, depends neither on keeping oneself entirely to oneself nor on absolute giving, but rather on an exchange, on a giving that is seen as always and necessarily leading to reappropriation. The question we should ask ourselves is why this reappropriation is not possible for Henriette herself.

What I have called Henriette's logic can be best seen in her agrarian improvements and her social theories. Critics do not normally pay much attention to the parts of the text where Henriette, no more the "turtle dove" or the chaste mother of romantic literature, discourses on mundane, practical issues. But it is precisely the anomaly of these passages within the narrative that should call our attention to their importance.[10]

Henriette makes two agrarian improvements, replacing share cropping with simple leases and instituting crop rotation. Both changes have a common goal: to avoid sharp fluctuations in income and instead ensure a stable, even if moderate, yield. Avoiding the extremes of both gain and loss is also, on another level, an elimination of competition and reduction of conflict. Whereas with share cropping, masters are in competition with their farmers and income fluctuates all the time, the lease plan eliminates both unpredictability (for the master) and conflict. The same principle can be seen in crop rotation: by giving up growing wheat every year, one gives up, or postpones, some gain, but one also avoids impoverishing the soil and the loss this entails. The giving up or delay involved in the "mise en quatre" is not a speculation, a gamble, that can lead to either great gain or complete loss; but neither is it a constant, perpetual giving up that avoids gratification altogether. It is, rather, a postponement, a delay, that guarantees a moderate gain.

It is not an accident that Henriette's main occupation is agriculture. Even though she is constantly associated with the world of nature (she is, after all, the lily of the valley), she does not promote or recommend a state of nature where plenty alternates with want, where one lets things take their natural course, at the mercy of an incomprehensible power, thus inevitably alternating between fortune and misfortune. Her entire enterprise is regulating nature and thus bringing it under human control. Agriculture itself is a control and regulation of nature, and Henriette's agrarian improvements are an attempt to safeguard against the "chances de l'agriculture" (135), that is, against what is still natural—unpredictable, unstable—in agriculture.

Henriette's social theories (presented in the letter of advice she gives Félix before he goes to Paris) apply the same principle of balancing profit and loss (that is, avoiding total loss) toward reducing conflict in society as a whole. The conflict between weak and strong, just like the fluctuation between loss and gain, entails the danger of total destruction, of complete loss. Set on preventing this possibility of total loss (without return, without reappropriation), Henriette proposes a mode of conduct that does not pit the weak against the strong, but that by a kind of averaging out, creates a system where everyone is useful and from which everyone benefits.

This mode of conduct is the opposite of gambling or speculation, that is, fluctuation between loss and gain. Whereas those who gamble see only their own interest, Henriette would have a system in which "tout s'arrange," and credits and debts end up balancing one another. Whereas those who gamble lose sooner or later, Henriette promises Félix that by following her advice he will always gain: "Je vous ai trouvé un meilleur usage du temps que vous dissiperiez au jeu; vous verrez que là où les autres doivent perdre tôt ou tard, vous gagnerez toujours" ("I have thought of a better use for the time you would dissipate at the gambling table. You will see that where others are bound to lose sooner or later, you will always win"; 152; *109*). This cannot, of course, mean that Félix will never incur any losses, only that losses and gains will average out so that finally there will be no absolute expenditure, no loss of self. This is why Henriette's theory promotes constant giving and at the same time insists that one must keep oneself to oneself.

Whereas those who gamble think that some people are important and others not, and "gamble" on those they deem important, in Henriette's model every person is important. As a young man, Félix may think that old women are useless; but Henriette encourages him to cultivate them, just as later on she advises him to stay with the King when his power is threatened by the return of Napoleon. People and things that may seem unimportant or superfluous will, at a later moment, in another place, prove to be significant. In other words, Henriette's theory implies an understanding of society as a structure where everything is functional, where "everything signifies," and where there is no unsignifying residue, no waste.

The governing principle of this mode of conduct is politeness, which means "forgetfulness of self." This cannot be mere pretense, sheer strategy, an empty form, or a "grimace"; but it cannot be an altruistic sacrifice either, since the whole system is predicated on absolute egotism. Rather, politeness presupposes a real forgetfulness of self by means of which the self gains back everything it has given out to others. The greatest danger to society, according to Henriette, comes from those who think that everything is owed to them whereas they owe nothing (young women and kings), that is, those who see themselves as outside the system of exchange and reciprocity, and who, by so placing themselves, increase the disparity between weak and strong.

Henriette's theory is "rational" in the sense that it insists on proper rationing, on equal and even distribution. Thus her agrarian reforms would not benefit farmers at the expense of landowners or vice versa, but improve the circumstances of both. If in her letter to Félix she is concerned primarily with the regulation of social relations, elsewhere she applies the same principle of equal distribution or of averaging out to the regulation of the emotions (142; *99*). The purpose of this self-regulation is to maintain a constant level of excitation, thus protecting oneself against both pleasure and pain, by opting (to use Freud's terminology) for "bound" pleasure—regulated, conservative, following "facilitated" routes. Speaking of her needlepoint, she says: "J'ai senti le besoin de régulariser la souffrance par un mouvement physique. J'évitais ainsi les atonies qui suivent les grandes dépenses de force, aussi bien que les éclairs de l'exaltation" ("I felt the need to keep a rein on suffering by some sort of physical movement. I avoided, in this way, the nervelessness that follows great expenditures of strength, as well as any periodical flashes of elation"; 142; *99*).

Whichever way we look at Henriette's theories, they involve an abolishing of both high losses and high gains, and aim at a regulated economy, based on give-and-take, on a loss and gain that cancel each other out. Her principle of "politeness" is not geared toward ensuring Félix a meteoric social success (which can only lead to an eventual catastrophic fall). It promises a more modest, well-regulated success designed precisely to avoid the oscillation between "high" and "low." This is the career that, following her advice, he achieves: his post in the King's service is "place de confiance, sans faveur éclatante, mais sans chance de disgrâce" ("a post of trust, without conspicuous favours, but without risk of disgrace"; 178; *136*). Henriette's knowledge of the future is not a magic gift, nor is it a speculation about the future; it is a reasonable prediction, possible once one assumes society to be a rational and regular structure of relations.

Indeed, Henriette sees society as a structure of relations among parts, regulated by a certain number of fixed rules. Her view is decidedly "synchronic"; she does not concern herself with the origin of society and its development over time: "J'ignore si les sociétés sont d'origine divine ou si elles sont inventées par l'homme, j'ignore également en quel sens elles se meuvent" ("I do not know if social communities are of divine origin or if they are man's invention. Nor do I know in what direction they tend" 156; *114*). This synchronic perspective is fully compatible with a view of the system as self-regulating, as reducing as much as possible fluctuation and conflict, in other words, as self-perpetuating. Historical change, then, comes from outside the system and hence must be irrational. We see here the same resistance to change that we find in Félix's "nature." By seeing the Restoration as a "coup de baguette," both Félix and Henriette declare history to be the realm of nonreason. While refusing to become the plaything of irrational history (Henriette says that she did not do anything to bring this change about, nor did she desire it), Henriette can tame the effects of history by bringing them within the pale of her reasonable system. Thus, the effect of the Restoration on her family is that of an "averaging out" by present gains of the losses incurred during the previous period. Her advice to Félix during the Hundred Days is not a "speculation" about the irrational course of history but a "prediction," since it is based on the principle that no person and no act are useless, and that a reasonable, moderate loss is bound to eventually bring about a reasonable, moderate gain.

VI

Several critics have suggested that the society Henriette describes or prescribes may have been possible in court, during the *ancien régime*, but certainly not in 1836 (the time *Le Lys* was written) or even 1815 (the time in which it is set).[11] To see how different modern, postrevolutionary society is from the one imagined by Henriette, all one has to do is read Balzac.[12] The world *he* shows in his novels is the world of the market economy, a world governed by gambling and speculation, whose rhythm is precisely that of fluctuation between high and low. Balzac always describes the oscillation between "splendeurs" and "misères," and the life of his characters is basically the life of Lucien de Rubempré, that is, the life of a commodity in the market or the life of an article of fashion, marked by a meteoric and arbitrary ascent and a catastrophic, just as arbitrary descent.

But it is a mistake to see Henriette as believing in a world that *Balzac* knows to be defunct. Henriette is not so naive as to think that the world in which she lives is really a perfectly well regulated machine that strives toward homeostasis. Indeed, she clearly acknowledges the opposite—that society obeys the law of the jungle, and that the dynamic principle in both nature and society is not a reduction of conflict but on the contrary, a constant competition where the strong prevail and destroy the weak: "les faibles sont malheuresement méprisés par une société qui ne voit dans chacun de ses membres que des organes; peut-être d'ailleurs a-t-elle raison, la nature condamne à mort les êtres imparfaits" ("weak folk are unfortunately despised by a society which sees each of its members as nothing but organs—and perhaps rightly so, for nature condemns imperfect creatures to death"; 160; *118*). Society, then, resembles nature, nature that agriculture is meant to control, just as Henriette's agrarian reforms are designed to diminish social conflict between owner and worker. It is not the voice of society or the voice of nature that she expresses in her theories, but the voice of reason, which opposes both. Nature and society are similar, and Henriette, a woman and a mother, "mothering" the physically frail Félix into the social world, opposes *both* with her reason. In "delivering" Félix into the social world, Henriette protects him by her advice to ensure his survival, in the same way that she protects her sickly children against the brute force of nature. Her role as a mother is played against both nature and society, so that despite her constant depiction as "natural" (the lily of the valley) and as a social conformist (as opposed to Arabelle), Henriette is both anti-nature and anti-society in her most pronounced attribute—that of a mother. Her goal is not simply to protect the weak but to oppose, by reason, the brutality and blindness of sheer matter: "lutter contre une force aveugle . . . faire triompher l'intelligence du coeur sur la brutalité de la matière" ("battle against a blind force . . . making the heart's intelligence triumph over the brutality of matter"; 160; *118*).[13] Henriette both describes society as a jungle and prescribes the law of reason, which through forgetfulness of self eliminates conflict.

In this sense, Henriette does not ignore (nostalgically, anachronistically) the existing social order; rather, she proposes a mode of conduct by which social reality can be rationalized and improved. Can we say, then, that Henriette dies because her mode of conduct cannot, after all, be effective in modern society? This is not quite the case, since Félix, as we have seen, follows her advice and is successful. But Félix's success does not end up benefiting Henriette, so that her act of "giving" or of "self-forgetfulness" in sending him to Paris—"vous livrer au monde, n'est-ce pas renoncer à vous?" ("Is not handing you over to the world tantamount to giving you up?"; 156; *113*)—does not end up serving *her* interests too, as the motto "tout s'arrange" would imply. On the contrary, by the end of the novel, she is the "weak" creature, condemned to death by either nature or society; and she dies at Clochegourde, at her improved, well-regulated estate, and not in the mad world of Paris. This suggests that perhaps the rational society she tries to create is not, finally, all that different from the existing social world; it also suggests that perhaps Félix succeeds where she fails because they are not "equal" parts within a mutually supporting system but are positioned differently within this system.

I would like to propose that though the modern world appears as a nightmare of irrationality, unpredictability, conflict, and destruction, and the society Henriette prescribes and tries to implement is a model of rationality, order, and mutual support, on one crucial point they surprisingly converge: they both subscribe to the opposition between matter and reason. Warning Félix against the dangers of modern society, Henriette points out that "malheureusement les hommes vous estiment en raison de votre utilité, sans tenir compte de votre valeur" ("unfortunately, men will appreciate you in proportion to your usefulness, taking no notice of your worth"; 161; *118*). She turns to an analogy to drive home her point: "Pour employer une image qui se grave en votre esprit poétique, que le chiffre soit d'une grandeur démesurée, tracé en or, écrit en crayon, ce ne sera jamais qu'un chiffre" ("To use an image which will impress itself on your poetic turn of mind: whether the cipher is of an exaggerated size, traced in gold, written in pencil, it will never be anything but a cipher"; 161; *118*). Though Henriette regrets this state of affairs, though she seems to evoke a notion of "worth" or "value" as intrinsic to the individual, as independent of its relation (its utility) to others, her entire rational system of social relations is predicated precisely on the definition of value as relational, hence on the lack of importance of the individual, who is but the "material" support of this relational value.

We can see how much Henriette's diagnosis of modern society converges with a description of a rational-relational structure if we compare her metaphor to a metaphor used to describe precisely such a system—Saussure's famous chess metaphor for the system of language. "Take a knight, for instance," writes Saussure. "By itself is it an element in the game? Certainly not, for by its material make-up—outside its square and other conditions of the game—it means nothing to the player; it becomes a real, concrete element only when endowed with value and wedded to it. Suppose that the piece happens to be destroyed or lost during the game. Can it be replaced by an equivalent piece? Certainly. Not only another knight but even a figure shorn of any resemblance to a knight can be declared identical provided the same value is attributed to it." Hence, Saussure concludes, "in semiological systems like language, where elements hold each other in equilibrium in accordance with fixed rules, the notion of identity blends with value and vice versa."[14] Made of ivory or of wood, large or small, the knight in the chess game has no intrinsic value, no identity, except the one constructed through its relations to other pieces in the game, and in this it is similar to Henriette's "chiffre," which "tracé en or" or "écrit en crayon" receives its numerical value only through relations to other numbers and, in itself, is nothing more than a cipher. Just as Saussure's knight is totally replaceable since its value is determined solely by its relations to other pieces, so in Henriette's system, materiality—the color or size of the "chiffre"—is totally irrelevant. The system functions as a system only by bracketing the material.

This can be said with equal right about both the "jungle" of modern society and the well-regulated economy of Clochegourde. Matter for Henriette is that which reason has to oppose and control; devoid of reason, it is subject to violent fluctuations, carries in it the menace of complete loss and waste. Within the world of Clochegourde, it is the Comte, with his unreasonable character, his violent fluctuations of temper—"ses soudains changements d'humeur, ses profondes tristesses sans motif, ses soulèvements brusques, ses plaintes amères et cassantes, sa froideur haineuse, ses mouvements de folie réprimés, ses gémissements d'enfant, ses cris d'homme au désespoir, ses colères imprévues" ("his sudden changes of mood, his deep, unaccountable bouts of sadness, his bursts of temper, his bitter, cutting complaints, his hate-filled coldness, his spasms of madness instantly checked, his childlike whimpering, his cries of a desperate man, his unexpected fits of anger"; 190–91; *48*)—who embodies this menace. The Comte can thus be seen as a synecdoche for the irrationality of nature. And just as Henriette's reforms are designed to regulate nature, so they are designed to curb and control, neutralize and render null, the impact of the Comte's temperamental unpredictability and lack of reason, in order to ensure the stability of both her estate and her state of mind. By so organizing life at Clochegourde as to neutralize the effects of the character of the Comte, Henriette in fact makes him dispensable. His "mastery" is a fiction. Once his individual character, which is unreasonable, is neutralized, the Comte is just a pawn (or a knight) in a rational system that achieved its rationality by neutralizing him, and that can dispense with his particular existence once he has been neutralized.[15]

In opposing reason to matter, in attempting to neutralize the fluctuations and loss inherent in matter through rational structure, Henriette designs a rational society where value does not inhere in particular individuals any more than it does in the jungle of modern society against which she is trying to fight. And what her formulation makes clear is that what is dismissed or bracketed in both is not an abstract notion of "individual merit" or of the irreducible autonomy of the individual but rather the materiality of a body that, as a body, is subject to complete destruction and loss, can be and is brought to death.

VII

We still have to explain, however, why Félix manages to survive in Henriette's rational system (or in the jungle of society), whereas she does not. Since Félix and Henriette resemble each other in all respects except for their sex, we have to conclude that the materiality of the body is not totally bracketed, or that the body is not simply material.

The difference between the beautiful, young, and healthy Henriette who dies and the sickly males, especially the Comte and Félix, who are saved from death is highlighted by a certain similarity among them.[16] As the doctor explains to Félix, Henriette's real disease has the same symptoms as the Comte's imaginary disease: "elle avait les affreux symptômes que M. de Mortsauf vous aura sans doute décrits, puisqu'il croyait les éprouver" ("she had the terrible symptoms which I dare say Monsieur de Mortsauf must have described to you since he believed to have them himself"; 260; *220*). It is not simply that the Comte fails to notice in his wife the very disease he imagines in himself, but that somehow Henriette really dies of the Comte's imaginary disease, dies "instead" of him.

But Henriette's disease is more than a realization of the Comte's imaginary disease; it is also a literalization of Félix's figurative disease. In the crisis that the revelation of his affair with Arabelle introduced in his relations with Henriette, Félix tries to explain his predicament to Henriette and thus justify his acts. He explains to her that in men, after a certain age, carnal desire can no longer be subdued by sentiment as it was during childhood. He continues:

> Privé de la nourriture qui le doit alimenter, le coeur se dévore lui-même, et sent un épuisement qui n'est pas la mort, mais qui la précède. La nature ne peut donc pas être longtemps trompée; au moindre accident, elle se réveille avec une énergie qui ressemble à la folie. Non, je n'ai pas aimé, mais j'ai eu soif au milieu du désert. (230)

> (Deprived of the nourishment that should sustain it, the heart feeds upon itself and experiences a drained lassitude which is a kind of forerunner of death. Nature cannot be cheated for long: at the slightest accident it awakens with an energy akin to madness. No, I did not love, but I have thirsted in the middle of the desert; *188*.)

I will come back to this passage later on, but for the moment, I would like to stress that Félix's figurative description of his predicament contains all the elements of Henriette's literal sickness: malnourishment; unquenchable thirst; the madness that results from the "cheating" of the body, from the energy that circulates without object because of this cheating; the confusion or substitution of heart, stomach, and sex.[17]

Henriette literally dies from a disease that in the case of the Comte and Félix remained imaginary or figurative. Her death realizes their "illness"— she has become their symptom—and thus allows them to continue living. Meditating on Henriette's impending death and its effect on him, Félix says:

> J'étais hébété de douleur. . . . Je tâchai de me détacher moi-même de cette force par laquelle je vivais; supplice comparable à celui par lequel les Tartares punissaient l'adultère en prenant un membre du coupable dans une pièce de bois, et lui laissant un couteau pour se le couper, s'il ne voulait pas mourir de faim: leçon terrible que subissait mon âme de laquelle il fallait me retrancher la plus belle moitié. (271–72)

> (I was overcome with grief. . . . I tried to free myself from that force which kept me alive, a torment comparable to the one by which the Tartars punished adultery, by placing a limb of the culprit in a vice, and leaving him a knife to cut it off with, if he did not want to starve to death; a terrible lesson for my soul, compelled as I was to cut off its finest part! *231*.)

By detaching himself from the force that kept him alive, Félix paradoxically saves his own life; by cutting off a limb, by sacrificing his "plus belle moitié," he ensures that he will not die of starvation.[18] It is not clear whether we are in the society/nature of the jungle, where one creature kills the other to ensure its own survival and where individuals can be eliminated, since society "ne voit dans chacun de ses membres que des organes" (160), or in the rational system prescribed by Henriette, where "tout s'arrange," where her death is another act of self-forgetfulness and of giving.[19]

At any rate, Henriette dies of thirst and starvation, of lack of nourishment or the inability to take any nourishment. In her case, the lack of nourishment does not turn into nourishment. These "turns," as we have seen, are possible only when a literal sense is doubled by an imaginary or figurative sense (as when Félix's real mother is doubled by mother nature or when his real childhood is doubled by a metaphorical one). But for Henriette the lack of nourishment does not "turn"; it is not doubled or supplemented by an additional gift that will allow the lack to turn into a gain, the sacrifice of the force of life to become a possibility of life. She simply and literally dies of a lack of nourishment.

According to the text of *Le Lys*, desire is born of a lack (the lack of/in the mother, the lack of love, "the bitter breast")—for both men and women, for both Félix and Henriette. This lack cannot or should not be filled; hence both Félix and Henriette actively assume that lack and perpetuate it by foreclosing the consummation of desire through displacement and postponement. In elaborating his theory on the merits of frustrating desire, Félix can speak for both Henriette and himself: as long as desire is understood in terms of a lack that cannot or should not be fulfilled, there is no difference between males and females. But Félix also insists that for men—unlike women—this movement of displacement and postponement at a certain point has to be delimited: "Un amour sans possession se soutient par l'exaspération même des désirs; puis il vient un moment où tout est souffrance en nous, qui ne ressemblons en rien à vous" ("A love without possession is sustained by the very exacerbation of desire; then there comes a moment when everything is sheer suffering for us, who are so utterly unlike you"; 230; *188*). This delimitation is not only necessary; it is also possible since, for men, "puissance" is not only "potentiality," the mere possibility of the ever-deferred fulfillment of a lack, but also "potency," a positive trait, something that one may "possess": "Nous possédons une puissance qui ne saurait être abdiquée, sous peine de ne plus être hommes" ("We have a potency from which we cannot abdicate, on pain of ceasing to be men"; 188; *230*). We can recognize in this potency that one possesses and that cannot be abdicated the "gift of nature" that cannot be lost. The gift of nature is nothing else than Félix's "male nature." Defined as nature—as a given—phallic potency lies outside the series of substitutions and displacements, which it thus delimits. It is what all elements in the series refer to in the mode of displacement and substitution, but it is not in itself a substitute for anything (it is a given) and hence can never be wasted or lost. Thus, Félix's strategy of endlessly postponing the fullfillment of desire guarantees that desire is not wasted, is kept as pure potentiality; but since, according to him, this potentiality is (for men) also a potency, the displacement and postponement can at a certain point stop without leading to an end or death (indeed, must, to avoid death from "thirst" and "hunger"). It is through this doubling of "puissance" that Félix survives: he does not die from the consummation of desire, nor does he die out of frustrated sexuality. Without such doubling, substitution, postponement, and displacement remain unlimited, without term or, in other words, entail sheer loss (without gain), waste (without return). Let me now quote in its entirety the passage I have been commenting on for the last few pages:

> Un amour sans possession se soutient par l'exaspération même des désirs; puis il vient un moment où tout est souffrance en nous, qui ne ressemblons en rien à vous. Nous possédons une puissance qui ne saurait être abdiquée, sous peine de ne plus être hommes. Privé de la nourriture qui le doit alimenter, le coeur se dévore lui-même, et sent un épuisement qui n'est pas la mort, mais qui la précède. La nature ne peut donc pas être longtemps trompée; au moindre accident, elle se réveille avec une énergie qui ressemble à la folie. Non, je n'ai pas aimé, mais j'ai eu soif au milieu du désert. (230)

(A love without possession is sustained by the very exacerbation of desire; then there comes a moment when everything is sheer suffering for us, who are so utterly unlike you. We have a potency from which we cannot abdicate, on pain of ceasing to be men. Deprived of the nourishment that should sustain it, the heart feeds upon itself and experiences a drained lassitude which is a kind of forerunner of death. Nature cannot be thwarted for long: at the slightest accident it awakens with an energy akin to madness. No, I have not loved but I have thirsted in the middle of the desert; *188*.)

According to this passage, by not abdicating his male power (by keeping the gift, what nature gave him, his nature that cannot change), by precisely limiting the play of substitution (the displacements of desire), arresting the flow of energy, Félix can both satisfy desire—gain nourishment, quench his thirst—and survive satisfaction, survive consummation—escape death.

As Félix stated (and Henriette agreed), the circulation of affect without "inhibition" leads to "horribles affaiblissements," to a state where "notre puissance s'échappe tout entière sans aliment, comme le sang par une blessure inconnue" ("our entire strength leaks away without nourishment, like blood from an unknown wound"; 92; *49*). What stops this hemorrhaging, what stops this movement of displacement and substitution, what serves as a limit, is what is posited as being outside the system of substitution: the literal, the referential, the real. As we have seen, it is this positing of a term outside the system of substitutions (the gift of nature) that allows the system to come into being in the first place (it allows the play of figurative and literal; it allows lack of nourishment to "turn" into nourishment). But Henriette, though she too believes that the lack of an "inhibiting" factor leads to complete loss, does not realize that if the system she is proposing is truly one of unlimited substitution, there is no guarantee that her giving, her self-forgetfulness, will yield a return. At the same time, she does not realize that in society as it is, indifference to "individual worth," which, as we have seen, is the indifference to the materiality of the body on which the possibility of substitution is predicated, is in fact limited—by sexual difference.

One could, of course, argue that at least from Henriette's point of view, her death is a response to and a contestation of Félix's "theory" of the difference between the sexes. Already in her letter, in admitting the sexual arousal caused by his first kiss and her wish to have her resistance overcome, she counters Félix's discourse on the double nature of men by stating that women, too, are double or divided.[20] Now, by her death, she counters his argument that only in men sexual desire (nature), if repressed, returns with an energy "akin to madness": her sickness shows that this is the case with women too. The irony, of course, is that Félix does *not* go mad or die; only Henriette does. According to the text of *Le Lys* (and Henriette's death supports, rather than contests, this point), women and men are equal in being divided, subject to the return of the repressed, but only men have the power to turn this lack into a gain. This is precisely the gendered economy of *Le Lys*.

In describing *Le Lys*'s gendered economy, I have argued that it is produced through an equivocation. This equivocation is not simply that of a certain sliding in particular points in Félix's discourse (for example, the sliding from "puissance" as a virtuality to "puissance" as a power one possesses); it permeates his entire discourse on sexual difference, since it has to do with the very status of this discourse. We can say that since Félix's speech to Henriette, like his entire letter to Natalie, is a performance (or an extended performative—"excuse") designed to produce certain effects, his "theory" of sexual differences could be rightly characterized as "mere words." We then undermine the status of Félix's discourse as a discourse about the world, a discourse of truth (from which we could gain some knowledge). Félix's speech to Henriette and his entire letter, then, have no determined cognitive value, only rhetorical power—the power to posit and to affect others. But Félix's discourse can have its rhetorical effect, its power of persuasion, only if we (and the public within the text) forget this act of positing and (mis)take the posited limit for a given "nature," a "real" prior to and independent of the discourse, which is, then, "about" it. The rhetorical power of the discourse depends on the suppression of its rhetorical power; it both undermines and generates the assumption of its cognitive value.[21]

Since sexual difference is the grounds for Félix's "excuse" and the topic of his "theory," it may be useful to reformulate this point in psychoanalytical (and here, more specifically, Lacanian) terms. Félix's theory of sexual difference is organized around the phallus as a "master signifier" and shows how this master signifier functions within the rhetorical system of substitution and displacement. To use Žižek's formulation, we can say that Félix's discourse shows that the role of this master signifier "is purely structural, its nature is purely performative—its signification coincides with its own act of enunciation; in short, it is a 'signifier without a signified'"; and yet its functioning depends on its being (mis)taken for a "transcendent Guarantee," "a point of supreme plenitude."[22] The text of *Le Lys* allows us to read the tension between these two perspectives.

In reading the game of hide-and-seek between these two aspects of discourse or of the symbolic system, we have to keep in mind both elements in unresolvable tension: on the one hand, the symbolic system is created and sustained by a performative act of positing that is cognitively empty (does not "reflect" the "real") and arbitrary (the real does not include within it the mode of its own symbolization); on the other hand, since this act gives coherence and stability to a system of meaning, its status is obfuscated. Or, put differently again: on the one hand, "reality" as a constructed symbolic system produces the "real" as its effect, but, on the other hand, it is (mis)taken for a symbolization/representation of a prior "real." Thus the "real" is not outside the "symbolic" (spatially or temporally), a realm that has escaped symbolization and hence is totally inaccessible to us; rather, it is outside the symbolic in the sense of being produced by it as its ground and limit.[23] *Le Lys* enacts this production.

In *Le Lys*, then, Balzac has created a rhetorical text, a text whose power does not depend on its cognitive value, since whatever cognitive value it may have is produced by its rhetorical power—or so the text itself tells/shows us. The author of such self-authorizing discourse is not the omniscient observer of the "typical" Balzac text. Apart from the fact that he is far from omniscient, his ability to produce the text depends not on the particular qualities he may have (for example, the ability to observe, read, interpret), but rather on his power, a power assumed and generated by the discourse itself. In *Le Lys* this self-authorizing discourse is shown as perpetuating male power, but male power understood specifically as "word power." If in *La Peau* Balzac assesses literary discourse in relation to the discourse of knowledge par excellence—philosophy—in *Le Lys*, one can argue, he shows the proximity of literature to a discourse whose power is detached from truth value and whose epitome would be, for him, journalism. A few years later, in *Illusions perdues*, Balzac will describe, with a mixture of admiration and disapproval, the practice of journalists. Critics of *Illusions perdues* normally couch Balzac's attack on journalism in terms of the commodification or prostitution of literature: the trouble with journalists is that they are merchants of words, selling their merchandise to the highest bidder. If literature is to avoid such prostitution, it must define for itself a separate artistic sphere, outside the stock exchange (D'Arthez's "cenacle" in *Illusions perdues*; the idea of "art for art's sake" later in the century). But though this is undoubtedly one aspect of Balzac's relation to journalism, our reading of *Le Lys* allows us to understand his concern with journalism (and with literature's proximity to it) somewhat differently: as a concern with the purely rhetorical power of discourse, against which no quarantine may be possible.

CHAPTER 3

Beyond Oppositions, the Limit:
Stendhal's 'Abbesse de Castro'

Every reader of Stendhal is familiar with the underlying oppositions that structure his discourse: France and Italy, the nineteenth century and the Renaissance, passion and vanity, the red and the black. But readers of Stendhal realize quite quickly that these oppositions are not entirely stable. Stendhal's world is not simply dichotomous; it is also a world where vanity cannot be neatly separated from passion, where the spontaneous and natural hero repeats by rote the words of others. A first step toward explaining this curious mixture would be to insist on the ironic stance of a narrator who does not share the oppositional model constructed by his characters but rather undermines it, showing the illusory nature of such oppositions. No doubt, such irony is an essential element of Stendhal's texts, but it is not sufficient for explaining their particular nature because (among other things) the opposition between narrator and characters is itself unstable. Hence the possible conclusion that the world of Stendhal is not a world of oppositions but one of contradictions.

Where critics who hold that the aesthetic value of a literary work depends on its unity would either explain any contradictions away or see them as flaws, others would regard them as the points where the text produces knowledge. Marxist criticism on the whole attributes such contradictions to the represented social world and, more precisely, to its ideological construction. According to this view, the literary text, as a representation of social reality, consciously or unconsciously reveals these contradictions and thus provides a critical purchase on that reality; it produces knowledge of its object.

Recent critics, broadly defined as "new historicist," have questioned precisely this point.[1] They do not deny that the literary text (the novel in our case), as a representation of the social world, shows its contradictions, only the claim that by so doing the novel differentiates and distances itself from the world it represents. This supposed distance of the text from reality, it is argued, is merely a "ruse" of literature: by presenting itself as a representation of social reality, the novel hides the fact that it itself constitutes a social practice, similar to the ones it represents. No more seen as offering us the possibility for a critical distance toward social reality, the novel is regarded as complicit with power. The locus of this complicity is not the thematic content of the text (which very often includes a social critique) but rather the specifically literary means used for representing this reality.

In *The Novel and the Police*, D. A. Miller makes explicit the two points on which his Foucauldian interpretation differs from the Marxist tradition. First, he would stress "the positivity of contradictions": "Contradiction may function not to expose but to construct the ideology that has foreseen and contained it."[2] The text, rather than consciously exposing or unconsciously betraying the contradictions in the represented world, thus producing critical knowledge of it, is actively participating in the construction of this ideology by "putting into place" these contradictions. The emphasis on literature as a social practice, on a par with other practices (rather than a representation of social practices), receives its particular flavor from an argument about what all social practices do: they "put in place" and "put to use" prevailing structures of power; they contribute to the perpetuation of a power that has already foreseen and contained any "oppositional," "demystificatory," or "subversive" aspect they may have.

The second point has to do with form. As I briefly indicated in the Introduction, Miller argues that in the Marxist tradition (or at least in a certain Marxist tradition), what allows the literary text's distance from prevailing ideology is "artistic form."[3] But for Miller himself, it is precisely through its form (whatever that form may be) that the literary text shows its resemblance to other social practices.[4] Though as a representation of social reality the novel can "register" many different things (thus producing at times a contradictory text), through its form it always performs one and the same thing. What the novel in its form "relays" is thus not only independent of *what* it registers but also independent of *how* it registers it. The novel as practice, according to this logic, is equal to the performative function of form, which is abstract and always the same, since it is equally independent of content and form.

By abstracting literary practice from both its content and its form, by positing that it, like all social practices, can do only one thing, Miller not only puts into question the privileged status of literature (or of art in general) as in one way or another above, outside, social practices.[5] More importantly, he denies the very possibility that a practice (literary or not) can articulate a position that is not always already caught in prevailing structures of power. In other words, he contests the possibility not only of critical distance but of freedom—freedom understood not as opposition but as a space of non-determination.

Such a dysphoric view of a world (or a text) of complete determination is symmetrically opposed to the euphoric view of a text (or a world) of complete indeterminacy (the openended, purely metonymical text). Stendhal's texts are very often seen as examples of openendedness since they notoriously lack closure. Thus D. A. Miller, in his earlier book *Narrative and Its Discontents*, locates Stendhal's "crucial values"—"freedom, spontaneity, being oneself"—in the deliberate failure of plots and closure, "in a constantly reenacted recovery of openendedness, that is, a blissful moment of release from the tyranny of narrative control."[6] Should we now simply reverse perspectives and see this openendedness not just as an illusion, but as the "ruse" of literature, the way in which it distances itself from the world of power only so as to better serve it?

In the pages that follow I would like to show how in Stendhal's *Abbesse de Castro* (1839) a sustained undermining of any kind of opposition renders the notion of freedom as opposition to power inoperative. But, I will argue, this undermining does not eliminate all possibility of freedom. Rather, through his practice as a writer and in the structure of his narrative, Stendhal articulates a notion of action that is not contained and foreseen by power—a concept of freedom that is not opposed to, yet is still distinguished from, power. This possibility of a certain kind of freedom depends on the notion of a limit—a limit to "openendedness." Through the use of a limit, Stendhal articulates in *L'Abbesse* not a world or a practice *outside* the play of power, but rather a strategy for differentiating, within social reality, between power and freedom. Though, as we shall see in the next chapter, this point will be problematized in *La Chartreuse de Parma*, it is important to mark its presence in *L'Abbesse*.

I

"Dès le milieu du XVIe siècle, la vanité, le *désir de parestre*, comme dit le baron de Fœneste, a jeté en France un voile épais sur les actions des hommes et surtout sur les motifs de ces actions. La vanité n'est pas de la même nature en Italie. . . . elle a une action plus faible" ("From the middle of the 16th century, vanity, 'le désir de parestre' as the baron de Fœneste calls it, has thrown in France a thick veil on the actions of men, and especially on the motives for these actions. Vanity is not of the same nature in Italy. . . . There its effect is weaker"; 556). In this quotation from the Preface to what became known as *Chroniques italiennes*, we find an all too familiar theme of Stendhal's: the opposition between France and Italy, between vanity and natural behavior. The interest of Italy, especially the Italy of the Renaissance, is that it affords us the possibility of seeing what in France remains covered by the thick veil of vanity; Italy, in other words, represents a promise of transparency.

When one talks about transparency, the savage is never too far away, and indeed the author of the Preface mentions, besides the French and the Italians, the natives of Ceylon called Riccaras, whose true stories ("récits véridiques") were told by a certain Captain Franklin. But the Riccaras' complete lack of vanity, complete transparency, makes them, paradoxically, totally incomprehensible: they are too different, if not from the author himself, at least from the human beings he encounters in his own country: "Ces Riccaras sont trop différents des hommes qui ont été mes amis ou mes rivaux" ("Those Riccaras are too different from the men who have been my friends or rivals"; 556). Italy stands precisely in the middle between the complete transparency that is savagery or lack of civilization and the thick veil of vanity that characterizes this most civilized of nations, France: "Je ne sais si l'on pourrait trouver hors de l'Italie . . . une époque assez civilisée pour être plus intéressante que les Riccaras et assez pure de vanité pour laisser voir le cœur humain presque à nu" ("I don't know if one could find outside Italy . . . a period civilized enough to be more interesting than the Riccaras and sufficiently free of vanity to enable us to see the human heart almost in its nakedness"; 557). From a categorical opposition—between the opacity of modern civilization and the transparency of savagery—we move to a middle ground where the differences are quantitative rather than qualitative, where it is a question of "assez" and "presque." If contemporary civilization masks the human heart in such a way that it is no longer accessible to us, and if savagery gives us a transparent image in which we can no longer recognize ourselves, our only chance of knowledge is to see the human heart through some kind of semitransparent veil. Italy is precisely this possibility and as such presents itself as an object of *reading*: since we have to see through or behind a veil, the simple act of seeing will have to be replaced by an act of reading, of interpretation. Because the Riccaras are completely transparent in their motivations, completely denuded of the veil of vanity, the truth about them transpires, is there simply to be seen, and the stories about their lives and habits are unambiguously "récits véridiques." In Italy, by contrast, signs do not yield their meaning immediately and yet their signification is not entirely opaque. Since the relation between motivation and action is veiled, interpretation will be necessary, but since this veil is thin, it will be possible.

And indeed when, with *L'Abbesse de Castro*, we move from the savagery of the Riccaras to sixteenth-century Italy, to the realm of semitransparency, what we encounter is precisely the necessity and possibility of reading:

> Beaucoup d'historiens, loués encore aujourd'hui par la littérature routinière des académies, ont cherché à dissimuler cet état de choses, qui, vers 1550, forma de si grands caractères. De leur temps, leurs prudents mensonges furent récompensés par tous les honneurs dont pouvaient disposer les Médicis de Florence, les Este de Ferrare, les vice-rois de Naples, etc. (563–64)

> (Many historians, praised even today in the hack literature of the academies, have sought to conceal this state of affairs, which, about the year 1550, was forming such great characters. At the time, their prudent falsehoods were rewarded with all the honors which the Medici of Florence, the Este of Ferrara, the Viceroys of Naples and so forth had at their disposal; *14*.)

The narrator is not the ethnographer Franklin, who sees and lets us see in a totally unmediated fashion; he is, rather, a reader of previous interpretations. His "raw material" is not a reality but accounts about reality; he does not see, or even interpret, human behavior, but rather interprets interpretations. Without getting into the complex question of the relation of the narrative-I to its sources, or the no less complex question of the relation of Henri Beyle to his own presumed sources,[7] it is sufficient for our purposes to say that the narrator of *L'Abbesse* presents himself not as a simple translator and editor, but rather as a critical, unbiased reader who can tell truth from falsehood. The narrator reads both the popular narratives and the official histories (the advice not to read the latter certainly does not apply to him), and through a series of oppositions (between oral and written, spontaneous and official, simple style and ornate rhetoric), he arrives at an interpretative judgment: the official histories, written by people in the pay of the tyrant and serving the interests of those in power, are false: they do not tell the truth, or not the entire truth. To these approved authors with their "écrits publiés sous la censure de [leurs] maîtres" ("publications issued under the official censure of their masters") are opposed the popular chroniclers who wrote "de petits poèms qui racontent avec chaleur la vie des brigands les plus renommés" ("little poems which narrate with ardour the lives of the most renowned brigands"; 562; *13*). These popular poets, rather than being at the service of the tyrant, wrote in opposition to him, and this guarantees the truth of their accounts. Telling the truth is possible only for those who are in the opposition; truth is possible only as a transgression of a law. The narrator can declare himself a champion both of the oppressed people and of truth.

II

The Preface to the *Chroniques italiennes* presents Italy as an intermediary point between absolute transparency and complete opacity. The very fact that the Riccaras are contemporary with modern France contributes to the construction of a logical (rather than historical) scheme, where, between two extreme points, one can find an intermediary zone called Italy, or even "italianity." But *L'Abbesse* does not describe such an intermediary stage. Rather, it *tells a story* that dramatizes before our eyes the passage from one extreme to the other, shows us the very process of the thickening of the veil. Hélène, who starts as a passionate character, becomes vain, is corrupted by civilization: "Nous allons, en effet, assister à la longue dégradation d'une âme noble et généreuse. Les mesures prudentes et les mensonges de la civilisation, qui désormais vont l'obséder de toutes parts, remplaceront les mouvements sincères des passions énergiques et naturelles" ("For we are now about to observe the gradual degradation of a noble and generous nature. Prudent measures and the falsehoods of civilisation, which for the future are going to assail her on every side, will take the place of the sincere impulses of vigorous and natural passions"; 629; *97*). If Hélène's conduct in the latter part of the story is not entirely comprehensible, or better, not entirely predictable, it is because of this veil of vanity obscuring the relation between motivation and action. Her passion, sincerity, and naturalness at the beginning of the story are expressed by the simplicity of telling the truth: "A quoi bon mentir? se disait Hélène. Est-ce que je ne l'aime pas de toute mon âme?" (" 'What is the use of lying?' Hélène said to herself. 'Do I not love him with all my heart and soul?' "; 576; *30*). The truth of this love is transparent to her, to Jules, and to all those around her. In the latter part of the story, by contrast, her conduct toward her lover, Bishop Cittadini, is characterized by a certain opacity of signs: she insults him constantly but, as one of the nuns says at the interrogation following the discovery of their secret affair, "Quand on se parle sur ce ton, c'est qu'il y a bien longtemps que l'on fait l'amour ensemble" ("When people talk in that tone, it means that they have long been making love to one another"; 644; *116*).

Thus Hélène's story repeats or dramatizes the larger course of history, presents the relation between the naturalness of the savages and the veiled behavior of the civilized as a transformation in time. Her story can be seen as an example of History, of world history conceived as a process of "degradation." In passing from the Preface to the story, from the general discussion of the customs of people (the Riccaras, the French, the Italians) to the particular story of an individual (Hélène at the beginning of the story, Hélène at the end of the story), we have moved from a logical, paradigmatic structure (a "synchronic" view in which time is suspended and both "savagery" and "civilization" are essentialized) to a temporal, diachronic sequence where properties are subject to change. Once we look at oppositions not as logical and immutable but as produced in time, it becomes possible to ask about their causes and history.

What, then, causes Hélène's degradation, transforms a natural and passionate woman into a vain one? The first part of *L'Abbesse* uses a scheme that is quite recurrent in Stendhal and that we can find in a simple form in many of the short stories he wrote well before the great novels.[8] This is the story of passion born in spite of or because of obstacles put in its way. Imprisoned in her house, guarded jealously by her tyrannical father and brother, Hélène is by definition desirable, an object of passion for Jules, who sees her from a distance, behind the walls of her house/prison. Her own passion for him is awakened by the opposition of her father and brother, and grows in proportion to this opposition. After their attack on Jules in the garden, Hélène's love for Jules increases: "Cette journée-là avança plus les affaires du jeune homme que six mois de constance et de protestations" ("This day did more to strengthen the young man's position than six months of constancy and protestations"; 576; *30*). Thus, though the first encounter between Jules and Hélène is due to chance, his winning her follows a certain logic. Passion in Stendhal defines itself in opposition to tyranny, and tyranny is tyranny because it attempts to put limitations on passion; every passion is the passion for liberty, for escaping a prison.

The oppositional origin of passion determines the course it will follow. Since passion is generated by tyranny, as an opposition to tyranny, the story of passion follows an inexorable logic, a law. In the conflict between tyranny and passion, passion is always destroyed; it is destroyed either by the force of tyranny—death of the lovers—or, if tyranny itself is for some reason eliminated, passion is eliminated too, is no longer passion, becomes, for example, vanity. The story of Hélène could have been the story of passion destroyed by tyranny: she could have been killed by her father the night of the attack on Jules in the garden; she could have been killed by her brother the night she and Jules, disguised as two monks, were met on the road by the two Campirealis. As the narrator repeats, and as Hélène herself says, this could have been the end of her story, and it would have been better for her; it would have also been a better story, because the story of passion opposed to tyranny is always the story of transparent, well-motivated actions. Tyranny, with its inexorable law, keeps the story on a well-defined course, where a certain beginning leads to a certain end in an undeniably logical way. Unfortunately, this is not what happens in this case. Into the inexorable law of tyranny (which is the law of logical, binary opposition) is introduced a certain contingency—the contingency, specifically, of temporality or of history. Rather than being killed by her father or brother, Hélène remains alive, and it is her brother and father who die. Whereas her death at the hands of either brother or father would have obeyed a strict logic and a necessity (that of the opposition between tyranny and passion), the death of the brother and father does not obey any logic, any necessity, any law, but is rather the result of a chain of circumstances. It is this death, however, this introduction of contingency, of not fully motivated or entirely predictable events, into the logic of opposition that gives the second part of the story its particular shape: from that moment on, tyrannical, physical power is replaced by manipulation through lies and money; the instruments of a primitive, if not savage, power are replaced by the instruments of civilization, and passion in Hélène gives way to vanity.

The relation between passion and tyranny is presented as a logical opposition: tyranny produces passion as its opposition, and from that point on, each reinforces the other by opposing it. The conflict between these two opposed powers cannot be resolved except through the elimination of one of them. It is here that we see the difference between the virtual story (what could have happened but did not) and the actual story told in *L'Abbesse*. In the virtual story, tyranny is so powerful that it ends up destroying passion (killing the lovers), and thus brings about the resolution (hence end) of the opposition. But in the actual story told in *L'Abbesse* (as elsewhere in Stendhal), it is the other possibility that materializes, the one in which tyranny itself is eliminated. And here the resolution of the opposition introduces a change, a transformation: when tyranny is eliminated, passion is no longer passion; it is transformed into vanity. The story continues, telling the history of this vanity, of this loss of passion. Properly speaking, we have a "story" only in this second case (which explains why the first one remains a virtuality); there is a story because there is a transformation, because a narrative element has been introduced into the logical opposition. The cause of this transformation—the elimination of tyranny—cannot be explained by the initial givens of the opposition; in this case, at least, the logical opposition does not include in its definition the possibility of its transformation. This is why the disappearance of tyranny, even when it is caused by the power of passion, cannot be considered the *logical* result of the conflict between these two forces and has to be represented as the unexpected consequence of a contingency, of the intrusion of time and change into what up to now has been a purely logical structure.

It would be idle to speculate on whether Stendhal chose, at a certain point in his career, to write "stories" because of a growing historical awareness (of change, of the intrusion of the contingent) or whether he became aware of this dimension of reality through his practice of narrative. What is nevertheless clear is that if he started out with a certain typology or grid predicated on a logical opposition of two terms (France and Italy, for example), "translating" them into a narrative not only has introduced transformation—the change in time of one term into its opposite (passion turns into vanity, savagery becomes civilization)—but also has shown that the opposition itself, under certain circumstances, may disappear. This means that, at least in *L'Abbesse*, narrative cannot be seen as a translation onto a temporal axis of a meaning that is atemporal (passion and vanity always oppose each other, and the story is but a narrative manifestation of this theme). Rather, the "narrative" aspect modifies the paradigmatic one and, as we shall see, is modified by it.

III

We have seen that in *L'Abbesse*, an initial opposition, logical or typological (between France and Italy, between tyranny and passion), is given a temporal inflection. This inflection allows for the construction of another opposition: that of before and after, past and present. In *L'Abbesse* the two main characters are not presented as constantly oscillating between two opposed states—for example, between understanding and misunderstanding (as are the main characters in Stendhal's earliest novel, *Armance*); nor are they seen as opposed to the world (as are Julien and Mathilde in *Le Rouge et le noir*). Rather, the opposition that defines the characters here is a temporal one, between a "before" and an "after"—between the Hélène and Jules of the beginning of the story, who enjoy perfect communication, and the Hélène and Jules of the second part of the story, who are either passive victims of the manipulations and lies of the outside world or themselves participants in some pretense and disguise (Hélène in her relations with Cittadini; Jules disguised as Colonel Lizzara).

This temporal opposition is always accompanied by a certain nostalgia for the past, for what was "before" and got lost over time (nostalgia for the Italy of the Renaissance, for passion, for tyranny). Since the opposition between before and after, with its accompanying nostalgia for passion and tyranny, has the force of a social critique of the present, and may even be construed as some didactic prescription for what the future should be, it is important to see that, like other oppositions in the story, it is both asserted and undermined. Though the personal story of Jules and Hélène follows the lines of passage from a before to an after, passage from, or the transformation of, passion to vanity, when we move to the larger historical context in which the personal story is couched and of which it is also a dramatization, things are different.

We should note, first, that the social and historical context in which the story of Hélène and Jules is couched is presented in static (paradigmatic) rather than dynamic (temporal) terms. We have already seen that the personal story emphasizes a transformation in time; when we look carefully at the historical context, however, we realize that we are not concerned with a moment of historical transition—we are not at a time of crisis, of revolution or restoration. The historical transformation either has taken place already— the passage from republic to tyranny—or is yet to come—the passage from tyranny to constitutional monarchy or democracy (the latter being the sociopolitical equivalent of vanity). I would like to propose that in the same way that the temporal aspect of the personal story works as a corrective for the tendency to view qualities as logically opposed essences (savagery and civilization, France and Italy), so the static or paradigmatic representation of the historical context acts as a corrective for the nostalgia and idealization of the past that the temporal aspect of the personal story generates.

Before we get to the treatment of the historical context of our story, however, we need to look briefly at its "prehistory," that is, the concept of the republic. In the opening pages, tyrannies are represented in negative terms— they are "les gouvernements atroces"—and the brigands, the heroes of the story, are represented as those who oppose tyranny, the first brigands being "les républicains les plus énergiques, ceux qui aimaient la liberté plus que la majorité de leurs concitoyens" ("the most energetic among the Republicans, those who loved freedom more than the majority of their fellow-citizens"; 564; *15*). As a result, it is all too natural to see the republic as an ideal form of government that has, unfortunately, degenerated into tyranny (later on to be further degenerated into democracy). This interpretation becomes even more attractive if we consider Stendhal's writings on the Italian Renaissance to be a hardly veiled commentary on French contemporary history, where Stendhal himself can play the role of one of those "energetic republicans who loved freedom." In other words, our tendency is to read Stendhal as an author who sees history as a process of degradation, nostalgically idealizing a past that is lost forever.[9]

But this is to misunderstand him. For though it is perfectly obvious, everywhere in Stendhal, that tyrannies are atrocious, they are also what gave "tant d'esprit et de courage aux Italiens du seizième siècle, et tant de génie à leurs artistes" ("so much spirit and courage to the Italians of the 16th century and such genius to their artists"; 561; *11*); and the collapse of the medieval republics is "malheur pour la félicité publique, pour la justice, pour le bon gouvernement, mais . . . bonheur pour les arts" ("misfortune for the general welfare, for justice, for good government, but fortunate for the arts"; 564; 15). For Stendhal, then, history is never a simple process of degeneration or progress; it is always both at the same time. Moreover, the republic gains positive value only at the moment in which it is threatened by tyranny; it is only then that, in opposition to tyranny, republican sentiments can be seen as passion, and precisely as a passion for freedom. Without the opposition to tyranny, republican sentiment, like any other passion, cannot exist: it is mere vanity, a product of "civilization."

In any event, the opposition between republic and tyranny is not my main concern, since it belongs to the "prehistory" of the text. In the story proper, the important opposition is between tyrants and brigands, and these, rather than following each other in a temporal sequence, are contemporaneous, are two opposing elements in a structure: "On peut dire en général que ces brigands furent l'*opposition* contre les gouvernements atroces qui, en Italie, succédèrent aux républiques du Moyen Age" ("Speaking generally, one may say that these brigands were the *Opposition* to the vile governments which, in Italy, took the place of the medieval republics"; 561; 11). Since temporal development has been replaced by logical or structural opposition, it becomes very hard to locate the brigands historically. Contradictory information is given about both their emergence and their decline. On the one hand, they are described as rising to power around the time our story begins ("Dejà, vers 1555, les brigands régnaient dans les environs de Rome"; "Already, around 1555, the brigands reigned in the neighborhood of Rome"; 567; 19) and declining toward the end of the story (when Jules Branciforte comes back from his forced exile in Flanders and is asked by Colonna to be his successor, he expresses his opinion that the days of the brigands may be over). On the other hand, the existence of the brigands reaches as far back as the Middle Ages and earlier ("Les premières histoires qu'on ait écrites en Italie, après la grande barbarie du neuvième siècle, font déjà mention des brigands, et en parlent comme s'ils eussent existé de temps immémorial"; "The earliest histories to be written in Italy, after the great wave of barbarism in the ninth century, make mention already of the brigands, and speak of them as though they had existed from time immemorial"; 564; 15) and stretches to the time of writing, the beginning of the nineteenth century ("même aujourd'hui, le voyageur regarde avec inquiétude au fond de la forêt; il a peur des brigands"; "even today the traveller peers anxiously into the depths of the forest; he is afraid of brigands"; 566; 17). The historical existence of the brigands, their rise and fall as a power at specific moments in European history, is obscured by this temporal breadth; this allows us to think of the brigands as a force that has always existed and will always exist, as the ever-present possibility, beyond historical determination, of opposition to official, institutional power.

But this opposition between the brigands and official power is more apparent than real. Even though we are *told* that the brigands constitute a republican opposition to tyranny and a popular movement, when they are actually *represented*, they appear as merely another power, all too similar to the one they presumably oppose. Thus, Alphonse Piccolomini and Marco Sciarra oppose the powers of the Pope but then negotiate with the powers of Venice; Fabrice Colonna seeks the Pope's legitimization in his battles against the secular power of the Orsinis; and so on. What we find here is not institutional power (Pope or secular government) opposed by some kind of underground, popular power, but a multiplicity of powers whose network of relations is complex and constantly changing. The reigning families who hold official power or are protected by it feel the need to secure their position by recruiting their own army, called the "bravi." In an example for the general state of affairs (which will then be dramatized in our own story in the incident of Bandini and the crucial battle of Ciampi, where Fabio is killed by Jules), we are told:

> Au seizième siècle, le gouverneur d'un bourg avait-il condamné à mort un pauvre habitant en butte à la haine de la famille prépondérante, souvent on voyait les brigands attaquer la prison et essayer de délivrer l'opprimé. De son côté, la famille puissante, ne se fiant pas trop aux huit ou dix soldats du gouvernment chargés de garder la prison, levait à ses frais une troupe de soldats temporaires. Ceux-ci, qu'on appelait des *bravi*, bivaquaient dans les alentours de la prison. (563)

> (In the 16th century, had the Governor of a township sentenced to death a poor inhabitant who had incurred the hatred of the leading family, one often found brigands attacking the prison in an attempt to free the victim; on the other hand, the powerful family, having no great faith in the nine or ten soldiers of the government who were set to guard the prison, would raise at its own expense a troop of temporary soldiers. These latter, who were known as bravi, would install themselves in the neighborhood of the prison; *14*.)

The *bravi* are paid soldiers, mercenaries or "soldats d'aventure," and as such seem opposed to the brigands, who act out of love of freedom, against oppression, with the spontaneous help of the people. But in fact the opposition between the two is not sustained in the text. Jules, the brigand, not only employs "bravi" but is repeatedly called "soldat d'aventure" himself. The followers of Prince Colonna are called "bravi" (570). When Ranuce tries to persuade Jules to join the forces of the prince, he tells him, "tu pourrais être parmi nous un brillant *soldat d'aventure*, et de plus faire ta fortune" ("you might be a brilliant soldier of fortune among us, and, what is more, make your fortune"; 581; *35*). When Jules reveals his secret to Hélène, he tells her, "*je suis brigand et fils de brigand*" ("I am a brigand and the son of a brigand"; 586; *42*), but when he thinks about it, he says to himself, "Que ne dirait pas le seigneur de Campireali s'il [me] savait *soldat d'aventure?*" ("What would not Signor de Campireali say if he knew him to be a soldier of fortune?"; 581; *36*). In one of the battles between the brigands and official power, a certain Ruiz d'Avalos is going to be attacked by the prince's men because he talked disrespectfully about the "soldats d'aventure de la compagnie Colonna" ("soldiers of fortune of the Colonna band"; 582; *37*). And public rumor has it that Hélène is married to the "soldat d'aventure qui avait eu le malheur de tuer son frère" ("soldier of fortune who had had the misfortune to kill her brother"; 598; *57*), but she is also called "femme du brigand" (602; *63*).[10]

Rather than being presented with an official, institutional power opposed by some popular underground movement, then, what we have are different powers, each recruiting its forces in parallel fashion from among the people. The conflict between the brigands and the government is not a conflict between passion and tyranny but a conflict between two passions, or two tyrannies, or at any rate, between two parallel powers whose difference is not intrinsic and qualitative but quantitative, and as such, subject to constant fluctuations.

IV

In the love story of Jules and Hélène, passion was seen as opposed to tyranny, as a power that acts against tyranny and hence is either destroyed by tyranny or, if tyranny itself is destroyed, transformed. In the sociohistorical context, the brigands are in a certain sense on the side of passion, since they are presented as opposing tyranny, as partisans of freedom; and yet tyrants and the leaders of the brigands are all too similar, and their men cannot be clearly distinguished. Earlier I argued that the love story of Jules and Hélène shows the "logical" opposition between tyranny and passion to be subject to historical transformation, brought about by contingencies. We see now that the description of the historical context further demystifies this opposition. What the account of the conflict between brigands and tyrants shows is that power does not reside in one person (or one group of people) whom others simply oppose, defining themselves by and as opposition; rather, we always find a multiplicity of competing powers, whose relations change constantly according to the circumstances.

If indeed the notion of oppositional relations (for example, between tyrants and brigands) is in a sense false, who is responsible for it? The Preface to the *Chroniques* gave us an answer: it is produced by the official histories, for political reasons. These histories, the narrator of *L'Abbesse* tells us, are false by omission: they hide facts (for example, "les empoisonnements et assassinats sans nombre ordonnés par la peur qui tourmentait ces petits tyrants"; "the countless poisonings and assassinations ordered by the fear that used to torment these petty tyrants"; 561; *11*), and thus construct a difference, an opposition, between tyrants and people. Official history "channels" aggression, violence, and passion, and attributes them to the people, thus opposing violence and order, savagery and civilization, people and ruler.[11] But when the narrator at a certain point (or more precisely, in a certain part of his text) wants us to believe in an opposition between savagery and civilization, he is not really different from the official historians he has rejected with so much confidence (whom he has indeed, opposed): he too is imposing an oppositional grid on a reality that is not so structured. In showing the similarities between tyrants and their supposed opposite, the narrator redefines the status of his own discourse: lies and falsehoods are not restricted to official power, producing, by opposition, a true discourse of the people; rather, there are different accounts of events, all interested, all competing for "the last word."

But this deconstruction of the concept of opposition generates, by its very articulation, a new opposition: that between an ideologically motivated "narrative" (*récit*), which constructs false oppositions (or which falsifies by constructing oppositions), and a reality, or history (*histoire*), where a multiplicity of forces exist in varied and complex relations.[12] The latter is the domain of contingency and chance, of indeterminate fluctuations in a complex play of powers, and finds itself structured in terms of oppositions only by the force of a narrative representation. This narrative has a social and political purpose: to limit the violence of all against all by "channeling" it, by giving it a limited, hence legitimate, object. If we return for a moment to our point of departure, we can say that, from this point of view, the semitransparency that characterizes Italy is not due to either that country's status as a "mixed form" between two opposed and immutable qualities or its historical situation as a moment of transition between two forms of social organization or two cultures; rather, this semitransparency is the result of the representation of a historical reality by a narrative that transforms it but through which one can still see it as it really is. The veil that is thrown "sur les actions des hommes et surtout sur les motifs de ces actions" would then be nothing other than the veil of narrative representation, under which one can still see reality—transparent and well-motivated actions. But this reality has also been characterized as the domain of contingency and chance, and it is narrative that, by polarizing forces, represents actions as motivated by a logic—the logic of opposition. Reality, or story (*histoire*), is thus aligned with savagery (the struggle of all against all), which is the domain of transparency, but is also associated with contingency and thus with a lack of clear motivation that up to now has been seen as characteristic of vanity, that is, of civilization. Similarly, narrative (*récit*) is the domain of opacity, of lies, of vanity, but is also the source of oppositional logic, of the well-motivated actions characteristic of transparent passion or the savage. In other words, with this last opposition (which has been generated through the deconstruction of previous sets of oppositions), we find the key terms of the text articulated as a set of contradictions rather than in a paradigm of oppositions. We cannot, in particular, think of the relation narrative/story as a variety of the opposition lies/truth (or its opposite).

V

In fact, in Stendhal the relation between narrative (*récit*) and story (*histoire*) cannot be reduced to a relation of falsification. Narrative for him is not a structure imposed on a history that exists in and of itself, falsifying it for ideological reasons; rather, it has the power to determine reality—it creates rather than interprets it. At the beginning, then, there is a narrative that the story cannot but reenact; the narrative is a destiny that gets accomplished in reality.

The story of *L'Abbesse*, like many other of Stendhal's stories, makes a prophecy its point of departure. The prediction or announcement of a destiny is a narrative, a previous text, that limits and determines the lives of the characters (the story) in the same way that the previous texts Stendhal uses for his novels and stories limit his plots. The story of the Campireali family is announced from the very beginning as a story of destiny; this is why the narrator can say that in this story, though he sees misery everywhere, he cannot locate culpability or fault in anyone (568). After all, a saintly monk of the convent of Monte Cavi "avait prédit au seigneur de Campireali que sa famille s'éteindrait avec lui, et qu'il n'aurait que deux enfants, qui tous deux périraient de mort violente" ("had prophesied to Signor de Campireali that his family would be extinguished with him, and that he would have but two children, each of whom was to perish by a violent death"; 568–69; *20–21*). This prediction is the first cause of all that follows or, to use the terms of *Le Rouge et le noir*, it is the "first step," and it announces death, the end that is going to follow. Between this beginning and this end, the entire story of *L'Abbesse* unfolds.

As with any story of destiny, where we know from the start what the end is going to be, *L'Abbesse* does not have true temporality (open toward the future, toward the unpredictable) and depends for every transformation on spatial change. Thus, Campireali, who cannot find a wife in his own country because of the prediction, attempts to avert destiny and goes to Naples to look for a wife. He there finds Victoire Carafa, "une femme capable, par son génie, de changer sa mauvaise destinée, si toutefois une telle chose eût été possible" ("a wife capable, by her intelligence, of averting his evil destiny, had such a thing been possible"; 569; *21*). But destiny cannot be averted, and its fulfillment takes, as always, the form of irony: Victoire Carafa, the one woman who could have averted destiny, becomes the tool for its fulfillment, since it is her manipulations and intrigues that bring about the degeneration and death of their daughter, Hélène.

The fulfillment of destiny through the ruse of irony gives the plot its shape, which is that of deferral (of death) and displacement (of aggression, of desire). To show her love for Jules, in response to the increased hostility of her father and brother, Hélène proposes that they spend the night in his deserted house at the outskirts of the town. Disguised as two monks, they encounter the old and young Campireali on the road. Fabio stops them for a moment and threatens to lift the hoods that cover their heads to get a better look at them. At this, Jules seizes his dagger, ready to kill Fabio to protect himself and Hélène. But the danger is averted, and the two lovers continue unharmed on their way to the house, where they spend the night. Just as they are about to consummate their love, Jules thinks that this is the occasion for him to make a true sacrifice to Hélène by resisting his desire; at the same moment, they hear the bells of the monastery ringing, and Hélène echoes his inner thoughts by, asking him to make a sacrifice to the Madonna. Thus morning arrives, and nothing has happened: nobody is killed; love is not consummated.

But what did not happen on that night, on that road or in that garden, will happen on other nights, on other roads or in other gardens. The battle of Ciampi, where Fabio discovers Jules's identity by lifting his hood up and insulting him, bringing about his own death, is thus the fulfillment of a destiny that was only momentarily averted the other night. Jules's attack on the convent of Castro, the battle and bloodshed in the garden of the convent, is a displacement of the sexual act, of the violation that has not taken place in the garden of his house.[13] Or, as we have already seen, since Hélène did not give herself to Jules, she will give herself to his degraded substitute (degraded because a substitute), Cittadini; since passion was not killed by tyranny—since Hélène was not killed that night on the road by her brother—it will be killed by vanity; she ends up, as she herself says, being killed by the manipulations and lies of her mother. Destiny cannot be averted; it can only be postponed. The detour one takes to escape it only ensures its fulfillment, which, though deferred, is no less inevitable.

There is no doubt that *L'Abbesse* is the story of the fulfillment of destiny in the ironic mode of deferral and displacement. The narrative (of destiny), rather than falsifying the story, determines it; it is a force that limits the freedom (of the characters, of the narrator) from both sides (beginning and end). To better characterize the relation between narrative and story, we can borrow, by way of analogy, the description of the *commedia dell'arte* given by the narrator in *La Chartreuse de Parme*: only the general sketch of the plot ("le plan seul de la comédie") is posted on the wall of the theater, and the actors make up the lines as they go along.[14] The same can be said of most of Stendhal's novels and stories. Typically, the main lines of the plot are predetermined, a given, borrowed from a previous text. On the level of narration, these predetermined lines are set, for example, by the newspaper account of the trial of Antoine Berthet in *Le Rouge*, the chronicle of the Farnese family in *La Chartreuse*, and the manuscript describing the transgression of the abbess and the bishop and their ensuing trial in *L'Abbesse*; on the level of the story, they are set by the piece of newspaper Julien finds in the church of Verrière, the various prophesies telling Fabrice of his future imprisonment and death, and the prediction about the destiny of the Campireali family. But within these predetermined lines, an "improvisation" takes place, whereby the characters and the narrator are free to "amplify," that is, to speak and act independently of the imposed plan. The feeling we have in reading Stendhal that the plot is infinitely expandable or infinitely contractable (that is, that there is no compelling reason why it is the way it is), that entire episodes can be eliminated or, conversely, enlarged, rendered with greater and greater detail—this feeling testifies to the fact that characters and narrator enjoy a great measure of freedom to create the story, that for most of the time, they are free to follow nothing other than their own will. Most of the energy of Stendhal's characters and narrators goes into this act of improvisation, and most of their—and the reader's—delight is in this "middle."

The text, then, consists of two elements: a source, another narrative that determines the main lines of the story, especially the end, and that functions as a destiny, that is, provides reason or motivation for actions; and a plot, a story that is unforeseeable and contingent, and where the characters act freely, without being determined by this narrative-destiny. This free and contingent plot cannot produce a necessary and well-motivated end and is hence always, in principle, interminable. If the characters (and narrator) are left free to act, they act in an unpredictable manner and act interminably;[15] the only thing that can bring their story to an end is an external intervention. Despite Stendhal's own characterization of the novel as a "mirror," this external determination does not originate in "reality" but stems from another narrative—be it some manuscript used by Stendhal or the narrator, or some prediction given to one of the characters. This intervention brings the story to its end, an end that consequently cannot be seen as produced inevitably by the series of events preceding it. The end is the result of the intervention of another element (of an elment of otherness) and is hence always a violent rupture. The story is neither a direct line between beginning and end nor a detour, a somewhat longer course toward the end. Between beginning and end, there is a "middle," which does not contain the end in a state of potentiality, ready to be realized later on. The middle is not subordinated to the end: the end is not its end and goal—it is a gratuitous play, absolute freedom.

We can use as an emblem for the entire story of *L'Abbesse* the state of affairs toward its end: Pope Gregory XIII has just died in 1585, and "le règne de désordre commença avec le siège vacant" ("disorder reigned as soon as the See was vacant"; 646; *119*). In this period between two orders, between two fathers, between two laws, there is no law. Everything is possible; all is chance and power play: "pendant le siège vacant, les lois étaient muettes, chacun songeait à satisfaire ses passions, et il n'y avait de force que la force" ("during a vacancy of the See, laws were mute, everyone thought of gratifying his own passions, and there was no force but brute force"; 647 *120*). But this period where everything is possible, where nothing is predictable, is only a "pocket of time" delimited at both ends by a power that can only be obeyed or opposed. Inside this delimited domain, all are free to "satisfy their passions." Since passion in Stendhal is always passion for freedom, the freedom to satisfy one's passions is in fact a freedom that has no purpose other than itself. This "freedom for freedom's sake" cannot be distinguished from absolute force, that is, from the sheer exercise of power, independent of any specific goal. What happens in this "pocket of time," in this "story" framed from both sides by the narrative, is, in other words, not just the exercise of absolute freedom but also the exercise of absolute power, unharnessed to any goal.

The figure who exemplifies this mode of action is Hélène's mother, who, as the narrator says, acts not out of a desire to reach a certain goal but out of the "manie de régner." Her actions become more and more extravagant, less and less "proper," in the sense that they are increasingly out of proportion to their presumed goal, since in fact they have no real goal other than the exercise of power (through manipulation, intrigue, plot).[16] Think of the elaborate scheme of writing a series of false letters imitating the handwriting of Jules and showing his passion for Hélène dying. But this is nothing com-

pared with the next scheme: subsidizing the marriage of Cardinal Santi-
Quatro's niece to Colonna's son in exchange for Hélène's nomination to the
post of the abbess of the convent, with the complex charade of multiple faked
lawsuits necessary for this transfer of money to take place. Yet for all its
complexities, even this scheme is relatively simple compared with the last
one, the plot to rescue Hélène from her prison by way of an enormous
underground tunnel, involving as its does the nightly spreading of incredible
amounts of dirt all over Rome. The number of people and the amounts of
money that all these projects require become larger and larger, and the purpose tends to disappear under the mass of letters, lawsuits, and finally, dirt.

VI

We see, then, that the narrative of destiny functions in the text of Stendhal in a very specific way: rather than imposing itself at every step as an
inevitability that shapes the story (or the narration), it functions only as
a limit. The narrative is a force that limits the story by imposing on it an
end and a finality it does not have in itself. How can we characterize this
narrative-limit? It is, first of all, totally arbitrary; the announced destiny is
presented neither as a consequence of past actions nor as a punishment. It is
announced one day, without any reason; it is a text that one reads by chance
(as in *Le Rouge*) but whose authority is never questioned. It is also, to the
extent that such a thing is possible in language, without any content.[17] The
only thing it announces is that there is a beginning (the "first step" of *Le
Rouge*), and even more explicitly, that there will be an end.[18] That this end
will be a violent one means only that it will not be an end produced by
internal causes, an organic or well-motivated end, a natural death, but will
instead come from the outside, the result of the arbitrary destiny-limit.[19] The
narrative-limit, then, is an arbitrary force, without meaning other than its
existence as an external limit, and whose existence as a limit is accepted
without question by both characters and narrator. This acceptance, however,
does not transform the limit into an "inner necessity"; nor does it endow it
with meaning. It remains external.

It is clear that in his literary practice, Stendhal could not operate without
this narrative-limit, and that at least in this sense, he created characters in his
own image. We can now understand better why. What the reading of *L'Abbesse* has demonstrated is the systematic undermining in Stendhal of the
notion of opposition, whether articulated logically (as the opposition between two coexisting terms) or historically (an opposition between a before
and an after), or whether it takes the shape of an opposition between reality

and representation. With this, the possibility of freedom as opposition to power has been undermined. Once the possibility of oppositional freedom is discarded, the only notion of freedom left is that of absolute freedom. But in itself the behavior we call absolute freedom cannot be distinguished from the absolute exercise of power; it is only when we see it as limited by an external force that we can understand it to be, in relation to this determining force, an exercise of freedom. One needs, then, to limit freedom in order to make it possible. Without such a limit, freedom will be indistinguishable from power or force, and it is this confusion that Stendhal seeks to prevent. The limit is what allows him to distinguish freedom from power (rather than oppose them). The narrative-limit in Stendhal is a literary device that allows one to define, in a world of contradictions (and not of oppositions), a certain possibility of freedom.

CHAPTER 4

The Prison House
of Parma

~

La Chartreuse de Parme (1839) was written at about the same time as
L'Abbesse de Castro, and many critics have pointed out its affinity with the
Chroniques italiennes in general and L'Abbesse is particular. Clearly, La Chartreuse can be regarded as the longest and most developed of the Italian chronicles; and yet some differences come immediately to mind, the most obvious
of which is that, in La Chartreuse, the material drawn from the old chronicle
has been transposed from the sixteenth to the nineteenth century.[1] Given that
in Stendhal's system of values, the opposition between the Renaissance and
the nineteenth century is as important, and of the same nature, as that between Italy and France, between passion and vanity, the "modernization" of
the chronicle must be of some consequence. If the nineteenth century is
separated from the Renaissance by a historical gulf that makes passion impossible, or more precisely, reduces passion to its parodic imitation, vanity, then
transposing a Renaissance chronicle to the nineteenth century would result in
a parodic representation. Just as the Prince of Parma models himself on, and is
ultimately a caricature of, Louis XIV, so, one can say, this modern novel
models itself on a Renaissance chronicle (which it copies and imitates) and
presents a parody of both passion and politics. The historical difference between past and present that calls for imitation also makes perfect imitation
impossible, and parody is the sign of this gap between model and imitation.

But the imitation of the past, even if imperfect and parodic, suggests that
the past is not entirely past (that is, not altogether different), that in some
sense it is still present. And indeed the present represented in the novel is not
in symmetrical opposition to the past. If the Renaissance is characterized by
the convergence of tyranny with passion (political, erotic, artistic), its op-

posite for Stendhal is "democracy in America," characterized by equality, mediocrity, and vanity ("le culte du *dieu* dollar. . . . [Le] respect qu'il faut avoir pour les artisans de la rue, qui par leurs votes décident de tout"; "the cult of the 'almighty dollar' and the respect that had to be shown to ordinary men of the working class who by their votes decided everything"; 115; *130*). The context for the novel, however, is not this American dystopia, but Parma.[2] And Parma can be seen as an intermediary space (or time), both (or neither) past and (nor) present.

Such middle ground is not unique to *La Chartreuse*. As we saw in the last chapter, even in a sixteenth-century "chronicle" like *L'Abbesse*, the tragic conflict between passion and tyranny cannot be for Stendhal a subject for a story (or the whole story); it is only a virtual story (what could have happened but did not) or the first stage of a story, which then follows a different course. This is because Stendhal writes a Renaissance "chronicle" but lives in the "post-Waterloo" world of weak fathers and constitutional monarchs, a world in which tyranny is inefficient or only a charade. To this extent, *La Chartreuse* merely makes explicit a temporal predicament that in some sense operates in all the *Chroniques*.

I would like to argue, however, that *La Chartreuse* does more than that. By transposing the ancient chronicle into the present, Stendhal shows the present to be inhabited by the past as well as different from it. This historical consciousness (which we will find again in James's *Awkward Age*) undercuts not only the nostalgic idealization of the past (as totally different from the present), but also the view of the present as in some sense "beyond" the past— a vantage point from which one can apprehend the past, turn the "pastness" of the past (its being irrevocably lost) into its knowledge. With both nostalgia and irony in some sense undermined, characters in *La Chartreuse* find themselves peculiarly situated in time, in a "middle" without a firm, or clearly defined, beginning and end. Thus, even though *La Chartreuse*, like *L'Abbesse*, has its story framed by a previous text, the transposition of this previous text into the present has brought the frame into the picture, the beginning and end into the middle. And thus the "freedom" or relative indeterminacy of the middle has been compromised. In what follows, I will argue that the limited freedom (or freedom made possible by a limit) of *L'Abbesse* is problematized in *La Chartreuse*. Since its possibility depended in part on a distinction between an external limit and the interior it limits, I will discuss the ways in which the dichotomy exterior/interior gets complicated in the novel. This will have to do primarily with the relation between the interiority of a subject and what is presented as exterior to it (masks, conventional customs, a previous or unknown narrative or text). My reading will start with an analysis of the text's parodic aspect, where the difference between past and present is predominant and where, concomitantly, masks, imitations, and conventional customs are seen as sheer exteriority. I will then move on to an analysis of the aspects of the text that show an interior space of freedom to be determined by what has been considered sheer exteriority, thus abolishing the line of demarcation.

I

The parodic aspect of *La Chartreuse* is most explicit in Fabrice's elaborate love affairs with Marietta and Fausta.[3] These episodes resemble the love stories Stendhal told in his early writings, as well as in *L'Abbesse de Castro*, where the woman is imprisoned by a cruel "tyrant" and passion is born out of opposition to this tyrannical power. But though Fabrice's situation here recalls that of Jules in *L'Abbesse* or of Pietro Buonaventuri and Stradella in earlier stories,[4] he is not the exemplary lover for the very simple reason that he repeatedly fails to feel any passion (and this is what accounts for the repetition of love affairs). Fabrice, we can say, is a parody of the passionate lover; he imitates the passionate lover, an imitation whose other name is vanity. The lack of passion is manifested, as always, by a feeling of boredom (213; *227*), which, together with vanity, constitutes the "modern" predicament. And it is this predicament that accounts for the tone of comedy, the charade of quid pro quo's that characterizes this part of the novel. After the elaborate comedy of errors at the church of Saint-Jean, la Fausta is "femme passionée," her jealous guardian, Comte M——, pulls out his sword, and the next day, the prison house seems more of a prison than ever with its windows "soigneusement fermées" (218; *233*). Everything goes according to the old plot of tyranny and passion reinforcing each other in their conflict—except that Fabrice does not feel any love: bored, "la plaisanterie commença à lui sembler longue" (218; *233*). We can say that the tone of comedy, as well as Fabrice's lack of passion and boredom, derives from the fact that in his time and place, all he can do is imitate, merely play the role of the passionate lover who rescues the tyrannically guarded woman, and that this imitation fails to produce passion, can produce only "amour vanité."

As we have seen, the story of passion's opposition to tyranny cuts across the line separating private from public, the erotic from the political. The passionate lover is both a "son" opposing a tyrannical "father" who holds the woman captive and a "liberal" opposing an oppressor and motivated by the passion for freedom. But in *La Chartreuse* this convergence of the erotic and the political, like everything else, undergoes a transformation. During much of the first part of the novel, Fabrice's actions are motivated by his fear of being sent to prison for political reasons—for his presence at the battle of Waterloo and his alleged spying for Napoleon. But this political transgression, his opposition to Austrian tyranny and his support for the man who freed Italy, is at a certain point forgotten. From a certain point on, Fabrice is not followed by an Austrian police force bent on sending him to the Spielberg for his political sympathies; rather, he is escaping the spies of the Prince of Parma, who wants to send him to the citadel for a petty "crime of passion"—the murder of the mediocre actor Giletti for the "love" of a little actress. Thus the relation between the public and the private, world history and individual story, is not one of mutual support: the latter is a parodic degradation of the former. When Rassi, following the Prince's instructions, attempts to "politicize" the murder of Giletti and treat it as a liberal plot against the Prince, the passion for freedom so celebrated in *L'Abbesse* turns into a fiction created by an unscrupulous politician for the sake of court intrigue. At the same time, it is obvious to everybody in Parma that Fabrice's imprisonment has very little to do with his murder of Giletti: "au fond, le meurtre de Giletti était une bagatelle, et l'intrigue seule était parvenue à en faire quelque chose" ("After all, the murder of a man like Giletti was a mere trifle, and intrigue alone had contrived to make it something of importance"; 251; 265 [see also 363; 376]). Fabrice is persecuted neither for a crime of passion (he does not really love Marietta; Giletti is too insignificant to count) nor for a political crime (his "spying" for Napoleon is just a lie; it is now forgotten; the liberal plot is just a fiction). His imprisonment and sentence stem from a complex comedy of intrigues involving several players (the Prince, Gina, Mosca, la Raversi), each motivated by various, often contradictory, desires.

Fabrice is neither a passionate lover nor a liberal fighting for the cause of freedom for the same reason that the Prince of Parma is not really a tyrant but just a parody of one, and the liberal opposition to his power, a parody of conspiracy and revolution. The parody of tyranny and of all forms of opposition is the other side of the imitation of models; it indicates that the past is different from the present, the model from the self that imitates it. What characterizes *La Chartreuse* in general is that no form of imitation (and we can include here masks, invented identities, lies, representations) "sticks." Rather than producing compelling illusions of reality, their fictitious nature always transpires (every mask is revealed, every lie is discovered, all representations are known to be fictions).[5] From this perspective, role playing, masks, fictions (which belong to the "present"), are always perceived as such: they are not "confused" with the models, with the past, and they remain external to the subject who adopts them.

II

The Prince of Parma is explicitly depicted as a parody of the absolute monarch: trying to imitate Louis XIV in the nineteenth century, he is inevitably a caricature, a mock monarch. The choice of Louis XIV as the model of the monarch suggests that what is lost forever for the nineteenth century, and what the Prince, through imitation, tries in vain to recreate, is the belief that kingship inheres in the person of the king. By imitating the gestures of Louis XIV, the Prince shows that royal attributes do not coincide with his own person, since he needs to borrow the gestures of another to assume the royal status he craves. The Prince is separated forever from the model he tries to imitate, and it is his imitation that shows this separation. But the Prince's failed imitation (failed because we can see under it the model with which it tries in vain to coincide) is not only a sign of nostalgia (the impossibility of capturing the past); it is also a sign of the present's ironic (enlightened) difference from the mystified beliefs of the past. If the Prince cannot be Louis XIV, it is because the Enlightenment that separates them has exposed the myth of the divine right of kings by arguing (and demonstrating) that the king is a king only because people stand in the relation of subjects to him. The difference between past and present yields nostalgia and a sense of loss, but also an ironic demystification of the illusions that characterize the past by a superior understanding possible in the enlightened present.

The Prince has some other, less obvious models besides Louis XIV: his Renaissance forefathers and their contemporaries. These Renaissance figures (who are described also in the chronicle on which the novel is based, as well as in other *Chroniques italiennes*) are tyrants who exercise brute force on all those around them to satisfy their own personal interests and pleasures. They imprison and poison their enemies and remain tyrants by virtue of their power and as long as their power is supreme (they can always be defeated by a stronger power, as in the story of the Duke of Milan and Vespasien Del Dongo; 168; *182*). This Renaissance myth of brute force intersects with that of the ancien régime through the image of the prison (Bastille, Castel San Angelo, Spielberg).

Though the novel presents the Prince as a "souverain absolu" (92; *107*) who, like the tyrants of the Renaissance, knows all his subjects-enemies personally,[6] who, like an absolute monarch, can imprison for no good reason (93; *107–8*), who never grants a pardon (111; *126*), he is only a mock tyrant, fearful of the (pseudo) liberals who may be hiding under his bed. True, the tyrants of the Renaissance were also tormented by the fear of their enemies (as we are told in *L'Abbesse*, 362); but the sixteenth-century chronicles convince us that they (as well as their enemies) had good reason to be so afraid. *La Chartreuse*, on the other hand, makes clear that the enemies of the Prince are paper tigers; and even though the Prince is said to be universally feared, his representation as a despot is not supported by the events of his reign set out in the narrative. True, the Prince has had two "liberals" who allegedly conspired against him hanged; but this conspiracy was only a fiction, its suppression a parodic imitation of a gesture, that even in the past was somewhat empty.[7] More important, these two liberals are not in any way present in the novel, except as disembodied initials. When Mosca tells Gina how Rassi convinced the Prince that he should hang the two liberals, he mentions that "l'exécution de l'un d'eux, le compte L..., fut atroce ("the execution of one of them, Count L——, was atrocious"; 106; *121*); after Fabrice's imprisonment, when Gina thinks she may need to buy Rassi's favors, she speaks of him as "ce monstre, encore tout couvert du sang du comte P. et de D.!" ("That monster still steeped in the blood of Count P—— and of D——!; 267; *281*), though a page earlier, she thought of one of these liberals as "ce pauvre L..."; and Ludovic, when ordered to flood Parma after Fabrice's escape, thinks of this as a revenge against the people of Parma, who were so sure "que monsignore Fabrice allait être empoisonné comme le pauvre L..." (that Monseigneur Fabrice was going to be poisoned like poor L——"; 372; *385*). Though P—— and D—— are mentioned several times as two dead liberals, they also seem to be alive and after a good job. When Mosca describes his plan to start an "ultra" newspaper, he mentions that "les graves personnages P. et D." are eager to become editors (118; *134*). Of course there can be more than one person with the initial P or D, more than two liberals killed, P——, D——, and L——; but my point is that this uncertainty indicates the insubstantiality of these characters within the novel.

The Prince's power over his citizens is symbolized by the prison house of Parma. But so far as we know, the Farnese tower, this transposed Bastille where aristocratic privilege is exercised without check or opposition,[8] this modern version of the dungeon of ruthless Renaissance tyrants, this citadel, holds only two prisoners: the one Gina meets during her first visit to the tower and Fabrice. The first, freed at Gina's intervention, probably deserved to be in prison ("cet homme se trouva un demi-coquin, une âme faible; c'était sur ses aveux que le fameux Ferrante Palla avait été condamné à mort"; "this man turned out to be a bit of a rascal and a weak character; it was on the strength of his confessions that the famous Ferrante Palla had been sentenced to death"; 112; *127*), and Fabrice (who is also freed thanks to Gina's intervention) can be considered wrongfully kept in prison only on the grounds that, as an aristocrat, he ought not to be punished for killing an insignificant and mediocre actor like Giletti. But it is Gina (and Mosca) who insist on this "old regime" aristocratic privilege: "La mort d'un être ridicule tel que Giletti ne lui [Gina] semblait pas de nature à être reprochée sérieusement à un del Dongo. Combien de Giletti nos ancêtres n'ont-ils pas envoyés dans l'autre monde, disait-elle au comte, sans que personne se soit mis en tête de leur en faire un reproche!" ("The death of a ridiculous creature like Giletti did not seem to her the sort of thing for which a del Dongo could be seriously blamed. 'How many Gilettis have our ancestors not sent into the next world,' she said to the Count, 'without anyone ever taking it into his head to re-proach them for it?' "; 201–2; *215*). In the circumstances, it is difficult to think of Gina as "liberating" the prisoners, since the grounds for this "liberation" are whim or privilege.[9]

Even before the last lines of the novel, then, the prison of Parma is "empty"—its horror, like the tyranny of the Prince, has the status of a fiction we are asked to accept without any "proof." Significantly, everything that has to do with the prisoners has the same status, can be characterized as stories rather than facts:

> Ces malheureux prisonniers de la citadelle sont au secret le plus rigoureux, et l'on fait des histoires sur leur compte. Les libéraux prétendent que, par une invention de Rassi, les geôliers et confesseurs ont ordre de leur persuader que, tous les mois à peu près, l'un d'eux est conduit à la mort. Ce jour-là les prison-niers ont la permission de monter sur l'esplanade de l'immense tour . . . et de là ils voient défiler un cortège avec un espion qui joue le rôle d'un pauvre diable qui marche à la mort. (94)

> (These unfortunate prisoners in the citadel are kept in the most rigorously secret confinement, and all sorts of stories are told about them. The Liberals assert that, following a bright idea of Rassi's, the gaolers and confessors have orders to make them believe that, once a month, one of them is led out to die. That day the prisoners are given permission to go up on to the platform of the huge tower, . . . and from there they see a procession wending its way with a spy who plays the part of some poor devil going to his death; *109*.)

But we cannot dismiss the Prince's representation as a tyrant as a simple misrepresentation; on the contrary, the novel suggests not so much that the Prince's power is a fiction as that a fiction is at the source of his power, a fiction that we have no reason to believe but that produces real effects.

The fiction of the Prince-despot created by the narrative has its equiv-alent within the novel in the legal fictions created by Rassi. In exercising power through the manipulation of the legal system, the Prince shows the kind of power he holds: a power to which others submit despite their under-standing of its true nature. Nobody in Parma believes in the legal fictions

Rassi concocts (even though he sometimes says the truth, as in the case of the murder of the Prince). Everyone takes them for fiction, but this "demystified" view does not prevent people from going along with the fiction. On the contrary. People go along with it, cynically and opportunistically, by choice.[10]

The prison, this symbol of the Prince's power—"cette fameuse citadelle de Parme, terreur de toute la Lombardie" (93; *107–8*)—is constructed precisely by means of such fiction. On the occasion of Fabrice's imprisonment, we read:

> Cette tour Farnèse où, après trois quarts d'heure, l'on fit monter Fabrice, fort laide à l'extérieur, est élevée d'une cinquantaine de pieds au-dessus de la plateforme de la grosse tour et garnie d'une quantité de paratonnerres. Le prince mécontent de sa femme, qui fit bâtir cette prison aperçue de toutes parts, eut la singulière prétention de persuader à ses sujets qu'elle existait depuis longues années: c'est pourquoi il lui imposa le nom de *tour Farnèse*. Il était défendu de parler de cette construction, et de toutes les parties de la ville de Parme et des plaines voisines on voyait parfaitement les maçons placer chacune des pierres qui composent cet édifice pentagone. Afin de prouver qu'elle était ancienne, on plaça au-dessus de la porte de deux pieds de large et de quatre de hauteur, par laquelle on y entre, un magnifique bas-relief qui représente Alexandre Farnèse, le général célèbre, forçant Henri IV à s'éloigner de Paris. (290–91)

> (This Farnese Tower, to which, after an interval of three quarters of an hour, Fabrice was conducted, had a very unattractive exterior; it rises some fifty feet above the platform of the great tower and is adorned with a number of lightening conductors. The Prince, who, in a fit of anger at his wife's conduct, built this prison visible from all the country round about, had the singular desire to persuade his subjects that it had stood there for many years: that is why he gave it the name of the Farnese Tower. It was forbidden to make any reference to this building; yet from all parts of the city of Parma and from the plains around it, people could clearly see the masons laying each of the stones which compose this pentagonal edifice. In order to prove its antiquity, there was placed above the door, two feet wide and four feet high, which forms its entrance, a magnificent bas-relief representing Alexander Farnese, the famous general, forcing Henri IV to withdraw from Paris; *304–5*.)

The Prince who constructed the tower sought to legitimize his actions and his power by claiming that the tower/his power had been there all along, was hence not "constructed." The people see this act of legitimization for the fiction it is, but they go along with it, and thus make it, and the Prince's power, real. To say that the people go along with this fiction because the Prince has the power to imprison them if they do otherwise is true, but this "truth" shows the clear circularity of the argument: it is their acceptance of the fiction that allows the Prince to have the power to ensure that they accept it.

As opposed to Louis XIV or the Renaissance tyrant, the rule of the Prince of Parma is made possible neither by a myth in which the subjects truly believe nor by brute force. We can say that the people of Parma behave *as if* the construction of the tower dated from the fifteenth century, *as if* Rassi's legal fictions were true, *as if* the Prince were Louis XIV or Cesare Borgia, though they know full well that this is not the case.[11] And it is this "as if" behavior that gives the Prince his power and produces, finally, a belief in that fiction.

III

The discrepancy between action (external) and belief or disbelief (internal) that characterizes the people of Parma is spelled out as a deliberate mode of conduct in the advice Fabrice receives at various points in his life. This advice always consists of the injunction to follow a certain mode of behavior he clearly does not believe in (or rather, to follow it whether he believes in it or not). Thus when, back from Waterloo, Fabrice escapes to Novare to avoid being arrested by the Austrian police, the canon Borda advises Gina:

> Il fallait que dans son exile à Romagnan Fabrice [ne] manquât pas d'aller à la messe tous les jours. . . . Il ne devait fréquenter aucun homme passant pour avoir de l'esprit, et, dans l'occasion, il fallait parler de la révolte avec horreur, et comme n'étant jamais permise. . . . [En] générale, montrer du dégoût pour la lecture, ne jamais lire. . . . Enfin . . . il faut surtout qu'il fasse ouvertement la cour à quelqu'une des jolies femmes du pays, de la classe noble, bien entendu. (86–87)

> (During his exile at Romagnano it was essential that Fabrice should . . . go to Mass everyday . . . should associate with no one who was reputed to have a mind of his own and, on occasion, should speak of revolution with horror and as something never to be permitted to occur. . . . In general he should show a distaste for reading. . . . And lastly . . . he must in particular pay court openly to one of the pretty women in the district—one of noble birth, of course; *102–3*.)

Borda may seem here to be advising Fabrice to act hypocritically, to appear the opposite of what he actually is in order to hide his true feelings and beliefs. But since we do not know what Fabrice really is, since he is more or less a collection of disguises and roles, this interpretation is somewhat questionable. And indeed, when this kind of advice is repeated by Gina later on, in her much cited invocation of the "rules of the game," it becomes clear that something quite different is at stake. Gina tells Fabrice: "Crois ou ne crois pas à ce qu'on t'enseignera, *mais ne fait jamais aucune objection*. Figure-toi qu'on t'enseigne les règles du jeu de whist; est-ce que tu ferais des objections aux règles du whist?" ("Believe or not, as you choose, the things they teach you, *but never raise any objection*. Imagine that you are being taught the rules of the game of whist; would you take objection in any way to the rules of whist?"; 117; *132*.) Gina has used the same analogy before to describe life at court: "Une cour, c'est ridicule . . . mais c'est amusant; c'est un jeu qui intéresse, mais dont il faut accepter les règles. Qui s'est jamais avisé de se récrier contre le ridicule des règles du whist? Et pourtant une fois qu'on est accoutumé aux règles, il est agréable de faire l'adversaire *chlemm*" ("A court . . . is quite a ridiculous thing, but it is amusing. It's a game that interests you, but in which you have to conform to the rules. Whoever thought of protesting against the absurdity of the rules of whist? And yet, once you are accustomed to the rules, it is delightful to beat your opponent by winning all the tricks"; 99; *114*). Thus, if one follows certain customs or modes of conduct, it is not out of hypocrisy, not to hide one's true feelings or beliefs, but because these are the rules of the game; these rules, customs, or ways of behavior are arbitrary, are things that one cannot, and indeed is not asked to, believe in. Hence, obeying rules one recognizes to be contingent or arbitrary leaves one free to believe whatever one wants ("crois ou ne crois pas"). To behave "as if" one believed is not to wear a mask, pretend to be other than one is, but to create a private space where a free self can exist.

It is by pointing out that belief in the rules is not necessary that this reasoning can present itself as "enlightened," as superior to the "superstitions" of the ancien régime. But this does not mean that for Gina a different social order, for example, the republic, is less arbitrary: "ne tombe point dans la vulgarité de parler avec horreur de Voltaire, Diderot, Raynal, et tous ces écervelés de Français précurseurs des deux chambres. . . . Ce sont gens depuis longtemps réfutés, et dont les attaques ne sont plus d'aucune conséquence" ("Do not indulge in the vulgar habit of speaking with horror of Voltaire, Diderot, Raynal, and all those hairbrained Frenchmen who ushered in government by two Chambers. . . . They are people long since refuted and whose attacks have ceased to be of any consequence"; 117; *132*). Gina is not an advocate of either the monarchy or the republic; she exposes the arbitrariness of all social rules, suggests that one can use these rules for one's own advantage, and implies that what is most important in this attitude is the possibility it offers for a private, interior space of freedom of feelings and beliefs—a freedom that can exist only under these circumstances of arbitrary laws, obeyed without any belief in them.

Thus in spelling out for Fabrice how he should conduct himself in the

theological academy of Naples, Gina describes a way of life that also holds
true for her, in the court of Parma, and, as we have seen, for the citizens of
Parma at large. But the religious context in which Gina gives her advice alerts
us to the possibility that her enlightened reasoning may turn into something
like its opposite. Because Gina, in telling Fabrice to follow certain rules
whether he believes in them or not, says something quite similar to what
Pascal, for example, says about religious behavior.[12] But whereas, according
to Gina, obeying arbitrary rules leaves one free to think and believe as one
pleases, is indeed the guarantee of such freedom, the religious-Pascalian perspective can be seen, surprisingly, as the demystification of this cynical reasoning: it is by obeying without believing that one starts believing. Doing
without believing does not determine sheer external obedience; it determines the internal space of thought and belief as well. If both the parodic
perspective and its enlightened correlative present a certain behavior as sheer
exteriority (the mask does not stick, obeying the rules leaves one free to think
what one wants), here interiority is produced by actions (or practices) that
can no longer be seen as simply external.

Thus Fabrice, in his first meeting with the Prince, expresses the most
"ultra" sentiments:

> Les mots *liberté, justice, bonheur du plus grand nombre*, sont infâmes et criminels: ils
> donnent aux esprits l'habitude de la discussion et de la méfiance. Une chambre
> des députés *se défie* de ce que ces gens-là appellent *le ministère*. Cette fatale
> habitude de la *méfiance* une fois contractée, la faiblesse humaine l'applique à tout,
> l'homme arrive à se méfier de la Bible, des ordres de l'Eglise, de la tradition, etc.,
> etc.; dès lors il est perdu. (128)

> (The words *Liberty, Justice, the Good of the Greatest Number*, are infamous and
> criminal; they form in people's minds a habit of argument and mistrust. A
> Chamber of Deputies *mistrusts* what these people call *the Ministry*. This fatal
> habit of *mistrust* once contracted, human weakness applies it to everything. Men
> come to mistrust the Bible, the Canons of the Church, traditions, and so on;
> from that moment they are lost; *143*.)

The Prince interprets Fabrice's words as sheer hypocrisy, as the clever
playing of a role dictated by Gina. But the narrator explicitly states that this is
not the case: "En croyant Fabrice l'élève de sa tante, le prince se trompait. . . .
Fabrice croyait à peu près tout ce que nous lui avons entendu dire; il est vrai
qu'il ne songeait pas deux fois par mois à tous ces grands principes" ("In
supposing Fabrice to be his aunt's pupil, the Prince was mistaken. . . . Fabrice
believed practically everything that we have heard him say; it is true, however,
that he did not think more than twice in the month about all these great
principles"; 129; *144*). These *are* Fabrice's opinions even though we cannot

quite see them as the expression of private, "authentic" beliefs. It is his following certain rules of conduct (for example, Borda's advice to speak of revolt always with horror and as never permissible) as if he believed in them that takes the place of belief, generates his belief, "saves" him the trouble of believing.

In this respect Fabrice is not much different from Mosca, who plays the role of the courtier with ironic detachment (he tells Gina "je m'habille comme un personnage de comédie pour gagner un grand état de maison et quelques milliers de francs"; "I dress myself up like a character in a comedy to keep up a great establishment and gain a few thousand francs"; 91; *106*) and yet shows, in the crucial episode of the pardon letter, the extent to which being a courtier has engaged his entire being. The determining power of the supposedly external "rules of the game" can also explain Gina's and Mosca's reluctance or inability to leave Parma. As Gina puts it, "Je serai plus libre sans doute à Rome ou à Naples, mais y trouverais-je un jeu aussi attachant?" ("I should doubtless be freer in Rome or Naples, but should I find there so fascinating a game to play?"; 120; *138*). Mosca and Gina lose their freedom by following the very rules of the game that were supposed to guarantee it, just as the citizens, in following the fictions created by those in power as if they believed in them, end up supporting this power, thus making it "real." The characters' acts and behavior expose the illusion that underlies Gina's reasoning, which is in fact "the principal illusion of the Enlightenment, . . . that we can preserve a simple distance from the external 'machine' of social customs."[13]

IV

Gina's instruction is not the only force shaping Fabrice's identity. Complementing her view of what Fabrice should be is that of Blanès, who sees Fabrice's future. Through the mediation of Blanès, Fabrice sees his destiny as already inscribed, the end of his life as already determined. This writing in the sky is as arbitrary as Gina's rules of the game. Nowhere in Blanès's predictions is there a hint that what will befall Fabrice is in some sense a punishment (or a reward) for what he has done, for what he is. Destiny here is not retribution. This is why the imprisonment Blanès predicts for Fabrice precedes, rather than follows, a "crime," which, moreover, will be committed by someone else (152, 153; *167*, *168*).

The destiny spelled out in the sky is arbitrary, but unlike the rules of the game, which, according to Gina, one chooses to follow out of rational consideration, it is not "chosen." Indeed, it cannot even be entirely known. Even

Blanès who reads this destiny in the sky cannot claim to really know it. Blanès is not a divine oracle; he is a human being subject to certain weaknesses that may distort his reading. As he himself puts it, "nous sommes toujours faibles, et il faut toujours faire entrer cette faiblesse en ligne de compte" ("we are all of us weak vessels, and we must always take this weakness into account"; 152; *167*); and yet it is not at all clear how the observer can master the effects his own weakness has on his calculations. Blanès is thus tormented by the possibility that a certain "faute" (meaning both an error in calculation and a moral failing) has impeded him from knowing the truth (or the entire truth) of Fabrice's destiny.

Moreover, Blanès recognizes that revealing the future constitutes an intervention that may change everything: "Toute annonce de l'avenir est une infraction à la règle, et a ce danger qu'elle peut changer l'événement, auquel cas toute la science tombe par terre comme un véritable jeu d'enfant" ("Every foretelling of the future is a breach of the rules, and contains this danger, that it may alter the event; in which case the whole science falls to the ground as a child's game"; 153; *168*). If he nevertheless feels the need to announce the prophecy to Fabrice, it is, one can presume, in order to warn him against committing a crime after his escape, in which case everything in his calculations will change: "Si tu as la faiblesse de tremper dans ce crime, tout le reste de mes calculs n'est qu'une longue erreur" ("If you are weak enough to get yourself implicated in this crime, all the rest of my calculations are but one long mistake"; 153; *168*). In trying to ensure the fulfillment of the destiny he reads (or maybe misreads) in the sky, Blanès puts himself in a self-contradictory situation: he reveals the future to prevent an action that, if committed, will change the future, but revealing the future may change it. We can consider the destiny written in the sky to be fulfilled exactly and completely only if we bracket the interpreter (whose interpretation may be inaccurate because of human weakness) and the subject (whose knowledge of the future may change the future); destiny is fulfilled only if totally unknown—or destiny is that which, unknown, is fulfilled—an "unconscious" fate to which the individual is the unwitting subject. And it is because the subject follows this destiny blindly, unknowingly, that it can be considered necessary, inevitable. The individual does not choose to follow the arbitrary and contingent in order to create a space of freedom; rather, he follows unknowingly an arbitrary fate to which he is, whether he wants it or not, subject.

Gina's and Blanès's views of the individual's life are not so much opposite as complementary. Whereas the life Gina charts out for Fabrice has no goal other than itself, Blanès's prophecies involve primarily the goal of Fabrice's life (prison) and its end (death: "tu mourras comme moi, mon fils, assis sur un siège de bois, loin de tout luxe, et détrompé du luxe, et comme moi n'ayant à te faire aucun reproche grave"; "You will die, my son, like me, sitting in a wooden seat, far removed from all luxury, and with no illusion about it. And like me, without having any great reproach upon your soul"; 152; *167*). The coincidence of goal and end (prison and death) is expressed in the novel by the conflation (or confusion) of the Farnese tower (goal) and the charter-house (end). As in *L'Abbesse*, prophecies determine the arbitrary end and goal of a middle that has no goal outside itself. But the way these two are related in *La Chartreuse* suggests that the freedom or arbitrariness of the middle cannot be clearly separated from the necessity of the end; rather, the necessity that has been banished from the private space (so that this space can be perceived as a space of freedom) returns in the shape of impersonal, external destiny.

V

The purpose of Gina's instruction is to create a certain identity for Fabrice, to distinguish him from others. Since Fabrice can be neither a soldier nor a doctor, nor yet a lawyer, the life he is in danger of adopting is the "vie de café" (115; *130*). If Gina objects to this kind of life for Fabrice, it is not because it is without goal and socially unproductive; after all, the mode of conduct she defines for him on the model of the game of cards is equally without a goal (other than the game itself) and is strictly geared toward the pleasures and interests of the individual. Rather, it is because Fabrice would then be no different from a thousand other young men about town. To fashion Fabrice into a singular young man, Gina, with Mosca's aid, appeals to a peculiarly prerevolutionary, indeed aristocratic, notion of singularity—that of noble ancestry. Without his ancestors, Fabrice is just a common man like many others (since the time in which one could distinguish oneself by merit alone—the time of Napoleon—is gone). His uniqueness can come only from following in the steps of his ancestors Ascagne and Fabrice del Dongo, being (or rather, being believed to be) a del Dongo. Unlike the parodic imitation of a model, where the gap between model and imitation cannot be closed, here the assumed role "sticks": Fabrice never doubts his being a del Dongo; his identity as a del Dongo is never exposed as a mask, a false representation. Concomitantly, the difference between the past (the Renaissance ancestors) and the present disappears.

The genealogy of the del Dongo family, where the life of these ancestors is told, is the fictive representation within the novel of the chronicle that is at the novel's "origin," and in his life Fabrice will follow in the steps not only of the archbishops of the del Dongo family but also of his other, textual "ancestor," Alexandre Farnese.[14] Both provide Fabrice with a mode of conduct—that of the powerful aristocrat who for contingent (historical) reasons finds within the church the position from which to exercise his power. This cynical view of the church is not particularly modern since, as the chronicle shows, it characterizes the attitude of the cardinals and popes of the Renaissance. Similarly, Alexandre Farnese, who started as a libertine, ended up, as Fabrice will do, a pious man; and in both cases a doubt is raised whether this is a genuine change or just a pretense.[15] The present cannot be opposed to the past (libertine present vs. pious past or libertine past vs. pious present). In following Gina's advice, Fabrice does not attempt to imitate in the present a model from the past (an attempt that necessarily fails), nor does he follow an arbitrary mode of conduct without believing in it. Rather, he lives out a story set out independently of him—in the genealogy, in the sky, in the chronicle; he follows a destiny that determines (not altogether consciously) his entire identity and being.

We see, then, Fabrice assuming a certain role—the one Blanès reads in the sky, the one Gina shapes for him in her advice, both coinciding with the figure of his "origins" or ancestors, the cardinals del Dongo and Alexandre Farnese. As we have seen, part of the instructions Fabrice receives is to engage in insignificant love affairs. In going through the motions of a lover, Fabrice is following a script in which he does not believe (he is following Borda's advice; he is following Gina's advice to play the game whether he believes in it or not), and hence his actions are dissociated from feeling: playing the role of the exemplary lover, he feels no love, and feeling no love, he keeps playing the role of lover to different women. To that extent, his falling in love with Clélia is "out of character," constitutes a deviation from the role prescribed by Gina.[16] But this "deviation" just confirms how acting "as if" (Gina's advice) ends up constituting one's most intimate core. This process, however, is an unconscious one: Fabrice is completely unaware of the fact that, in loving Clélia, he fulfills a role carved out for him by his model (Alexandre Farnese had loved a woman named Cleria, whom he held prisoner).

The intrusion of this model into the novel (Fabrice cannot know that his "ancestor" is Alexandre Farnese; he cannot read the chronicle, only its analogue, the genealogy) is made possible through the mediation of Blanès and the key word *prison*. While Fabrice is followed by the Austrian police for his alleged spying, Fabio Conti is followed by the police of Parma for reasons that are never made clear. The police, quite improbably, mistake Fabrice for Fabio (thus anticipating the future, when Fabrice too will be followed by the police of Parma, for reasons that, as I have said, are never absolutely clear). Fabrice, then, is "identified" with Fabio and assumes this identification (imposed by others) to the extent that he finds Clélia, who travels with Fabio, a charming prison companion. In identifying with Fabio (whose name can be read as the Italian version of the French Fabrice) and later on falling in love with Clélia, the companion of a prisoner, Fabrice assumes the role/identity of a prisoner and plays it not to the admiring eyes of Gina but to the "sky"—the "absolute other" where his fate as prisoner has been determined. To the extent that Blanès's prophecy is analogous to the chronicle detailing the origins of the Farnese family (as two texts where the fate of the character is already written unbeknownst to him), Fabrice simultaneously recognizes himself in Fabio the prisoner, fulfilling Blanès's prophecies, and "recognizes" Clélia as the Cleria the chronicle has "predicted" for him. This latter recognition is not, and can never become, conscious. As in *L'Abbesse*, destiny comes from "another place" and retains its otherness; and yet here it is seen as determining the innermost feelings of the individual.

It is not accidental that we are dealing here with love: besides being what is "predicted" for every hero by the conventions of the novel, love in general cannot be the result of choice, though of course it cannot be imposed from the outside either.[17] Having Fabrice fall in love with Clélia when, brought as a prisoner to the citadel he meets her for the second time, shows that it is neither a matter of his choosing Clélia (which is impossible in love and impossible for him, since his love is predetermined) nor of her being chosen for him (which is also impossible). Rather, in loving her, Fabrice is in the position of having already chosen; he recognizes a choice that cannot be lived as a choice.

Fabrice's love for Clélia, then, is not a sentiment he freely chooses (and the prison that is its site should not be read as the paradoxical space of freedom). Just like his political opinions and religious sentiments, it can be seen as generated by conventional and arbitrary customs and practices, as belonging to a role he "borrows" from his ancestors, as predicted by the conventions of the novel or by the chronicle. This is why Fabrice's deep and genuine passion for Clélia is also, and at the same time, a continuation of the parody of the passionate lover in opposition to the tyrannical force of the father (rather than a stage "beyond" it).[18] Fabrice's love is both a parody of the exemplary lover and a genuine passion, is both imitated and authentic, comes from both outside and inside.

VI

As I have pointed out, the chronicle detailing the origins of the Farnese family is both outside the novel (for example, in an appendix) and represented within it, in the genealogy of the del Dongo family. Similarly, the model for

Fabrice, Alexandre Farnese, is represented within the novel in the figure of
the Crown Prince (who was imprisoned in the citadel, whose "model" is the
Castel San Angelo where, according to the chronicle, Alexandre Farnese was
imprisoned). The Crown Prince foreshadows Fabrice in one crucial aspect—
he too spent the best years of his life in prison (291; *305*). The Prince ended
up in prison because "fort différent de l'Hippolyte fils de Thésée, [il] n'avait
point repoussé les politesses d'une jeune belle-mère" ("much unlike Hyp-
politus the son of Theseus, [he] had nowise repelled the advances of a young
stepmother"; 290; *304*). Fabrice, however, has not committed incest on any
level, literal or figurative (love of a woman who belongs to another who in
some sense can be seen as a "father," since he "possesses"—keeps captive—the
woman): Gina is probably not his aunt, and at any rate, he does not recipro-
cate her (unavowed) love; Clélia is not yet married when Fabrice falls in love
with her, and his imprisonment, far from being a punishment for this love, is
what allows it to come into being; though Marietta's name, as Fabrice notices, is the same as his own (she is Marietta Valserra; 141; *156*), he is not in
love with her, nor does he really want to kill Giletti; and he prefers Bettina the
maid to her mistress, Fausta, the woman who belongs to the "father," Comte
M——. The similarity between the Crown Prince and Fabrice, then, has to
do not with Oedipality (which functions, rather, as a lure) but with the
"prison house of Parma," which is constructed for and around them (literally,
in the case of the Crown Prince; figuratively, in the case of Fabrice).[19]

In describing the construction of the tower-prison, the narrator underlines the fiction involved, so that we too, like the people of Parma, are not
duped into believing it is ancient. By attracting our attention to the construction and to the fact that it is visible to all, Stendhal shows the parodic
difference between past and present, the way in which the present attempts to
recreate the past but never quite manages to. The tower, then, can stand as an
emblem for the novel as a whole to the extent that it is a transposition of an
ancient chronicle to the nineteenth century, that it presents the modern
predicament as the failure to reproduce models from the past. At the same
time, as I have argued, this difference between past and present can be read
ironically (rather than nostalgically) as the superiority of present enlightenment over mystified belief in the past. Demystified about the political "superstitions" of the past, the citizens of Parma occupy an enlightened point of
view from which they can see the construction of the prison.

Still, the fact that Stendhal named the novel *La Chartreuse de Parme*
functions as a means of diverting our attention from the constructed prison,
of hiding it behind a charterhouse that we never see constructed, that we
indeed hardly see at all: seeing it would make its modern, constructed nature

visible since, as we have seen, Stendhal cannot recreate the past any better than his characters can, so that whenever he attempts to, the difference between it and the present becomes highly visible. Naming the novel *La Chartreuse de Parme* is analogous to the Prince's naming the tower "la Tour Farnèse"; the charterhouse gives the novel back the historical legitimacy that the prison house exposed as fiction. Moreover, by exposing the Prince's fiction, Stendhal hides his own. Because it is not really the Prince who constructs the Farnese tower on the model of Hadrian's Tomb in Rome (111; *127*), but Stendhal himself, in his text. And like the Prince, he does it in order to "backdate" his novel, give it the authority of the past, linking it to Alexandre Farnese (who, according to the chronicle, was imprisoned in the Castel San Angelo), just as the Prince linked his tower to another Alexandre Farnese, "général célèbre" depicted in the bas-relief on the prison door. By showing us how the Prince creates a fiction in which no one believes, Stendhal diverts our attention from the ficticity of the fiction he creates.

But the situation in which the characters' demystification generates our belief is also reversed, and this too happens in and around the prison. All the actions of Clélia, Gina, and Fabrice while the last is in prison have a particularly improbable, unrealistic flavor to them, as if here Stendhal is deliberately attracting our attention to the ficticity of his fiction. The communication by lights between Gina and Fabrice, the communication by way of the alphabets between Clélia and Fabrice, Fabrice's escape from prison, are all highly visible, and yet no one in Parma sees them, no one understands or overhears—and this in a city where everyone spies on everyone else, in a prison full of guards (365; *378*).

The unrealistic flavor of these scenes suggests that the narrator is constructing something in which we do not have to believe; but we continue to read as if we do believe it. Reading fiction, after all, is the prime example of continuing to behave "as if" one believed in something one knows is only a fiction. Our relation to the prison house of Parma is thus not different from that of the city's citizens: they sometimes see the obvious and are sometimes blind to it; we sometimes take the fiction for a reality and at other times see it for the fiction that it is. Just as their "as if" behavior does not set them free from the prison (since this pretended belief turns the fiction of power into reality), just as they, demystified, end up more mystified (since behaving "as if" ends up defining one's feelings and beliefs rather than securing a space of freedom), so it is with us, since in reading, we repeat both the characters' enlightened vision and their errors. This analogy and reversal suggest that, both in what he represents and in the way he goes about creating a representation, Stendhal manifests a complex understanding of his (and our) historical moment. On the one hand, the past is totally different from the present, irrevocably past, and this difference can be experienced either as a loss (nostalgia, failed imitation) or as a gain (ironic demystification of the past). On the other hand, the demystification of the illusions of the past generates its own particular blindness and hence does not simply take us a step ahead, beyond the past, toward a fuller and better understanding. The transposition of an old chronicle into a modern novel can then be seen as the emblem of a consciousness that is historical (since it is keenly aware of important differences between past and present) and yet resists a simple, linear narrativization of history.

CHAPTER 5

'Mansfield Park':
Representing Proper Distinctions

~

Mansfield Park (1814) is very often seen as an exception within the Austen corpus. Lionel Trilling has probably made the strongest case for this view, claiming that "alone among Jane Austen's novels, *Mansfield Park* is pledged to the single vision of the 'honest soul,' " that whereas the rest of Austen's novels judge self and society "as Hegel does, dialectically," the judgments of *Mansfield Park* are "uncompromisingly categorical."[1] Though here Trilling reads *Mansfield Park* as different from *all* of Austen's other novels in its rejection of dialectical becoming, the case is usually, and more easily, made by comparing it with *Pride and Prejudice*.[2] The thrust of such a comparison is to show that whereas in *Pride and Prejudice* opposites meet and reach a synthesis, as symbolized in the marriage of Elizabeth and Darcy, no synthesis occurs in *Mansfield Park*. Indeed, the possibility of such a synthesis—that is, of a marriage between Fanny and Henry and between Edmund and Mary—is explicitly raised in the novel, only to be unequivocally dismissed.[3] The rejection of the marriages with the two Crawfords allows the marriage between Edmund and Fanny to take place, and this marriage is certainly not the coming together of opposites. The celebration of the quasi-incestuous marriage between Fanny and Edmund would represent, then, not only the rejection of what is new, different, and foreign but, more seriously, the rejection of the possibility that one can move "through vanity and imprudence towards the new 'nobility' of autonomy."[4] Whereas the world of *Pride and Prejudice* can absorb new elements, changing them and being changed by them, thus reaching an "improved" state at the end of the novel, whereas Darcy and Elizabeth can move through the negativity of pride and prejudice toward a higher state of understanding, Mansfield Park is seen as intent on closing in upon itself, on refusing to be "improved" by the Crawfords' shortcomings and weaknesses, just as the Crawfords refuse to be "cured" by Mansfield Park.

Trilling's interpretation and evaluation of *Mansfield Park* are predicated on a larger, quite common scheme of intellectual history, where "archaic" ways of thinking are opposed to the "modern mind [committed] to the dialectical mode of apprehending reality."[5] More recently, this kind of dichotomization resurfaced as the opposition between "closed" and "open" form (where Trilling's "modern" commitment to dialectical thinking would probably fall on the side of archaic, "closed" form). And again Austen is situated on the nonmodern side. Unlike Stendhal, for example, Austen is seen as clearly valorizing "classification" over "transformation," an archaic notion of apprenticeship rather than a modern notion of "Bildung," closure rather than "narratability."[6] Thus D. A. Miller has argued that, in Austen, the instability of desire and of language, which generates the narrative, is viewed as a threat to the ideal state of "proper understanding expressed in proper erotic objects and proper social arrangements"[7] that is the goal or end of the narrative. Austen's novels, then, move toward effacing the elements that have made them possible. Closure is achieved at the cost of suppressing the "narratable"—the dynamic, destabilizing elements. From this point of view *Mansfield Park* is far from being an exception; indeed, it may be judged as the exemplary Austen novel.

Though Trilling and Miller are diametrically opposed in their evaluation of the status of *Mansfield Park* within Austen's work, they do agree on one point: that *Mansfield Park* (anomalously or typically) produces stable meanings by refusing or suppressing what is properly temporal—process in time as entailing transformation or/through negativity (instability of meaning, waywardness of desire, vanity, imprudence). Either the Crawfords as the dynamic force of the narrative have to be suppressed and banished for the novel to achieve "settlement" or their negative value (what needs to be overcome for growth and full understanding to occur) is refused, ignored, resisted.

I would like to suggest in what follows that the goal of narrative in *Mansfield Park* is indeed stable or fixed meaning, but that "fixity" here is not produced either by repressing or ignoring those elements that endanger it or by overcoming temporality, error, and change. Rather, the novel, through the representation of Fanny in her relation to the other characters, shows that what is fixed (and hence can serve as a measure, value, and means of evaluation) cannot be represented by itself, "as itself," as/in the present (for example, as a picture), but only through its difference from other things as made visible through time. Thus, it is precisely through time and narrative that stable meanings and fixed values are produced, and narrative is not simply the domain of error or instability that has to be resisted, suppressed, or overcome. My reading will show, then, that the novel is not so much concerned with the rejection of the process of becoming, in favor of the here and now (Trilling), or with the devaluation of narratability, in favor of closural settlement (Miller), as with the proposition that differences (or distinctions) can be properly represented only through narrative, and that it is only this, the proper representation of differences, that allows values to be recognized as true and legitimate.

I

A reading of *Mansfield Park* as a novel whose end consists of resisting or repressing the negative or the "narratable" would naturally place its *beginning* in the appearance of these elements: the arrival of Mary and Henry Crawford in Mansfield Park would be seen as what "incites" the narrative out of a state of quiescence. But *Mansfield Park* does not really begin with the Crawfords' arrival at the Mansfield parsonage. Others precede them, including, most importantly, Fanny, whose *difference* from the Crawfords would define the values of Mansfield Park. Her arrival in itself depends on (and follows in the order of the narration) various other events, such as the lucky marriage of Fanny's aunt to Sir Thomas Bertram of Mansfield Park, the far from lucky marriage of Fanny's mother herself, and the marriage of the eldest sister to the Reverend Mr. Norris, to whom Sir Thomas grants the Mansfield benefice. Thus, the world of Mansfield Park is presented from the very first chapter— and to the very end—as a world that absorbs new elements into it, such as Fanny and her two aunts at the very beginning, and Fanny's brother William and sister Susan at the end. This permeability to external elements suggests that Mansfield Park never was and never will be a homogeneous, unified, and stable world, opposed to an "other" (the Crawfords), which it eventually rejects. Rather, the world of Mansfield Park is constantly in need of constituting itself through a process of marking differences, making what the novel calls "proper distinctions."

The need to mark differences, with all the difficulties that involves, arises in the very first pages of the novel when the danger of marriage between Fanny and Edmund is discussed between Sir Thomas and Mrs. Norris. If Sir Thomas is opposed to such a marriage, it is because it will constitute an erasure of differences. Fanny is a poor cousin, not of equal social position, and thus is different from the family at Mansfield Park; a marriage between her and his son Edmund will erase this difference by making her, in fact, Sir Thomas's daughter.[8] Though Sir Thomas very clearly thinks that Fanny should be made to feel and think herself different from her cousins, he does not quite know how to treat—or better still, how to represent—this difference. He is aware that it is a difficult matter: " 'There will be some difficulty in our way, Mrs. Norris,' observed Sir Thomas, 'as to the distinction proper to be made between the girls as they grow up. . . . It is a point of great delicacy' " (9). Certainly there is no question in his mind of using crude, material signs of difference—Fanny is not to become a Cinderella, sitting by the kitchen ashes in rags. (It is only Mrs. Norris who thinks that the difference has to be thus expressed, and it is through her initiative that Fanny is "distinguished" by having no fire, no drawing or music lessons, no carriage, and so on.) Nor, however, can this difference be expressed through manners (he would "on no account authorize in [his] girls the smallest degree of arrogance towards their relation"; 9), since any such expression is a breach of manners. Sir Thomas insists that differences should not be erased but that they should be preserved in the minds of all those concerned, especially his daughters and Fanny: he would like "to preserve in the minds of [his] *daughters* the consciousness of what they are . . . and make [Fanny] remember that she is not a *Miss Bertram*" (9). The social difference has to be kept always in mind, but what, if any, outward expression of it is proper remains an open question. This tension between the importance of social differences and the difficulty in representing them indicates that, without in the least dismissing social distinctions as irrelevant, Austen (in this novel at least) suggests that they do not simply stand revealed.

In the end, the question of marking the difference between Fanny and her cousins resolves itself without Sir Thomas's assistance (and indeed mostly in his absence). Through the episode of the theatricals, for example, a difference between Fanny and her cousins becomes highly visible: whereas they are all eager to act, Fanny cannot and will not "act."[9] The novel insists in various ways that action reveals character, makes it manifest. This is the case with acting in the theatricals, but it is also true for action offstage, for example, during the visit to Sotherton. When Maria avails herself of Crawford's assistance in escaping the restraint of gate and fence, when she thus gains access to the pleasure grounds without waiting for lawful entry with a key brought by her future husband, Rushworth, her action is more than sheer action—it clearly reveals her desires and character and foreshadows her future. The scene at Sotherton is the most explicitly emblematic in the novel, since the characters themselves here point out the moral significance of the landscape and the figurative meaning of their words and action.[10] What this scene and the episode of the theatricals make clear is that action is an "index"—it manifests or makes known a character; more precisely still, action reveals the character's desires and shows them to be illegitimate. Both in the scene at Sotherton and in the episode of the theatricals, the other characters' activity stands in contrast to Fanny's passivity (in Sotherton she remains seated on a bench while others are roaming around); if their action reveals their character, it also reveals their difference from Fanny.

But making Fanny's difference reside in her passivity (as most critics do) tends to "confuse" her with her aunt, Lady Bertram. If, as we shall see, action reveals the inconsistency of character and the illegitimacy of desire, the complete passivity of Lady Bertram is judged too—it is considered socially and morally irresponsible. When Fanny refuses to act in the theatricals, she sees herself as momentarily occupying this position, but the difference between her and Lady Bertram becomes clear very quickly, since in spite of (or in fact because of) her refusal to act, she is "often very useful" (125). Unlike Lady Bertram, Fanny is not entirely passive, since she can act on behalf of others.

This last characterization is also problematic, because it tends to "confuse" Fanny with her other aunt, Mrs. Norris. Though in one sense Mrs. Norris is the opposite of Fanny, being "the spirit of activity" (4), to the extent that they both act on behalf of others, they can be seen as similar.[11] It is clear that in some respect Mrs. Norris functions in the novel as Fanny's double. Only in this way can we account for their fierce antagonism, for the fact that the ascendancy of the one is the fall of the other, that at the end of the novel Fanny inhabits the parsonage in which Mrs. Norris used to live;[12] only in this way can we account for the otherwise ridiculous incident in which the butler announces that Sir Thomas wishes to speak with Fanny, and Mrs. Norris exclaims, almost hysterically:

> Stay, stay, Fanny! what are you about?—where are you going?—don't be in such a hurry. Depend upon it, it is not you that are wanted; depend upon it it is me; . . . but you are so very eager to put yourself forward. What should Sir Thomas want you for? it is me, Baddeley, you mean; I am coming this moment. You mean me, Baddeley, I am sure; Sir Thomas wants me, not Miss Price. (246)

This "doubling" does not mean that Fanny is another Mrs. Norris, but rather that Mrs. Norris represents one of the modes of being from which Fanny needs to be differentiated.

If Mrs. Norris is the "spirit of activity," her activity is of a peculiar kind: it is "pure" activity in the sense that it has no goal or motivation outside itself. We can take as its emblem her plan of adoption for Fanny, at the very beginning of the novel. When the question arises of how to help Mrs. Price and her growing family, Sir Thomas, characteristically, sends "friendly advice and professions," the indolent but good-natured Lady Bertram sends money and baby linen, and Mrs. Norris "wrote the letters" (5). Nothing that is "in" the letters, in terms of content (advice) or matter (baby linen and money), comes from her, only the form that conveys them, the "pure letter." Mrs. Norris's "expensive charity" involves neither expense nor charitable feelings on her own part (the money and feelings come from others, from Sir Thomas and Lady Bertram).

One may argue that Mrs. Norris's action on behalf of Fanny differs from her actions on behalf of her other nieces, especially Maria. But this is not the case. When the Bertram girls make their début in society, Mrs. Norris is all too happy to take the position of a caring mother (instead of Lady Bertram), not only without being the real mother but also without investing in this position anything of her own. It is true that the lack of investment in this case is presented as purely monetary (rather than emotional), since the point is made that she does not have to incur any of the expenses involved in bringing the girls out (she is "mixing in society without having horses to hire"; 27). But Mrs. Norris's love of money has been explicitly presented as having taken the place of maternal feelings (her concern for money, which "has begun as a matter of prudence, soon grew into a matter of choice, as an object of that needful solicitude, which there were no children to supply"; 7), and so we can say that her "activity" as a mother is again pure form, involving neither material expense nor emotional content. What she thus achieves is a "post of . . . honorable representation" (27): her "post" is that of a representation of a mother, but this representation is pure or empty in the sense that there is nothing "present" to be re-presented.[13] Mrs. Norris's action does not reveal her desires, is not nourished (or "financed") by her inner resources. Nor does her action cover or hide secret desires. It is "empty" or "pure" action. This emptiness is for a long time misinterpreted by the inhabitants of Mansfield Park as selflessness, as the sacrifice or effacing of self in the interests of others; hence the possible confusion between Mrs. Norris and Fanny. Such an interpretation is of course deluded: not only does this "selfless service" cost Mrs. Norris nothing, but she is the ultimate beneficiary of her supposedly altruistic services, since she lives more or less at the expense of her rich brother-in-law. And rather than effacing herself, she reaches through her action, as we have seen, a position of high visibility.

We see, then, that the action of all the young people reveals their characters and shows their desires to be illegitimate; Lady Bertram's passivity is the result of her being too indolent to have any wishes or desires; and Mrs. Norris's activity on behalf of others does not represent either her concern for them or her own wishes and desires; it is a simulacrum of action, pure "representation," empty and highly visible. Fanny, by contrast, does not act though she does have strong wishes and desires; she acts only on behalf of others—always the messenger, the go-between, the prompter—but this activity does not make her visible. Her desires remain hidden and when made visible at the end of the novel, through the actions of others, they are seen as the most appropriate and legitimate desires.

We see here how in and through the course of the novel, various characters become "known." It should be clear from the previous analysis, however, that they become known not because the "veil" of their (false) appearance has been lifted to uncover their (real, hidden) self. The young people's action is not a false appearance but a manifestation of their character, as is Lady Bertram's passivity. And Mrs. Norris's action on behalf of others neither reveals selflessness nor hides a self, since it is sheer and empty form. The novel, then, does not explain "knowledge" through an appeal to the dichotomy reality/appearances (which presupposes, or entails, the possibility of knowing a character in isolation and at a "present" moment). If the "true self" is not immediately visible, it is not because it is double or split, nor is its becoming visible the result of a demystification. Rather, characters become known through differences and similarities unfolded over time. The sorting out (of truth and error, the fixed and the changeable, the legitimate and the illegitimate, what is valued and what, by means of this value, is judged to be faulty) occurs through time, through the unfolding of narrative.

II

Whereas other critics have seen the plot of the novel as generated by the arrival of a new and foreign element into the closed world of Mansfield Park, I would like to propose that the novel is structured around a return—Sir Thomas's return from Antigua.[14] This return brings to an end the theatricals and the lovemaking they made possible; it also brings Maria's marriage to Rushworth and Edmund's ordination closer, thus separating Maria and Henry and Mary and Edmund. Hence Sir Thomas's return is perceived by the characters as putting an end to all that was new and exciting in their life. Edmund, looking back at those past days and weeks, tells Fanny, "The novelty was in their being lively.—Yet, how strong the impression that only a few weeks will give! I have been feeling as if we had never lived so before" (149), and Henry says that then "we were all alive" (170). Sir Thomas's return, then, brings the end of "life"; it is a kind of death. Certainly this is the way Maria sees her impending marriage with Rushworth, and Mary Edmund's approaching ordination.

The return of Sir Thomas brings something to an end and does not start something new, since it is, precisely, a turn back. Though Edmund sees this turn back as purely regressive—"I believe our evenings are rather returned to what they were, than assuming a new character" (149)—this is not quite the case. Sir Thomas's return functions in the novel as a hinge, as a reflexive moment that allows the characters to turn back, and this turn back entails a transformation. Transformation in *Mansfield Park* is not the disruption of a previous equilibrium by the intrusion of a new element, nor is it the establishment of a new equilibrium through the modification of the existing elements. Rather, transformation in *Mansfield Park* has the reflexive form of a return, a turn back. We shall see in a moment what this transformation involves and how it comes about. For now let me insist that, according to the reading I am proposing, the marriage between Fanny and Edmund, which is made possible through this "return," is not the mark of resistance to transformation and to difference (as in the readings I sketched out at the beginning of the discussion); rather, it is the result of a transformation that reinterprets the first part of the novel. And, as I will show, this reinterpretation or rewriting does not depend on either suppression in the service of closural settlement or a moment of "conversion"—the death of the deluded self and the birth of a new, superior understanding.

Though Sir Thomas certainly returns from Antigua to his home in Mansfield Park, it is not at all clear what causes the "re-turn" or the change that follows his coming back. The last pages of the novel describe Sir Thomas's changed views—"Sick of ambitious and mercenary connections, prizing more and more the sterling good of principle and temper"—and oppose them to his previous views, "his early opinion on the subject" of marriage between Fanny and Edmund (358); but the novel does not provide us with a clear account of the process of change and its mechanism (as both *Pride and Prejudice* and *Emma*, for example, do). Did Sir Thomas change his worldview and understanding of things while in Antigua? Did he come back home the same and find such an improved Fanny that his appreciation of her changed? Or is it finally Fanny herself who changed while he was away and hence can now interpret differently her uncle's attitude toward her, an attitude that in itself has not changed at all? There are indications that any of these things may have happened, but the final cause of the change remains highly vague. Thus, without any clear and decisive "transformation" on the part of any of the characters involved, the return of Sir Thomas marks a change. Its end result is that the marriage between cousins—which was the "end" Sir Thomas dreaded, which Edmund did not even imagine as a possibility, and which Fanny did not dare to hope for—not only takes place but is seen by all the inhabitants of Mansfield Park as the most appropriate end to the preceding chain of events. Though Fanny has not changed the world of Mansfield Park or been changed by it, by the end of the novel, she is no longer considered a foreign, alien element; following the "re-turn," she finds in Mansfield Park an expression of her true nature (as her visit to her home in Portsmouth makes clear), and in her, Mansfield Park in turn sees clearly its own values.

How can we distinguish this change in the characters' understanding from the "conversion" experience, or the "prise de conscience" of, say, Elizabeth Bennet? The difference can be stated as follows: unlike Elizabeth, Fanny has known herself all along but has remained unknown to others, since she can be known only as difference. If the change in *Pride and Prejudice* is in the state of Elizabeth's understanding (of herself and of others), in *Mansfield Park* the only thing that happens is that Fanny, through no action of her own (since she cannot act), becomes known, and this brings about a change in others—for example, in Sir Thomas or in Edmund—which is only a change in their knowledge or understanding of her, is simply the other side of her having become known. Fanny does not change, nor does Edmund: what does change is Edmund's (or Sir Thomas's) understanding of Fanny, a change of which neither she nor they are the direct agent. One could say that Edmund's understanding of Fanny changes not because he or she has changed but because everybody around them (Mary, Henry, Maria) has changed. But this is not quite accurate, because Mary, Henry, and Maria have not changed; they have merely revealed themselves to be what they are (and have always been). Mary, Henry, and Maria act according to their characters, and these actions make them visible; and when they become fully visible, one sees them as they are. Fanny herself does not act and thus remains invisible, unknowable; it is only the action of others that, in revealing them, also reveals her—reveals her as different from them.[15]

As the scene of the visit to Sotherton and the episode of the theatricals make amply clear, action in this novel reveals character; more precisely, action reveals characters to be wanting in consistency. Henry, who is the best actor and who can fill any role, is also characterized, in his flirtation with Maria and Julia, as "short of consistence" (89), whereas Fanny, and Fanny alone, as Edmund says, in refusing to act, has been consistent (142). Thus the action of others reveals them to be inconsistent, marred by contradictions, lacking firmness and adherence to principles; their action also reveals Fanny to be what she is—different from them in that she alone is consistent. There is no essential quality in Fanny, something inherent in her, that can be grasped as present in her, in the present, and that makes her the representation of true, legitimate, and unchanging values. Rather, it is through her absolute difference from others and her equally absolute consistency (sameness with herself) that she is finally recognized as the yardstick by which everything in the world of Mansfield Park can and should be judged.

As a representation of the values of Mansfield Park, Fanny can be defined only negatively—as different from the others. Those others, on the other hand, define themselves through their actions, and yet their importance is not in what they positively are, but in the difference between them and Fanny that their action lets us see. This mixed form of characterization suggests that, though Austen does not abide by the "archaic" view of social distinctions as predicated on positive qualities, inherent to certain individuals or a class, neither does she see social identity in the "modern" way as purely differential (as Balzac did through Mme. de Mortsauf—whose old-fashioned and conservative character should give us pause about calling this view "modern"). Moreover, whereas both these views imply that differences and values can be perceived at a present moment, Austen's mixed form depends on or entails the introduction of a temporal dimension: it is only through time that Fanny can be seen as consistent, always identical to herself and hence different from others. Fanny's difference from others is made visible not through her embodying an inner self in a material sign (which will be a representation of false difference or a false representation of difference) or through her own actions (since action shows the liability of principles and values to change in the face of concrete situations). Rather, it is made visible through time. Far from rejecting narrative as the realm of error and instability, far from valorizing the here and now, Austen sees in narrative, or transformation in time, the appropriate means for representing values (which are the basis for social distinctions) as what remains unchanged over time. Understood this way, *Mansfield Park* is not the story of how changes occurred or failed to occur within a small closed world. Rather, it is the story of how values that have always existed and have not changed come to be recognized; it is the story of how differences become visible (that is, do not remain subjective, invisible to others, purely within the mind), get to be known without, however, being embodied in material signs, which only create false differences. It is, in other words, the story of how legitimate (and legitimizing) representations are generated.

What defines Fanny most clearly is her unchanging and unwavering love for Edmund. If this love remains a secret throughout the novel, it is not because it is hidden behind false appearances, but because Fanny remains until the end invisible. Even as late as the ball Sir Thomas gives in honor of Fanny, the ball that erases all social differences between her and the family at Mansfield Park (209), even then, no onlooker can suspect that Sir Thomas "had been bringing up a wife for his younger son" (212). At the point when Henry is courting Fanny, Sir Thomas, watching her, still cannot understand her

(277); and Edmund himself, even after his marriage to Fanny, does not suspect her long attachment to him until she tells him about it. It is true that in the novel it is usually Fanny who "sees" others, who understands their desires and nature long before everybody else. But the rest of the characters are not entirely blind: Sir Thomas, Edmund, even Rushworth, see and understand many things; and Mary is observant and sharp, and particularly interested in knowing who might love Edmund. Yet none of them, not even Mary, "see" Fanny, see her love for Edmund. Fanny remains unknown not because, like Lady Bertram, she has no meaning or because, like Mrs. Norris, she projects a false or empty appearance. Nor is it a matter of her meaning constantly changing, unarrested, as is the case with Mary; her meaning is fixed and has been fixed from the very beginning. But precisely as a fixed meaning she cannot be known through her own actions (hence she does not act); she can be known only as different, through the actions or inconsistency of others.

However, Fanny's reluctance to act, her desire to remain invisible, can be misunderstood. Edmund at a certain point says that Fanny is as fearful of notice as other women are fearful of neglect (150). In fact, Fanny is fearful of both notice and neglect.[16] She is hurt when she feels forgotten and neglected, as when Edmund forgets her on the bench at Sotherton and stays away with Mary in the pleasure grounds, or when he forgets her need for exercise and lets Mary keep her horse for a long time, or when during her visit home, her father and mother take her for granted. On the other hand, she is pained when she feels noticed: when Tom begs her to take part in the theatricals, saying she need not talk but "we must have you to look at," she is frightened; she is pained when her refusal causes almost every eye to turn on her (111); and at the ball, it is only her lack of understanding of her place that prevents her from losing "comfort by increasing the fears she already had, of doing wrong and being looked at" (202). Disliking to be visible and hurt by being neglected, Fanny favors a state in which being invisible does not entail being neglected or forgotten. Fanny, who participates in most scenes of the novel as a spectator, feels pleasure or pain not necessarily according to whether the scene she observes is painful or happy, not even according to whether what she watches is moral or not, but rather according to whether she feels neglected (forgotten because invisible) or hidden and protected by her invisibility. This is why she suffers in watching the scene of general and rather innocent merriment with Edmund and the Crawfords on horseback, and why she can derive "much innocent enjoyment" (125) from watching the theatricals, which involve immoral play according to her own standards and which are not really, as she knows better than anyone else, a scene of happiness, since "far from being all satisfied and all enjoying, she found every body to be requiring something they had not, and giving occasion of discontent to the others" (125).

Fanny would like not to be forgotten without becoming the focus of attention; she wants to be thought of without being directly visible; she wants, in other words, to be remembered. In being remembered, Fanny achieves the kind of representation where, without being materially present, her nature or meaning can still be apprehended.[17] We can perhaps say that with the return of Sir Thomas from Antigua, with the turn back this entails, Fanny is remembered. And the mode of representation the novel proposes as the only one that renders distinctions properly is a mode of representation—in language, in time, in narrative—with the same structure as memory.

III

We have seen that following Sir Thomas's return, the world of Mansfield Park can see the difference between Fanny, who alone was consistent, and the others who, by acting, have been short of consistency. Action makes something visible; it allows us to see and apprehend something, namely, difference or distinctions. Since these distinctions are the basis of moral and social life, the question of the proper way to represent them (so that the proper distinctions, rather than false ones, are made visible) is of crucial importance. I have been arguing that in *Mansfield Park*, Austen proposes that values cannot be represented in a direct or immediate way: Fanny herself cannot act and remains invisible. On the other hand, if the actions of others revealed only their character and desires, we would not be able to evaluate these characters and desires. The value of action or of any other representation is that by making something visible directly and immediately, it also makes visible its difference from something else that cannot be made visible directly.

The hinging of the novel on a moment of return, the fact that to be fully understood, Fanny has to be "remembered," indicates that narrative transformation is here neither a process of becoming, the overcoming of time as negativity (error, instability), nor an endless process of substitution (stabilized or not by the imposition of a limit). Transformation is, rather, the process in which what is unchanging becomes visible as difference. Though this process reaches an end—the recognition of past, unchanging values as true and legitimate—its dependence on time and transformation in time suggests that it will always need to start anew. It is this labor of continuity that the novel, as representation, performs. The novel, then, is not only an account of how values get recognized as legitimate but also the instrument through which such recognition or such legitimization takes place. Austen, I am arguing, sees the legitimization of past, unchanged values as the purpose of representations, and this purpose is best carried out through narrative since proper distinctions can be grasped only in time. Thus *Mansfield Park* is not a "static" novel, where time is frozen, transformations abolished or resisted, nor is it a narrative that aspires to annihilate itself, sees itself as, at best, the negative moment within a dialectic that leads one "beyond narrative." On the contrary, it is a novel that makes a strong case for the claim that meaning and values are produced in time.

The novel's equating of the representation of value with the representation of difference accounts for its implicit critique of two modes of realistic representation: the one associated with the theater and the one usually typified by pictorial art. This critique can help us understand the kind of representation the novel claims to be appropriate.

As I noted earlier, the objection to the theatricals is not that they are a false representation—that by acting, people pretend to be what they are not in real life, hide themselves, and so on—but that people (or at least amateur actors) reveal their true nature and desires by acting on stage.[18] One way of phrasing this objection is to say that in the theatricals something that should have remained private (for example, desire) is revealed—becomes public—by being put on stage in front of an audience.[19] This is, indeed, an objection that is raised within the novel, and that Edmund seeks to remove by insisting on the privacy of the performances (118). That this restriction is finally not sufficient to redeem the theatricals suggests that the objection to them should be phrased somewhat differently: all action is a representation of character, and the theatricals, by being a representation of action, are too transparent, or too faithful a replication of life. When Edmund, the clergyman in love, "plays the role" of a clergyman in love, the theatricals become a crude material revelation of character and desire (as action "in life" is), with no space left for reflection—for the difference that alone allows real values to be seen.

The novel's rejection of the representation of value as something present, visible and accessible in itself, directly represented in a material sign or through action (rather than as a difference), is made even clearer in its critique of the kind of realism associated with pictorial art. Pictorial representation seems at first best designed to capture that which is fixed and unchanging, and hence, in a novel whose heroine is praised for her fixity and consistency, ought by rights to be the model type of representation. But for Austen in *Mansfield Park*, representations that are simply fixed run the risk of being nothing but the manifestation of prejudice, received ideas, and stereotypes. This is a different kind of "realism" than the one associated with the theatricals, and it too is finally rejected. Throughout the novel pictorial representations are characterized as false; Sir Thomas's representation of Henry Crawford's character is called a "picture" (Fanny feels "almost ashamed of herself, after such a picture as her uncle had drawn, for not liking Mr. Crawford"; 239), as is his representation of Fanny's character and sentiments (Fanny's "heart was almost broke by such a picture of what she appeared to him"; 241–42). Even when pictorial representations are not "referentially" false as in these cases, they are condemned as having no capacity to instruct, as being, despite their realism and their "representativeness," false to real life. Even though some of the arguments against realism one can tease out of the novel are the all too common ones, claiming the inability of this kind of representation to instruct, dwelling on its amorality if not immorality, they deserve our attention, since they have the function of pointing out the kind of representation the novel claims to be legitimate.

The character who is repeatedly associated with pictorial art is Mary. Mary draws verbal sketches that, though "true to life," are finally rejected as lacking any power to produce knowledge. Her first sketch draws vividly the "broad distinction" between a girl who is "out" and a girl who is not (38). This distinction is between two states, each of which has a certain fixity by virtue of its universality, and each of which can be captured directly in a sketch through the representation of a material detail: "A girl not out, has *always* the *same* sort of dress; a close bonnet for instance, looks very demure, and *never* says a word" (38; emphasis added). Tom, who at least at this point in the novel is totally lacking in moral standards and social wisdom, is the active interpreter of this representation. His "reading" is interesting in its combination of a somewhat naive self-centeredness (he takes the picture to reflect directly his own experience) and crude referentiality (he claims the sketch is in fact a portrait of someone he knows: "I see what you are at," he tells Mary. "You are quizzing me and Miss Anderson"; 38). These two points are logically related: referential reading depends on the reader recognizing something as the referent for the sign, depends on that referent being part of the reader's own world, own lived experience, and hence is in some sense "self-centered" or narcissistic.[20] Mary "paint[s] too accurately for mistake" (38) and in what she paints, readers (or at least, a certain kind of reader) can recognize themselves and their own experience. This, as we know, is one of the most common understandings of "realistic" representation. Balzac, in the first pages of *Père Goriot* presents this "recognition" as the guarantee of the truth of his realistic art: "But you may be certain that this drama is neither fiction nor romance. *All is true,* so true that everyone can recognize the elements of the tragedy in his own household, in his own heart perhaps."[21] Walter Scott, in his praise of Austen's *Emma,* goes so far as to hail her as the originator of this mode of representation: "The narrative of all her novels is composed of such common occurrences as may have fallen under the observation of most folks; and her *dramatis personae* conduct themselves upon the motives and principles which the readers may recognize as ruling their own life and that of most of their acquaintance."[22] In *Mansfield Park*, however, such realistic representation, which is typically associated with pictorial art, is dismissed, in this first case indirectly, through the sheer triviality of Tom's reading. If all a "true-to-life" sketch can teach us is what we already know from our direct experience, then such representation may be amusing but has no other value.

Later on in the novel, Mary draws "an amusing sketch" of the services at the Sotherton chapel in older times: "Cannot you imagine with what unwilling feelings the former belles of the house of Rushworth did many a time repair to this chapel? The young Mrs. Eleanors and Mrs. Bridgets—starched up into seeming piety, but with heads full of something very different—especially if the poor chaplain were not worth looking at" (67). The audience for this sketch now consists of Fanny and Edmund, so that the stakes have been raised. What allows us to characterize the "sketch" as particularly pictorial is its dependence on a material detail that functions synecdochically to represent the whole—the close bonnet and demure smile in the girl who has not yet come out, and the young ladies "starched up into seeming piety" for the chapel services. The detail allows the reader to recognize the sketch as in some sense true (Edmund says, "You have given us an amusing sketch, and human nature cannot say it was not so"; 67), but the sketch is dismissed as not serious; merely depicting something "as it is" does not show us (through difference) how we should judge or evaluate it.

The most explicit condemnation of realistic representation of the kind Mary practices comes in connection with her sketch of a clergyman. "A clergyman," she says, "has nothing to do but to be slovenly and selfish—read the newspaper, watch the weather, and quarrel with his wife. His curate does all the work, and the business of his own life is to dine" (84). Edmund strongly objects to this description as a representation based on common opinion: "I suspect that in this comprehensive and (may I say) common-place censure, you are not judging from yourself, but from prejudiced persons" (85). Mary does not contradict him but defends her characterization on the ground that the opinion of the majority is the equivalent of truth: "I speak with what appears to me the general opinion," she says, "and where an opinion is general it is usually correct" (85). What the majority thinks is true, and this general truth can be represented by a sketch, which, through some revealing traits, creates a stereotype, that is, a general and unchanging representation. At the same time this representation—a "picture," fixed and unchanging—fixes that stereotype and so transforms it into truth. Thus there is a complicity between this mode of representation (the fixed and unchanging representation of a material detail) and the view that what renders a judgment true, and what constitutes values, is common opinion. This mode of representation depends for its truth value on common opinion, on stereotypical understanding, and in turn legitimizes it by presenting it as fixed and unchanging, hence true.

In critiquing this mode of representation, *Mansfield Park* reflects on its own status as a novel, distancing itself from certain ways of writing (or reading) and arguing for the value of others. The critique of "pictorial" novelistic representation can be seen most clearly in Mary's last sketch. Having been told that Edmund is visiting a friend with three grown-up sisters, she questions Fanny about their accomplishments and then says:

> But it is very foolish to ask questions about any young ladies—about any three sisters just grown up; for one knows, without being told, exactly what they are— all very accomplished and pleasing, and *one* very pretty. There is a beauty in every family.—It is a regular thing. Two play the piano-forte, and one on the harp—and all sing—or would sing if they were taught—or sing all the better for not being taught—or something like it. (219)

This sketch is based on, or is a representation of, common opinion or clichés one is likely to find in novels. Indeed, *Mansfield Park* begins with such a "cliché": Sir Thomas has married one of the three Miss Wards, Maria, who is undoubtedly the "beauty" that, according to Mary, can be found "in every family." Mary's ironic attitude toward this commonplace should be distinguished from the way in which the novel distances itself (by reflecting upon itself) from the mode of representation that grounds truth in the general and the fixed (that is, the commonplace). Mary's irony, her refusal to arrest meaning on one final signified, has its limit in what conventionally and arbitrarily fixes signification—common opinion.[23] The novel, by contrast, rejects both Mary's irony and the kind of fixity that arrests it. In its negative characterization of sketches, *Mansfield Park* says that the legitimization of values—which, I would claim, the novel takes to be the task of representation—cannot depend on our recognizing them as our own (as Tom does) or on a simple appeal to the majority, since social conventions or values when properly understood are not prejudices or stereotypical modes of behavior.

The combination of cliché and irony in Mary's last sketch can be interpreted in various ways. One can say that Mary's irony is fixed by the arbitrary and congealed "truth" of the commonplace, since boundless irony can be arrested only arbitrarily. One can also say that Mary's plurality of meaning is only superficially incompatible with stereotypical thinking: the fixity of common opinion does not mean that common opinion is monolithic, that it is one "opinion"; rather, it is made of many contradictory opinions, and these inner contradictions do not prevent it from (indeed, may assist it in) falsely presenting itself as the representation of unchanging, fixed truth. Any of the descriptions included in Mary's sketch (the three girls of our cliché novel "all sing—or would sing if they were taught—or sing all the better for not being taught") can be presented as a truth based on common opinion, generalizable, unchanging. Whichever way we interpret this conjunction of the fixity of the commonplace with the undecidability of irony, it is important to note that it exists already in Mary's own representations. True, by the end of the novel Edmund, for example, would "arrest" Mary's complex and undecidable meaning by reducing her to the commonplace temptress of cheap novels. But since Mary's understanding of herself and others is already inhabited by the cliché, we cannot quite say that she stands for an undecidability and plurality of meaning—for narratability—that the novel arrests, represses, or rejects in favor of closure and "settlement," through the agency of a conventional character such as Edmund.[24] In other words, the conservatism of the novel resides not in its suppression of narratability, the dynamic force of narrative, but in its use of narrative and temporality for the legitimization of existing values.

That Mary herself evokes the commonplace alongside a destabilizing irony indicates that the novel does not separate and oppose the grounding of meaning from the instability of meaning. On the contrary, their combination shows that even for a character like Mary, the instability of meaning is clearly circumscribed within a fairly narrow field of possibilities. Thus the difference between her ironic use of language and the irony practiced by the novel does not turn on the issue of fixity or lack of fixity of meaning; what is at issue is how the fixing of meaning is produced. As a character who is acutely aware of the instability of meaning within an utterance or a signifier, as a character who delights in sketches, Mary shows herself to be always living in the present—she has no memory and in fact has no use for it. Her point of view, if you will, is always synchronic, and within this synchronic system, she recognizes the need for an arbitrary limit to arrest the instability of meaning. With Mary, in other words, we are back to the problematic of *Le Lys*: the need for a limit to stabilize meaning, the status of the limit as both arbitrary (or sheer functionality) and full of meaning. Our own understanding and evaluation of Mary will finally depend on whether we emphasize the instability of meaning or the need for a limit, the arbitrary nature of the limit or its tendency to be taken as truth. But the novel claims that these two aspects of Mary cannot be separated and circumvents the whole issue of ambiguity by proposing that it exists only when we (like Mary) look at signs "synchronically"; a "historical" perspective, through memory, will allow us to see "fixity" not as something produced by arbitrary limiting but as that which has remained consistent in time. Hence the novel dismisses as prejudicial (or conversely, as liable to generate nostalgic narratives of loss) the synchronic irony practiced by Mary and opts for a different kind of irony.[25]

This is simply a narrative irony resulting from temporal unfolding: meaning, unambiguous and self-identical, is there, in a certain sign or object, but can be grasped, or read, only in and through time. The true meaning of the sign, the novel proposes, can only be "remembered" because true meaning has been defined as what remains unchanging over time and made visible as such by the change of other signs. Any attempt to read the sign as a full presence (or in the present) will result in an error.

A simple example of this irony is Edmund's statement, offered as an explanation of Henry's behavior, that men often court a sister or a friend of the woman they really love before, and as a means of, realizing their true object of desire. Edmund offers this explanation as a way to render Henry's flirting with Maria harmless—this is just a means for Henry's coming to understand his love for Julia. Obviously, as an explanation of Henry's behavior this statement is totally wrong. It is also a generalization, a cliché (probably a novelistic one—if there were no wrong choices before the true one, there would be no novels), and as such, it can be countered by other clichés (for example, about love at first sight); as a cliché, then, its truth value is indeterminate. But in one way this statement is true: though Edmund does not know it at the moment, he is describing the way he will take toward understanding his love for Fanny. The "detour" Edmund took with Mary has not been useless (even though it brings him back to his point of departure), and *Mansfield Park*, according to my reading, is not an instance of the devaluation of narrative. But by suggesting that *Mansfield Park* does not depend for its meaning on a devaluation of narrative, I do not intend to propose that it values "becoming." The novel is not the story of a dialectical resolution (failed or not) of the opposition between consistency (Fanny) and action (Mary, Maria, Henry) or between value (unchanging) and narration (of change). The "plot" of the novel is not that of a changed Edmund who, improved by his having gone through the moral and epistemological negativity represented by Mary (error, confusion, instability), can fall in love with Fanny. Rather, the plot as a process in time allows a "return," a turn or a glance back, that makes meaning (which has always been there and has never changed) visible in the only way that does not falsify it—as a difference. The ironic discrepancy between what Edmund says (which is false) and the meaning of what he says (which is true) is produced by time, and it is only as a "remembered" statement that we can grasp its truth in a way that parallels Fanny's value becoming visible only when she is "remembered."

I have been arguing that, according to *Mansfield Park*, meaning needs time in order to be made visible, and that this "need" for time should not be understood as simply instrumental: we should not think of the narrative as merely an ad hoc performance aimed at making visible and readable a meaning that is outside time, or as a means of expression somewhat perversely chosen since it is the least suited to express the intended meaning. Narrative, history, and time are for Austen the proper means for disclosing the stable and unchanging meaning she valorizes since, the novel proposes, what is stable and unchanging can be grasped only as difference, requires the turning back of memory. Meaning is not produced through an accurate depiction or an acting out of the here and now (the theatricals) or through the representation of what the majority thinks (consensus or prejudice of the sketch). Rather, meaning here is what has emerged unchanged through time; this is what is used to judge everything else, to give meaning to everything else. Only a novel, and an ironic novel at that, can represent this process of the production of values and meanings. What legitimizes representations according to *Mansfield Park* is time, and the novel is the representation of this process of legitimization. Its claim to truth is not predicated on its accuracy or on its being grounded in the opinion of the majority but on the fact that it shows us how legitimate values, "proper distinctions," are produced.

CHAPTER 6

Staying at Home with
Emma Woodhouse

All of Jane Austen's novels end with marriage, and this signifies, as critics have long recognized, that, for her, comic resolution depends on social integration. The novels represent socialization as a process of internalizing and legitimizing social conventions and customs. By choosing a socially and economically proper spouse, the heroine recognizes as her own desire, as her own choice, what social conventions have deemed appropriate; and by so doing, by internalizing these conventions and customs, legitimizes them.[1] The marriage at the end of the novels signals the completion of this process of socialization.

But what of a novel that *opens* with marriage, as *Emma* (1815) does? Marriage itself, as an action, means always the same thing (the lawful joining of two people); but its narrative *function*, to use Vladimir Propp's term, is not always the same and in fact depends on its place in the sequence:[2] a marriage at the beginning of the narrative does not have the same function as a marriage at the end. And indeed, if marriage at the end of the novel means closure, resolution, and hence the cessation of narrative transformation, marriage at the beginning of the novel means something quite different: not only does the marriage of Miss Taylor upset the routine of the Woodhouse household, but it is declared to be "the origin of change" (3).

I would like to suggest in what follows that by examining the notion of marriage as (also) the origin of change, rather than as (only) its cessation, we can better understand both the need for legitimizing conventions and the way legitimization is carried out in *Emma*. I will argue that in *Emma*, Austen is concerned with the "confusion at rank" but sees this confusion (the inability to perceive or draw differences) as the other side of instituting differences, judgments, and values. In other words, as in *Mansfield Park*, narrative error (confusion) is not separate from closural truth. This is the case, I will argue, because in *Emma* Austen presents both understanding and desire as produced within social relations, where confusion is inevitable.

As we shall see, social relations are marked by confusion since they involve a certain amount of imitation. In analyzing structures of imitation in *Emma*, I will evoke René Girard's theory of mimetic desire but will insist on the difference between Girard's and Austen's understanding of mediation. I will finally argue (with the assistance of Thorstein Veblen) that this difference can be attributed to the way each conceives change. Ultimately, Girard's economy of truth and error, where the state of demystification ("vérité romanesque") achieved by author and critic is a transformation, recuperation, and transcendence of the state of error ("mensonge romantique") that was the experience of the characters, can be seen as dependent on a teleological view of history (either progress or degeneration, either utopian or regressive). By contrast, Austen's view that confusion, or a lack of difference, is inseparable from the marking of difference can be seen as dependent on a nonteleological view of history (and this is one of the things she has in common with Veblen). Though this nonteleological view of change can be put to many different uses, and in Austen is used for a conservative purpose, it is important to dwell on it, since it is one of the ways her conservative narrative differs from that of other authors, for example, Dickens.

I

What, then, is the change that marriage in *Emma* gives rise to? Following her marriage to Mr. Weston, Miss Taylor leaves Hartfield, her home of many years, and removes herself to Randalls. Matrimony entails leaving home, and "leaving home," as opposed to "staying at home," is repeatedly equated in the novel with sociability. As long as we associate the "critique" of marriage (and of sociability as that which marriage causes and figures) with Mr. Woodhouse, we can dismiss it as the rather amusing, eccentric trait of an old, weak, idle man. But Mr. Woodhouse's opinions on this issue are echoed, and in a much more vigorous way, by his son-in-law, John Knightly, who is young and strong, a successful barrister in London. It is John Knightly who criticizes most explicitly sociability, understood precisely as leaving one's home:

> "A man," said he, "must have a very good opinion of himself when he asks people to leave their own fireside, and encounter such a day as this, for the sake of coming to see him. He must think himself a most agreeable fellow; I could not do such a thing. . . . The folly of not allowing people to be comfortable

at home—and the folly of people's not staying comfortably at home when
they can!" (87)

Similarly, we read:

That a man who might have spent his evening quietly at home after a day of
business in London, should set off again, and walk half a mile to another man's
house, for the sake of being in mixed-company till bed-time, of finishing his day
in the efforts of civility and the noise of numbers, was a circumstance to strike
him [John Knightly] deeply. (235)

Marriage can serve as a figure for sociability because it breaks out of the
home circle, opens it up toward larger circles, involves it with "mixed company."[3] Thus the marriage that opens the novel and is the "origin of change"
exhibits another aspect of sociability, its potential for the in-mixing of heterogeneous elements. Miss Taylor, a governess without any relations or connections the novel cares to mention, does very well for herself in marrying the
wealthy Mr. Weston, formerly in trade but now the owner of a considerable
estate. Even though Emma insists that Miss Taylor fully deserves this good
fortune, and even though the novel, as we shall see, backs this judgment, this
is still clearly a marriage involving "inequality" or "disparity." As such it
foreshadows all the other uneven marriages—proposed, wished for, or actually taking place—in the novel.[4] Miss Taylor's marriage is the origin of change
because it serves as the model for other marriages, all of which break away
from the homogeneity of the home into "mixed company," allowing (at least
potentially) for what the novel calls a "confusion of rank."

The figures who prefer sociability to staying at home—Mr. Weston,
Frank, Mr. Elton—are all characterized as indifferent to this confusion of
rank. Frank, at the moment of planning for the ball at the Crown, one of the
high points of social life in Highbury, is thus judged by Emma:

He seemed to have all the life and spirit, cheerful feelings, and social inclinations
of his father, and nothing of the pride or reserve of Enscombe. Of pride, indeed,
there was, perhaps, scarcely enough; his indifference to a confusion of rank,
bordered too much on inelegance of mind. He could be no judge, however, of
the evil he was holding cheap. (152)

Frank's sociability is lauded when opposed to the pride and reserve of the
Churchills; but it ends up being condemned when seen as bordering on an
"inelegance of mind." Such inelegance brings him close to the objectionable Mr. Elton and defines his fault as the inability to judge or to discern
differences.

Frank himself is not aware of his confusion of rank because his shortcoming (like his father's and like Mr. Elton's) is that he does not *see* differences (as

Mr. Elton does not, when he presumes to propose to Emma). Emma, on the other hand, as many critics have noted, constantly draws distinctions, "discriminating" between the manners of different people, judging them all against some ideal of proper behavior: Elton lacks "elegance of feature" (25), Weston's open-heartedness is a bit excessive (249), Frank does not have enough pride (152), Jane shows too much reserve (129), Mrs. Elton has ease but no elegance (208), and so on. Critics who impute most of the "class distinctions" in this novel to Emma disagree whether Austen shares Emma's class consciousness (in which case the novel is marred by class ideology) or not (in which case Emma's class distinctions are an example of snobbishness, for which she is reprimanded by Austen, who views society as a collective whole).[5] I contend that Emma's ability to discriminate and see differences is not really separate from the confusion of rank of the other characters, and that Austen, through the character of Emma, shows how the confusion of rank can be used for reaffirming differences.

Emma's conduct is initially marked by a certain contradiction.[6] Intent as she is on making distinctions, her object in educating Harriet is to improve Harriet's mind and manners by making her aware of differences: "I think, Harriet, since your acquaintance with us, you have been repeatedly in the company of some, such very real gentlemen, that you must yourself be struck with the difference in Mr. Martin" (23); when Harriet declares Frank to be similar to Mr. Elton, Emma is upset (169–70), as she often is when she feels that she is not succeeding in changing Harriet's way of thinking—is not succeeding in making her see differences. But in fact Harriet at the beginning of the novel is all too aware of differences ("Certainly he [Mr. Martin] is not like Mr. Knightly. . . . I see the difference plain enough"; 23), and it is her awareness of Mr. Elton's difference, of his "superiority," that makes it hard for her to imagine he would love her ("It is so much beyond any thing I deserve"; 56). It is rather Emma who, by making Harriet her close friend and by fantasizing about her marriage first to Elton and then to Frank, shows a remarkable indifference to a confusion of rank. At the same time, the education in differences Harriet receives does not teach her to see differences (either because she could see differences to begin with or because she constantly fails to learn anything); on the contrary, it results in her having "the presumption to raise her thoughts to Mr. Knightly!" (325), in her dreaming of a marriage of the greatest disparity, the grossest confusion of rank. This paradox suggests that the novel does not construct a simple opposition between characters who discern differences and those who are indifferent to the confusion of rank. There is something in the very articulation of and insistence on differences that makes indifference possible and, conversely, there is something in this very indifference that makes the redrawing of differences possible.

By the time the novel ends, several things have happened. To begin with, two marriages have taken place. The first is as close as possible to a pure replication of the marriage that opened the novel: Jane Fairfax, whose fate if not married would have been to serve as a governess, marries Frank Churchill, Mr. Weston's son, just as Miss Taylor stopped being a governess by marrying Mr. Weston himself. The similarity between the two marriages is highlighted ironically when Mr. Woodhouse, just before Mrs. Churchill's death and the revelation of Frank's engagement to Jane, remarks to Emma: "You know, my dear, she [Jane] is going to be to this new lady what Miss Taylor was to us. And I hope she will be better off in one respect, and not be induced to go away after it has been her home so long" (303). Since it is a close replication of the act that opened the novel, this marriage cannot serve as a model for figuring what has changed through the entire plot of the novel; instead of allowing us to read transformation, this subplot marks a repetition. I will come back to the function of this marriage later on.

The second marriage, of Emma and Knightly, is altogether different from Miss Taylor's: not only does Emma marry her social equal; she also marries the one man who would allow her not to leave her home (both literally and symbolically). Had Emma chosen to marry Frank (who in a sense is as much a part of her "home," as much her "brother" as Knightly is, since he is the stepson of her surrogate mother), she would have had to remove herself from home, just as Jane does at the end of the novel. As Mrs. Weston puts it, "The difficulty of disposing of poor Mr. Woodhouse has been always felt in her husband's plans and her own, for a marriage between Frank and Emma. How to settle the claims of Enscombe and Hartfield had been a continual impediment." The marriage to Mr. Knightly, on the other hand, is not only generally "suitable and unexceptionable" but also "in one respect, one point of the highest importance, so peculiarly eligible, so singularly fortunate," since no one "but Mr. Knightly could know and bear with Mr. Woodhouse, so as to make such arrangement desirable!" (367–68). Through her union with Knightly, Emma can accept marriage, the figure of sociability, while avoiding the confusion of rank associated with leaving the home. The marriage of Miss Taylor and Mr. Weston at the beginning of the novel is not simply *different* from the marriage of Emma and Knightly at the end of the novel: rather, we can say, the second marriage embodies a critique of the sociability present in and figured by the first one.

It is important to note that the novel does not propose either a way of overcoming (or abolishing) the confusion of rank or a way of mediating between the claims of the home and the claims of the larger society. Frank, Mr. Weston, and Mr. Elton are indifferent to the confusion of rank because of an excessive preference for society at large over the home. But Mr. Wood-house's preference for home is also excessive (to the point of being comic), and John Knightly's love of home, though positive in itself ("there was something honorable and valuable in the strong domestic habits, the all-sufficiency of home to himself"; 74–75) is too strongly linked to his "faults of temper" (280) to serve as a model. Does this mean, then, that what the novel finally sets out to discover is a synthesis between the two attitudes, each of which is rejected when presented in the extreme, that is, without its opposite? Not at all. We become suspicious of the plausibility of such a commonsense approach, of such a "golden mean," once we see that its champion in the novel is the entirely objectionable Mrs. Elton. When Mrs. Elton inquires about the possibilities for "exploring" around Highbury, and Emma responds that "we are a very quiet set of people . . . more disposed to stay at home than engage in schemes of pleasures," Mrs. Elton first declares, "There is nothing like staying at home," then goes on to say: "Yet I am no advocate for entire seclusion. I think, on the contrary, when people shut themselves up entirely from society, it is a very bad thing; and that it is much more advisable to mix in the world in the proper degree, without living in it either too much or too little" (212). With so banal an expression of the idea of the golden mean, from the lips of such a sponsor, it is impossible to think that the novel argues for a compromise between two opposed but equally important values. Rather, through the figure of Emma, the novel describes *the process* by which the confusion of rank, always latent in the society with which the novel deals, is used for a redrawing of differences and a reaffirming of the values that allow one to make distinctions ("judge") and condemn confusion.

This helps us to understand why the novel as a whole "indulges" in the same confusion of rank as its characters. Critics have remarked that *Emma* represents a much greater variety of social positions than we usually find in Austen.[7] But the presence of a broader social spectrum should not be understood as merely Austen's mimetic accuracy, as a reflection of the social reality she sets out to represent. It *is* a "reflection," but in another sense: within the novel the Coles, the Eltons, Harriet, and others function as "mirrors"; in reflecting the conduct of their social "betters," they enable the latter to become fully conscious of their values. Since these values are what allows one to make distinctions, becoming fully conscious of them will entail reevaluating the "reflection" or the "model" as a "copy"—that is, as imitation, which, qua imitation, is different from, indeed inferior to, the original. This reevaluation is clearest in the case of Elton: early on, Elton's manners are seen as almost perfect ("he was really a very pleasing young man, a young man whom any woman not fastidious might like"; 25), but by the middle of the novel he is presented as having no manners at all. This "transformation" is not the result of a development in Elton's character. Elton is a "model" or a "pattern" of good behavior (24) because his behavior is an imitation, and he himself is a "copy." Once he has fulfilled his role as a "reflection," he can be recognized and dismissed as a fake.[8]

Thus if the marriage that opens the novel is the origin of change in the sense that it is the model for other possible marriages, other acts of sociability with their potential confusion of rank, it begins another process as well, another change, different yet hardly distinguishable from the first one, whereby this confusion of rank allows the main subjects of the narrative to become fully conscious of the values that institute rank. The main narrative transformation in the novel is that of becoming conscious, and the novel entertains a notion of change that is sharply circumscribed:[9] there is little change in the world outside the subject of consciousness (the confusion of rank is *not* eliminated), nor have the values of this subject undergone transformation or development (so that the confusion of rank is judged differently); the subject has simply become conscious of what it has been all along.[10] As we shall see, reflection, the process that allows the *prise de conscience*, occurs in *Emma* through interpersonal relations, through sociability itself. Sociability, then, with its constant danger of a confusion of rank (since society is always what is outside the home, heterogeneous, "mixed," etc.), is both the illness and the cure, the danger and the means of warding it off: seeing her "home" reflected in Harriet's "sociability" and "confusion of rank," Emma can re-affirm the values of the "home" and hence redraw the difference between herself and Harriet. She can now marry.

II

How, then, does the coming into consciousness take place in *Emma*? To describe the process of transformation *Emma* dramatizes, it would be helpful to use *Pride and Prejudice* as a foil. Let me make clear, however, that my choice of *Pride and Prejudice* as the term of comparison, rather than *Mansfield Park*, does not imply that I consider the one the paradigmatic Austen novel and the other an anomalous one. It is simply that, from the perspective that interests me here, *Mansfield Park* occupies an intermediate position between *Pride and Prejudice* and *Emma*; hence *Emma*'s specificity can come into sharper focus by comparing it with the earlier novel. We can describe the intermediate position of *Mansfield Park* schematically as follows: *Mansfield Park* is similar to *Pride and Prejudice* in the sense that both depend for their meaning on a center that is fixed and unchanging: Darcy's portrait, which, fixed, can fix Elizabeth's wayward judgment, and Fanny, who, identical to herself and different from others, can serve as a yardstick. But unlike *Pride and Prejudice, Mansfield Park* situates this fixed term within social relations: it is through Fanny's difference from others that her status emerges. In that, the novel is similar to *Emma*.

That said, let us now see what distinguishes *Emma* from *Pride and Prejudice*. As in *Pride and Prejudice*, so in *Emma* the heroine visits the well-managed estate of the man she is to marry and learns there a certain truth about him and herself: Elizabeth's visit to Pemberly has its counterpart in the strawberry-picking party at Donwell Abbey. Even though Emma does not reach full recognition of her love for Knightly during this visit (as Elizabeth does during the visit to Pemberly), both scenes can be seen as dramatizing the process of understanding, but with important differences.

On the most elementary level, we should remark that the visit in *Pride and Prejudice* dramatizes understanding as the discovery of something new: Pemberly belongs to a different world from Elizabeth's (she has to travel there). But Donwell Abbey is not only just a mile away from Emma's own home, in the same parish, in the same closed world; it is also a place she is merely revisiting. The visit to Knightly's estate emphasizes that, in *Emma*, we are concerned not with a discovery of the new, but rather with re-discovery, or with the coming to consciousness of what has always been there but was not recognized before.

In her visit, then, Emma does not see anything new, does not discover another world, but rather sees her world, which is also Knightly's world, in a somewhat different way. This difference, however, is not that of a changed attitude. Unlike Elizabeth, who in Pemberly, through Darcy's portrait, sees a different Darcy or sees Darcy differently (or sees Darcy seeing her differently, thus seeing herself differently),[11] Emma's walk through Knightly's estate only brings to her consciousness the appreciation and respect she has had for Knightly and his world all along, from the start, as long as she can remember. She does not experience something new, nor does she see the old in a new way; she simply becomes conscious of what she has always "felt" or "sensed" in an unreflected way.[12]

The possibility of consciousness and reflection depends on mediation. Whereas in *Pride and Prejudice* it is Darcy's portrait that mediates between Elizabeth and the real Darcy, standing for him, allowing him to be seen as he could not be seen before, in the visit scene in *Emma* it is Isabella who functions as a mediator: it is by identifying with her that Emma becomes conscious of the value of Knightly and the world he represents:

She felt all the honest pride and complacency which her alliance with the present and future proprietor could fairly warrant, as she viewed the respectable size and style of the building, its suitable, becoming, characteristic situation . . . and its abundance of timber in rows and avenues, which neither fashion nor extravagance had rooted out.—The house was larger than Hartfield, and totally unlike it, covering a good deal of ground, rambling and irregular, with many comfortable and one or two handsome rooms.—It was just what it ought to be, and it looked what it was—and Emma felt an increasing respect for it, as the residence of a family of such true gentility, untainted in blood and understanding.— Some faults of temper John Knightly had; but Isabella had connected herself unexceptionably. She had given them neither men, nor names, nor places, that could raise a blush. These were pleasant feelings, and she walked about and indulged them till it was necessary to do as the others did, and collect round the strawberry beds. (280)

It is by implicitly identifying with her sister Isabella and becoming fully conscious that Isabella, in having married John Knightly, has chosen well that Emma starts being aware that her own marriage to the elder Knightly would be the right choice for her. The visit thus foreshadows the last scene of revelation, where Emma, discovering that Harriet loves Knightly rather than Frank Churchill, becomes conscious that this is precisely what she herself has always felt but never quite knew she did. In the later scene it is Harriet's love of Knightly that functions as the medium, allowing Emma's unreflected judgments to become fully conscious.

The differences between the mechanisms of mediation and reflection in the two novels are obvious: in *Pride and Prejudice* Elizabeth needs to see *Darcy* reflected in his picture to discover the truth about him (and herself) that she never knew before. In *Emma* Emma needs to see *herself* reflected in others (and more specifically, see her relations to those around her reflected in their interrelations) to become conscious of her own values and desires. Whereas *Pride and Prejudice* emphasizes the difference between Elizabeth and her sisters and between Darcy and other possible suitors, the later novel shows that Emma, though "handsome, clever, and rich," lives in a world where her strengths and weaknesses are reflected everywhere in figures that duplicate and mirror her.[13] And it is through these mirrors and reflections that she finally comes to see herself and commit herself to a certain way of life.

By making Darcy truly known only through his portrait, *Pride and Prejudice* presents him as similar only to himself, as unique and different from all those who surround him (Collins, Wickham, Bingley). Knightly, too, is declared to be different from and superior to all other men—and from the very beginning of the novel (e.g., 23). Emma, then, does not discover Knightly's superiority; rather, through the process of the novel, she is brought to reaffirm this difference. The need for reaffirming exists because the world of *Emma*, unlike that represented in *Pride and Prejudice*, is a world of reflections and replications where differences are hard to maintain. The structures of mediation we have seen functioning in *Emma* erase differences by making visible patterns of replication, whether the simple one of imitation (Harriet) or the more complex ones of representing one's self in and through the other (Emma's portrait of Harriet), forming the other in the shape of the self (Emma's education of Harriet), and so on.

Since desires in the novel are mediated by a third party (Isabella, Harriet, Jane, Frank), the subject of desire is not autonomous but rather defined by imitation. As we know from Girard's analysis of triangular desire, the world of imitation and mediated desire is also a world of rivalry.[14] But though we can describe what happens in *Emma* in terms of structures of rivalry (between Emma and Mrs. Elton over who will lead the ball at the Crown, between Jane and Emma over Frank's attention, between Mr. Woodhouse and Mr. Weston over Miss Taylor's time and attention, etc.), what is consistently played down in the representation of these relations is the violence that attends (at least potentially) rivalry. Indeed, this violence is so played down as to make it somewhat inappropriate to speak of these relations as instances of rivalry at all. Why is this the case, and what does this tell us of the status of mediation in the novel?

When Emma, through Harriet's mediation, discovers her own love for Knightly, she is left with the unpleasant problem of how to remove Harriet from the scene, how to dispose of her, how to eliminate the mediator who has become a rival. This is one of the few moments in the novel in which we come close to violence in the sense that the need to eliminate the "double" is acknowledged. But we should immediately notice the obvious ways in which this situation differs from the situation of imitation and rivalry we are used to in other novels (and in Girard's theorizing about them). First, Harriet's status as a model (like Elton's status as a "pattern") is rather complicated. On the one hand, one can say that she is not a model at all, since the novel insists that it is she who imitates Emma (the novel speaks of Harriet's "habits of dependence and imitation"; 68); it is Emma who shapes and forms Harriet (including, and especially, Harriet's desires). On the other hand, this shaping consists of creating a reflection that allows Emma to recognize herself in the mirror image, to see herself as the mirror image of that mirror. Remember also that though Harriet is literally a "model" when Emma draws her portrait, this portrait, presenting an improved version of Harriet, in fact represents Harriet's own model (Emma) and makes visible the process by which Emma improves Harriet, by which Harriet *becomes* an imitated (represented) version of Emma. As even Elton understands, rather than representing Harriet, the portrait self-represents Emma both as the model and as the artist. This is quite a complicated hall of mirrors, and even though it creates some confusion, or an erasure of differences (so that Emma can mistake Elton's courtship of her for homage paid to Harriet), and results finally in a rivalry over the same object (Knightly) that necessitates the removal of a "double," what is insisted on vigorously is that the mediating agent, the so-called model, is created by the subject itself, from whom finally the model receives its ability to mediate and reflect.

Representing the "model" as a "copy" may suggest that mediation is reciprocal or, in other words, that the desires or values of both the subject and the mediator are produced through the process of mediation itself. The novel attempts to contain the threatening implications of such an understanding of social relations by positing that values and desires existed in the subject prior to and independent of any process of mediation, whose function is thus limited to making the subject conscious of these values and desires. The mediator, as we have seen, is a mere tool. This crucial judgment is conveyed through a discrediting of the mediator, which, in turn, explains the under-playing of rivalry.

Thus, for example, when Mrs. Weston suggests that Knightly may be in love with Jane Fairfax, Emma expresses her objections by identifying with Isabella—she speaks her desires through Isabella, taking the place of Isabella, championing, as Isabella would have done, little Henry's right to inherit Donwell:

> Her objections to Mr. Knightly's marrying did not in the least subside. She could see nothing but evil in it. It would be a great disappointment to Mr. John Knightly; consequently to Isabella. A real injury to the children—a most mor-tifying change, and material loss to them all;—a very great deduction from her father's daily comfort—and as to herself, she could not at all endure the idea of Jane Fairfax at Donwell Abbey. A Mrs. Knightly for them all to give way to!— No— Mr. Knightly must never marry. Little Henry must remain the heir of Donwell. (175–76)[15]

As we have seen, during the visit to Knightly's estate, Emma, again modeling herself on Isabella, continues the process of identification that will bring her to Knightly and make her in effect Isabella's rival, the one who will take the es-tate away from little Henry. There is room for only one mistress in the Abbey, and once Emma discovers her desire to be that mistress (through her identifi-cation first with Isabella, then with Harriet), she has no recourse but to oust Isabella and her children from the Abbey (as she has to dispose of Harriet).

But the novel does not allow us to describe what happens as an "ousting" or even as a struggle over Donwell Abbey between two sister-rivals.[16] Emma, having recognized her love for Knightly, can laugh at her previous championing of Henry's rights, which she now recognizes for what it really was—an expression of her own desire to marry Knightly and provide him with an heir (353). This recognition is the last we hear of Henry's rights, but that brushing off cannot be ascribed to Emma's selfish complacency. In presenting both Isabella and John Knightly, the narrator insists on their various shortcomings.[17] Diminishing the stature of the mediator (John and Isabella here, Harriet or Frank elsewhere) weakens his/her status as a rival (equal or superior to the subject), reduces him or her to a smooth surface in which the subject can be mirrored and see itself. So, though the marriage of Isabella and John Knightly functions as a mediating agency for Emma's recognition of the appropriateness of her own marriage, both Isabella and John Knightly can be easily dismissed from the triangle (once they have fulfilled their function), since they have been presented all along as inferior in temperament, understanding, or status (John is the younger brother, after all). Thus again the "removal" of the rival is not allowed to be seen as an act of violence since the rival is not, in any serious sense, a rival. It is true that imitation or identification is in itself a way of curtailing violence: aggressive as it may be, identification is still a far cry from actual murder. Rivalry in short yields to, or becomes, mediation. Austen, we can say, goes one step further: acknowledging mediation (the subject is not entirely autonomous), she circumscribes its disruptive power by insisting on the fundamental inferiority of the mediator, who derives whatever qualities define him/her from the subject.

Indeed viewing the rival-mediator in any other way would be, according to the novel, to share in Emma's confusion. It would be misplaced interpretative zeal to sympathize with the plight of Harriet (who, having been led to recognize the superiority of Knightly, has to make do with his man, Martin), just as it would have been misplaced heroism in Emma "to entreat [Knightly] to transfer his affection from herself to Harriet, as infinitely the most worthy of the two" (338). It was precisely Emma's "confusion" that caused her for a moment to think, "Harriet is my superior in all the charm and all the felicity it [gentleness of heart] gives. . . . I mention no names; but happy the man who changes Emma for Harriet!" (207–8). We, like her, are asked to recognize the difference between the two, to recognize that Harriet is not a serious rival, since far from desiring autonomously and creating desire in Emma, she imitates Emma, is "created" by Emma, and hence is merely a mirror or (self-) portrait in which Emma can see and know herself. Mediation creates the possibility of confusion, of loss of difference; but the novel insists that this confusion is also what enables the redrawing of differences.

   Many critics insist on attributing these mirroring relations to Emma's egotism, her selfish imagination, her will to power over her world, and so on.[18] But once we realize that Harriet is only one of many mirrors, that Emma's world is full of replications and reflections whose existence is independent of her vision and will to power, we should see that the novel is not as much interested in Emma's character and psychology as in the social context in which she is situated. Austen, in other words, depicts a world in which relations of imitation and mediation are everywhere and unavoidable. Even Knightly, for all his good sense and integrity, is not independent of such relations and thus shows us their inevitability. Though he has known Emma ever since she was a child, it takes his jealousy of Frank, the sight of Frank flirting with Emma, to make him realize that he loves her. Once again, however, the novel circumscribes the scope of this mediation: Knightly's love has existed prior to and independent of Frank's relation to Emma but needs Frank's mediation to become conscious.[19] Though this in itself reduces Knightly's "autonomy" by making his cognitive ability dependent on jealousy and on identification with an inferior rival (Frank), the novel accepts this as the lesser of two possible evils, as what finally allows it to argue for the existence of values and desires prior to mediation. Rather than being presented as a serious rival—whose flirting with Emma has transformed her into a desirable love object in the eyes of Knightly—Frank is presented as a tool, and having completed his job, he, just like Harriet, can be dispensed with. This is why he is united with Jane, thanks to the timely and totally unexpected death of Mrs. Churchill, just as Mr. Martin renews his suit to Harriet exactly when he is needed. Austen's lack of concern with the probability of these events signals that, in *Emma*, the mediator is purely instrumental; he or she is not allowed to either incite violence or destabilize the love between subject and object.

   We can summarize this point by saying that, whereas *Pride and Prejudice* proposes that a subject can recognize certain values and accept them through the mediation of fixed representations (whose function is to give certain conventions their status as truths), *Emma* argues that all representations of value are produced through social relations of imitation, and that it is in others that we see ourselves (rather than, ideally, in our portraits). But the inequality of these relations of mediation (moral in the case of Frank, social in the case of Harriet) and the insistence on the "model" being a "copy" allow one to understand the mediator as a tool designed to help the pronounced "subjects" of the narrative (who are socially, economically, and morally superior to their mediators) become conscious of the values they have always upheld. The novel, then, makes two points simultaneously. It admits that values become visible only through intersubjective relations of mediation and imitation that tend to erase all differences (sociability and its confusion of rank). But in insisting that these values exist before becoming visible, it also argues that imitation and reflection are the means by which this problem is overcome. Rather than diagnosing the relations of imitation and replication as dangerous to the values of the society and a source of potentially violent competition, *Emma* presents them as instrumental to the grounding of the prevailing values. The novel forecloses our reading of the relation between subject and mediator as one where the two compete on the status of a subject, where the slave becomes the master's master. Rather, by reducing Harriet to a blank page, Frank to an irresponsible puppy, Martin to a person we hear much about but never directly hear—that is, by reducing the subjectivity of the classes that, through their imitation of the manners of the gentry function as their reflection—the novel can propose that this reflection, far from being the cause of incipient strife and potential change, functions to reassert and reaffirm society's values.

III

It would be entirely reasonable to claim that Austen's circumscribed view of change is related to her espousal of the point of view of the gentry, or, as one critic puts it, to the fact that, unlike "the greater novelists of the nineteenth century [who] all focus on the 'slave,' " Austen focuses on the "master," and "the self that sees itself as the master cannot change; this self can only reaffirm itself in its domination over others."[20] I would like to suggest, however, that Austen's representation of the way past values get reaffirmed and perpetuated does not deny historical change but indeed assumes its inevitability. If this underside of her conservatism is not readily apparent, it is because the concept of change that informs her understanding of social relations is, as I noted earlier, a nonteleological one.[21]

Though Austen shows how economic change can lead to a confusion of rank (the Coles are the clearest example), she does not ground this confusion in historical transformation. Just as she does not propose, in *Emma*, by what means such confusion might be either eliminated or reevaluated, she does not invoke a past in which this confusion did not exist or did not matter. Thus what we call her "conservative" tendencies do not depend on a narrative of loss and restitution (of the kind we find in Dickens's *Bleak House*, for example), and her closure does not require a return to a pre-narrative state where, presumably, no confusion existed. We have seen something similar in *Mansfield Park*, where, I have argued, we cannot think of that small world as having been, in the past, impermeable to foreign elements, stable and homogeneous, or as having reached such a state at the end, through the exclusion of the Crawfords and Fanny's marriage to Edmund. The world of Mansfield Park has always required, and will always require, a work of perpetuation, a labor of reproduction, the constant reaffirming of the values by which it can claim "distinction." Similarly in *Emma*, Austen sees the confusion of rank as the result of the very existence of rank (hence, not as a "deterioration" of a state of "pure" rank distinctions). The insistence on rank requires making social differences visible, creating representations that will function as signs of this rank. Such signs in Austen's world are manners. But since manners are *conventional* signs of rank, rather than, as we shall see, a natural extension of character (they are "symbols" rather than "indices," in C. S. Peirce's sense of these terms), they can be imitated. Imitation can compromise the distinction of rank by allowing people like the Coles to behave with the utmost propriety and thus presume to establish themselves as equal to the Woodhouses. It is the conventionality of the marks of difference, then, that produces the confusion or abolition of difference. The confusion of rank that results from the conventional nature of signs makes it urgent to show or discover how or why certain differences could and should be maintained. Insisting on the conventional nature of the signs of rank allows Austen both to account for the confusion of rank and to indicate by what means it can be contained, and differences redrawn.

Austen could have solved the problem of imitation or confusion in another way, by claiming that manners are not conventional signs of rank but indices of personal worth (or morals) that are inimitable. On the whole, the novel does not take this route (and here, again, the difference from Dickens, in a novel like *Oliver Twist*, is striking). This is particularly clear when we look at the women in *Emma*. As I have suggested before, the novel attenuates the "disparity" in the marriages of both Miss Taylor and Jane Fairfax, and it does so by claiming that their "property" of sound principles, good sense, accomplishments, and knowledge makes them more than the equals of their husbands. These virtues, however, are not innate; both acquire them through their association with the privileged, that is, through their ability to learn or imitate the manners identified with rank. This point is made most clearly in the case of Jane, who "had fallen into good hands, known nothing but kindness from the Campbells, and been given an excellent education. Living constantly with right-minded and well-informed people, her heart and understanding received every advantage of discipline and culture; and Col. Campbell's residence being in London, every lighter talent had been done full justice to, by the attendance of first-rate masters" (125). Miss Taylor's situation is more complicated. As a governess, she is supposed to have formed Emma rather than being formed herself by her association with the Woodhouses (we know nothing of her life before she came to them). But this may be the reason why the novel insists on the very little improvement Emma has received from her governess. We are told, indeed, that Miss Taylor did not do much to shape Emma: she never managed to make Emma read as much as she wanted; Emma mostly had her own way; and in any disagreement between them, Emma was very seldom the one to yield. Emma's indignation at Mrs. Elton's being "astonished that the person who had brought me up should be a gentlewoman" (215) could be given a somewhat different inflection now: having spent so many years as Emma's governess, Miss Taylor could not help emerging from their association as a perfect gentlewoman. But this association had little or no effect on Emma's formation or transformation. Her transformation occurs when, through the mediation of others, she recognizes her true values in her love for Knightly (who in this sense, and only in this sense, can be said to be the one who has formed her).[22] Manners are not presented as a natural expression of character; they are the conventional signs of rank, acquired by the imitation of a model or reaffirmed by recognition through reflection.[23] Thus Mr. Woodhouse, despite his personal aversion to matrimony, can still live by the code of manners that gives privileged status to a bride. As the conversation between him and Emma makes clear (216), this code has nothing to do with Mr. Woodhouse's personal feelings or views; he is merely adhering to convention, and in so doing, he makes himself known as a perfect gentleman.[24]

Austen thus does not see present social reality, with its relations of mediation and replication, as resulting from a "loss" brought about in and through history but sees it rather as the result of the very conventionality of the signs and representations that regulate social relations. We can better link the understanding of social representations as conventional to a particular view of history and change if we analyze it against the background of another theory of social relations that it seems to resemble. We have seen already that "mimetic desire" exists in *Emma* but functions in a way quite different from Girard's model. I would like to argue that Girard's view of mediated desire depends on a certain view of history, and that a different view of history produces an understanding of social relations that only superficially resembles Girard's. In my analysis I will use a possible "confusion" between Girard and Austen in order to articulate important differences. My purpose in insisting on these differences is not to promote the idea of the irreducible uniqueness of *Emma* (or any other novel) but to emphasize, on the one hand, the specificity of the social context and, on the other hand, the multiplicity of formal possibilities available within this context and with which the novelist, as a practitioner, negotiates various needs, imperatives, and contradictions.

As we have seen, the differences between the structure of mediation we find in *Emma* and the structures of mediation described by Girard are basically two. First, in Austen the desired values or objects are not presented as becoming desirable through the process of mediation; rather, the process of mediation allows their preexisting desirability to become conscious and their preexisting value to be reaffirmed. In other words, the process of imitation does not explain the origin or generation of certain values, merely their perpetuation. Second, for Girard the important relation is that between the subject and the mediator: the mediator, whom the subject sees as quasi-divine since he/she (supposedly) desires autonomously, is what the subject (who imitates) wants to be; hence what is highlighted is the rivalry and violence between subject and mediator. In *Emma*, as I have demonstrated, the mediator is presented as a mere tool, which can be disposed of once it has accomplished the task of reflection for which it is necessary. The violence is underplayed, since the mediator, rather than being in some sense superior or equal to the subject, is always morally and/or socially inferior and derives his/her power to reflect from the subject him/herself. These two "deviations" from the Girardian model can be easily read as ideological justifications, as mystifications ("deceits" in Girard's terms) designed to hide the constructed nature of values and the incipient violence that results from imitation. Such a diagnosis increases the explanatory scope of the Girardian model but reduces our ability to see what may be at stake in a particular articulation of a specific text. Rather than subsuming *Emma* within the Girardian model, I would like to highlight its specificity by proposing that the differences we have observed between the novel and Girard's model are indicative of two ways of understanding narrative and the role of representation in social relations.

Girard's analysis of desire depends for all its points and stages on the hypothesis of a divine mediator, that is, of a mediator who is intrinsically different from the subject who imitates it. The structures of mediation where the mediator's divine autonomy is only an illusion of the subject cannot be understood except as resulting from the loss of the divine mediator. Girard's postulation of a divine mediator as an origin dictates a history of loss (of that divine mediator), presents history as degeneration, where God is replaced by men who merely play the role of god for each other. All the permutations Girard so carefully and eloquently describes (reduction of distance between subject and mediator, internal vs. external mediation, reciprocal mediation, etc.) cannot be understood except as substitutions for the lost divine origin, as strategies for recuperating this loss.[25]

In the world where the Girardian subject finds itself, objects of desire are in themselves devoid of all value and become valuable (desirable) only to the extent that they are infused with value through mediation. To present things otherwise is for Girard not only "deceit" but idolatry: in a world centered around God, to believe in the autonomous value of objects is to treat creatures or creation as if they were not fundamentally different from the creator. Thus, though Girard's analysis of mediation may give us an accurate description of human desire in modern, "consumer society," we should not forget that from his point of view the problem is not that objects are made desirable by and through the imitation of a model but that the model is false. The consumer society is for him only an extension of a fallen world.

But for Austen the world with all its "confusion of rank" is not deteriorated and fallen. What interests her is not origin per se but the way in which society can perpetuate traditional (hence, for her, legitimate) values even in the face of internal contradictions that such perpetuation entails. She is not telling a narrative of loss, either nostalgic or utopian; rather, she is shaping a narrative that emphasizes the means for perpetuating an existing set of values and that carries out the minute, continual task of social reproduction. This social, secular interest, and the claim that social relations are regulated by conventional signs (rather than in terms of the relation to a lost God), make Austen's point of view quite different from Girard's. In order to make the difference more explicit, let me oppose Girard's understanding of social relations to another theory to which, I will claim, Austen's practice is closer: Veblen's theory of the leisure class.

Veblen's concerns are in some sense quite similar to Girard's (which allows us to bring them together): with his notion of conspicuous consumption, for example, he proposes that goods are valued not because of some intrinsic quality they have (their ability to promote what Veblen calls "the fullness of life") but rather because their consumption indicates the wealth of their consumer and places him in invidious relation to his peers. Veblen pays a lot of attention to "self-respect," which, he insists, is based on the respect of one's neighbors; and the role of "emulation" is one of his major points.[26] But in Veblen, as in Austen, imitation or emulation depends on the existence of conventional representations. As he puts it, "esteem" (the respect of the other, on which self-respect depends) "is awarded only on evidence,"[27] and the evidence is not some inherent virtue but a representation—hence the importance of "conspicuous" wealth or leisure.

Veblen's world is one of goods that contribute to survival, that are life-enhancing in the most immediate sense. And when objects are desired that are not functional in this sense, it is not because they were infused with value by a mediator—divine or not—but because they have been transformed from objects of use to representations. In "conspicuous consumption," the consumption of objects is secondary to their conspicuousness—their function as signs. Consumption (or possession in general) is not the goal (as it is in Girard, for whom every consumption is ultimately modeled on the Eucharist, on becoming one with the mediator); the goal is rather the conspicuous display of goods that have been turned from objects of consumption into signs. Hence when conspicuous consumption is "emulated," it is not subjects that are imitated (as in Girard) but conventional signs. In short, Veblen does not attribute to human subjects the desire either to be (the other) or to possess (what the other possesses); rather he sees human subjects as availing themselves of signs that conventionally represent prestige.

The conventional nature of signs of prestige and their social function as representations (rather than as objects infused with value) can be seen even more clearly in the case of conspicuous leisure, since Veblen distinguishes leisure from the signs that make it conspicuous—manners and learning. Leisure in itself is a kind of sign; it is an index of prestige, since it is an "evidence of the pecuniary ability to afford a life of idleness."[28] But a large amount of leisure is spent in privacy, not in the presence of the public who is to be impressed "with that spectacle of honorific leisure." Consequently, leisure has to be translated into, or represented by, marks that can then be viewed by others and that function as signs of past leisure. Such signs are manners and learning. Thus Veblen sees manners and learning not as the natural results of a life of leisure (or as indices) but rather as the arbitrary representations of this kind of life. His ironic treatment of manners and learning can be linked to his materialism—his valorization of material survival, compared to which other things are superfluous (hence his ironic treatment not only of manners but also of religion, taste, culture, and civilization in general). His irony is a way to reject the devalorization of the material and the physical as animal and subhuman, a refusal of a concept of the properly human as a craving for divine autonomy or for reciprocity (desire for the desire of the other, desire for recognition). But the effect of this materialist irony is to make manners and learning "strange"—that is, to denaturalize them, to show them as arbitrary signs that have been "naturalized" only by their repetition through emulation.[29]

We see, then, that the conventional nature of signs of prestige is double-edged: on the one hand, their conventionality explains their perpetuation within a culture, the fact that they exist beyond their original purpose and value to "enhance life." (Veblen always insists that conventional signs of prestige, such as manners, have an original function different from their function as conspicuous signs.) The conventionality of signs is thus a conservative force. Yet at the same time, the very fact that they are conventional means that they are always subject to change, as "natural" signs would not be. This double nature of arbitrary or conventional signs means that the system of representation they constitute will change in time, but the change will be unsystematic (nonteleological).[30]

We have seen that Austen does not represent history as either progress or degeneration. Clearly her view of history is linked to her defense of the "status quo" on the grounds that "this is the way things have always been." But in Austen's case the claim that past conditions will perpetuate themselves depends not on the premise of their "naturalness," but on the postulation that social relations are regulated by conventional representations. And it is this understanding of social relations that explains the inherent instability of her represented world (marriage, sociability, the confusion of rank, are there before the beginning and after the end), as well as the constant need for a labor of continuity, in and through novelistic representation. Though Austen emphasizes one side of the picture—the way in which the conventionality of signs of rank allows for their perpetuation—the other side is always at least implicit. Whereas Girard's theory presents us with a narrative of loss that can be made up only through utopian restoration, Austen's narrative (with some help from Veblen) allows us to read both the anachronistic, regressive perpetuation of social representations and their inherent liability (or availability) to change.

CHAPTER 7

The Case Against Plot in 'Bleak House' and 'Our Mutual Friend'

In the last two chapters I have argued that, for Austen, narrative (and by implication being in time, in history) is the domain of both error and truth. The point I wanted to make was not that Austen's novels are more "open" than they seem at first (either because closure can never be fully achieved or because she is, consciously or unconsciously, subverting her official conservative ideology). Rather, what I tried to show was that, in Austen, the stability of meaning ("fixity") needs to be produced, and that though the production here is indeed reproduction (of existing social relations, of past, unchanging values), reproduction too involves labor and transformation. Indeed, the differences we have noted among Austen's novels suggest that reproduction can take different forms, and these different forms produce different meanings (or reproduce meaning with a difference).

The same can be said of the novels of Charles Dickens. Though his novels differ from Austen's in relying heavily on what I have called a narrative of "restoration"—where knowledge and stability are gained through the erasure of narrative and the restoration of a "pre-narrative" state—that model does not account for all of his novels or even for the entirety of certain texts. If the previous two chapters implicitly relied on an opposition between Austen's concept of narrative and another view, attributed to Dickens, a closer look will show this opposition to exist within the work of Dickens, and even within one text. In what follows I would like not only to demonstrate this claim but also to reflect on its significance. What does it mean that the work of an author, and indeed a particular text, articulates different economies of narrative? How is this related to the undeniable historical and cultural specificity of certain modes of narrative?

I

As I suggested in the Introduction, one way to link formal and historical analyses of narrative is to affix a particular cultural function to specific formal structures. Thus Franco Moretti borrows Iurii Lotman's notion that every narrative text has to include both elements of classification and elements of transformation, and uses it to chart out the history of the European Bildungsroman. Premodern texts, such as Goethe's *Wilhelm Meister* (but also the entire English tradition, from Fielding to Dickens), Moretti argues, valorize the element of classification, whereas modern texts, such as the novels of Stendhal, Pushkin, or Balzac, emphasize transformation and devalue classification.[1] The historical and cultural inflection that Moretti adds to Lotman's formal argument in fact involves two interrelated claims: first, that the varying proportion of the two elements from text to text is not an accident or a question of the irreducible particularity of an individual author but is historically produced and determined; and second, that by analyzing how narrative texts from different cultures and periods value one element at the expense of the other, one can chart a history of narrative that will make manifest broader historical and cultural changes.

But how exactly should we understand the claim that particular formal choices are historically produced and determined? I would like to use Moretti's discussion of the English Bildungsroman as an occasion for reflecting on this issue. In order to do so, a more detailed analysis of his argument is necessary.

As I have noted, Moretti defines the English Bildungsroman in contradistinction to its European counterpart. The innovation of the European Bildungsroman, from Goethe's *Wilhelm Meister* to Stendhal's *Le Rouge et le noir* to Balzac's *Illusions perdues*, is its positive valuation of youth—of exploration, of interiority, of mobility and transformation. But the English Bildungsroman is defined, paradoxically, by a negative attitude or resistance to all these features that constitute not only the Bildungsroman but, through it, the modern concept of Bildung (as opposed to more archaic concepts of apprenticeship and initiation). Youth and its formative experiences are devalued. Speaking about *Tom Jones*, Moretti comments:

> The young hero's numerous erotic exploits are the very opposite of what we call "experiences." They are mere digressions, also in a narrative sense, and they will never shed a different light on, nor force Tom from, the straight and narrow path of asexual love, of *childhood* love. Contrary to *Wilhelm Meister*, in the English novel the most significant experiences are not those that alter but those which

confirm the choices made by childhood "innocence." Rather than novels of "initiation" one feels they should be called novels of "preservation."[2]

This positive evaluation of innocence and of choices made in childhood over the choices and changes of youth—which are seen as mere errors—entails a negative evaluation of narrative and plot (and implies a very specific view of history).

Whereas in the continental Bildungsroman the plot is generated by a conflict between the protagonist and the world around him, in England, "between the insipid normality of the hero, and a stable and thoroughly classified world, no spark will ever flash";[3] neither the hero nor the world can generate a plot or a narrative. In fact, as far as the hero and his world are concerned, they would rather not have either plot or narrative: "the plot affects them as a merely 'negative' force. Plot is violence and coercion, and they only agree to take part in it to avert the total disappearance of the violated order: to prevent the consummation of the *unnatural* marriages between Blifil and Sophia, or Uriah and Agnes." The plot gets generated neither by the hero nor by the world but rather by a villain or a monster who, as an anomaly in a highly classified social system, "generates plot merely by existing." The hero only reacts to this plot generated by the villain; he "fights back," and the end of the story is his victory. Plot is dismissed as a mere aberration or a nightmare; the reign of innocence and order is restored. Or more precisely, *legitimate* order is restored. The plot the villain generates for his or her own advancement consists of the usurpation or obfuscation of the legitimate rights of the hero or heroine. The discovery of identity and of inheritance that terminates so many of these novels (a dénouement virtually nonexistent in the European Bildungsroman) is the discovery of a *rightful* inheritance and of the heroes' identity as "people endowed with rights." As Moretti puts it, "They have been deprived, we could say, of the right to have rights; restoring it to them is nothing more than an act of justice."

If the English Bildungsroman is suspicious of Bildung—of the changes and transformations of youth, of plot, of history—it is because of its strong commitment to a notion of *justice* based on rights, legal continuity, and legitimacy. This is the way Moretti summarizes the analogy between the English novel and a concept of justice:

> The false testimonies of the villain and the sincere confessions of the hero; the cult of innocence and the all-pervasive opposition of "right" and "wrong"; the firm belief that it is possible to tell a story in an entirely "natural" and unquestionable fashion, that in so doing the meaning of events will automatically reveal itself, and that its evaluation will as a matter of course be unanimous....This is

not a novel—it is a trial. It is the popular view of how a trial should melo-dramatically emphasize the "simplicity" of justice.[4]

Moretti's argument is that this popular view of the simplicity of justice func-tions on the level of ideology, that is, participates in the symbolic legitimation of the existing order.

Further on, Moretti links the "culture of justice" that he has recon-structed from his literary examples to certain historical events and to the historical understanding of these events. Thus, his argument starts with the specificity of literary form that is his concrete given and moves back through the intermediary concept of "culture" or "ideology" or "symbolic form" to historical events (in this case, the English Revolution). Moretti is careful to insist that the culture of justice did not have to take the specific form it took in the English Bildungsroman. It is a matter rather of a specific form receiving its meaning and becoming functional within a particular culture. The form or structure of the plot of the English Bildungsroman was not the inevitable product but rather the expression (or performance, practice) of a certain ideology.

And yet Moretti's analysis already shows us that this is not quite the case. When he understands the English Bildungsroman as a certain negation of its European counterpart, when he sees it as suspicious of Bildung and transfor-mation *because* of its commitment to a certain notion of justice, he shows that the "culture of justice," even as an ideological construct but especially as a plot construction (in the valorization of preservation, restoration, classification), cannot be fully understood, either by an author or by a reader, without such a concept as transformation (thematized as change, Bildung), which is in some sense its opposite. Since each concept is necessary for an understanding of the other, together they define a whole field of possibilities, within which every text makes particular choices. This field of possibilities is not an abstract, logical or formal construction; rather it defines the specific cultural context in which the text's meaning is produced. Thus a text cannot "express" or "prac-tice" a certain ideology without, at the same time, thinking through the implications and consequences of different possible ideological constructions. This is not a question of deliberate choice but a result precisely of the fact that ideological constructs in a literary text need to be formalized (or that formal structures always acquire ideological meanings).

In the following pages I would like to elaborate on this issue by contrast-ing two of Dickens's novels, *Bleak House* (1853) and *Our Mutual Friend* (1865). My argument will proceed in two steps. First, I will analyze the model of narrative implicit in each novel; to bring out some of the differences between these two novels, I will exaggerate their adherence to opposed plot models. Following that, I will look at *Our Mutual Friend* in some detail in order to show how each of its various plots can be understood as a different combination of elements in the field of possibilities generated by those two models.

II

At the symbolic center of *Our Mutual Friend* are the dust mounds. On a level that is still close to their literal meaning—to their material existence— the mounds embody a certain contradiction. Being literally heaps of waste, they negate by their very existence the notion of waste. They are waste that is anything but wasted; they are waste that is made to be the opposite of waste, that is being recycled so that there will be no waste left, no residue. The mounds stand for—not so much symbolically as literally and materially—a very specific kind of transformation, a transformation that does not leave a residue, where what on one level is considered residue or waste can be seen, on another level, as similar to raw material, that is, functional and productive. The mounds that fill up the yard of Harmony Jail at the beginning of the novel are totally removed at the novel's end. But they are not made to disappear; they are simply recycled, carted away to another place where they will be transformed and used, transformed by being used. Having clear material existence and implying constant transformation, the dust mounds represent an economy that should not be confused with the economy of speculation, shares, and paper currency, represented by the Veneerings.[5] The economy of speculation, having no material existence and involving no productive transformation whatsoever, is merely a parody, or travesty, of the economy of recycling. I will return later to this difference.

The emblem of the economy of recycling is Jenny Wren.[6] "You can't tell me the name of my trade, I'll be bound," Jenny says to Headstone and Charley in the chapter where we first meet her. " 'You make pincushions,' said Charley. 'What else do I make?' 'Pen-wipers,' said Bradley Headstone. 'Ha! ha! What else do I make? . . . I only make pincushions and pen-wipers, to use up my waste' " (*OMF*, 272). In fact, the material Jenny uses for making pincushions and pen-wipers is not simply "waste" but waste of waste, the left-overs from her main product, doll's clothes, which are themselves fashioned from waste material. "I made acquaintance with my guests," Riah explains to Fledgby when the latter sees Lizzie and Jenny on the rooftop, "through their coming here to buy our damage and waste for Miss Jenny's millinery. Our waste goes into the best of company, sir, on her rosy-cheeked little customers" (*OMF*, 333). Thus Jenny uses waste to make her dolls' dresses and the waste of waste for her other goods in a process of production that, being entirely based on waste, does not allow any waste and thus involves complete and total recycling.

What is somewhat puzzling in this process is not the complete recyclability without residue but the productive origin of waste, the first moment in which, out of raw material, is generated besides a main product, waste that can then be recycled. In the basket Jenny has just purchased for two shillings are "strings of beads and tinsel scraps" (*OMF*, 332), but we are never told what Pubsey and Co. produces that leaves strings of beads and tinsel scraps as waste. Pubsey and Co. is called "a counting house" (*OMF*, 628), and the only business we see Fledgby and his man of business, Riah, engaged in is money-lending and trafficking in bills. The principle of complete recyclability, of no waste or residue, that characterizes Jenny's production assumes a world of constant processing, of constant transformation, hence without beginning (origin of production) or end (a residue that cannot be recycled). We cannot put our fingers on a primary production in the same way that we cannot locate an irreducible waste that cannot be recycled, transformed, and re-produced again. We are always in the midst of a process; everything is always already (but never merely) waste.

At the symbolic center of *Bleak House* is the court of Chancery and its parodic equivalent, Krook's rag and bottle shop. Like old Harmon, Krook is a dealer in waste. Our first introduction to his shop is through Esther's eyes:

> A shop, over which was written, Krook, Rag and Bottle Warehouse. Also, in long thin letters, Krook, Dealer in Marine Stores. In one part of the window was a picture of a red paper mill, at which a cart was unloading a quantity of sacks of old rags. In another, was the inscription, Bones Bought. In another, Kitchen-Stuff Bought. In another, Old Iron Bought. In another, Waste Paper Bought. In another, Ladies' and Gentlemen's Wardrobes Bought. Everything seemed to be bought, and nothing to be sold there. (*BH*, 38)

The similarity to and difference from *Our Mutual Friend* is obvious. Here too are heaps of waste, but here the waste is only accumulated and never sold, never recycled. Krook, as Bucket summarizes it, "was . . . buying all manner of pieces of furniter, and books, and papers, and what not, and never liking to part with 'em" (*BH*, 636).

The opposite of recycling is hoarding; whereas recycling is a constant process, hoarding leads to an end: spontaneous combustion. Since there is no outlet and no movement, things are bound to implode and "combust." The intransitive, self-reflexive nature of Krook's hoarding is made to be the ob-vious material representation of the court of Chancery, of "the one great principle of the English law, [which] is to make business to itself" (*BH*, 416). The closed system that feeds on itself, "inborn, inbred" (*BH*, 346), necessarily reaches a point of self-annihilation. The spontaneous combustion of Krook, the financial exhaustion of the Jarndyce suit, the death of Richard who has worn himself out, all are manifestations of the inevitable (because internally determined) finality of a process that takes place within a closed system.

It may seem perverse to insist on "finality" in a novel where the characters' major source of frustration is precisely its opposite, the feeling, as Jarndyce puts it, that "through years and years, and lives and lives, everything goes on, constantly beginning over and over again, and nothing ever ends" (*BH*, 73). But the characters' frustration is not really the result of the endlessness of process within Chancery (since suits do come to an end), but rather the result of their own inability to determine the course of that process and bring it to an end. The feeling of endlessness is the expression of a feeling of passivity and futility. The end, inevitable but also meaningless, does come; what follows this end (whether by combustion or by entropy) is precisely waste, an irreducible residue, which, as residue, is useless and meaningless: the bags full of papers that are carted out of Chancery at the end of the Jarndyce suit; the oil, soot, and junk left at Krook's shop.

The dust mounds and Krook's shop, then, do more than function as symbolic objects with clear thematic resonance. Implicit in the representation of each is a different notion of transformation, of plot, of temporality, and of what constitutes beginning, middle, and end, causality, motivation, and logic. In contrast to the constant process of recycling, without beginning or end, that we find in *Our Mutual Friend*, the plot of *Bleak House* has a marked, catastrophic end and a marked, simple beginning. If we take the Jarndyce suit as standing for Chancery and thus for the novel as a whole, we should note that one has to assume the issues involved when the suit was first brought were clear and obvious. Only with time did the case become an entangled mess: "This scarecrow of a suit has, in course of time, become so complicated, that no man alive knows what it means" (*BH*, 3). On a first level, then, the entanglement of plot is the result of sheer temporality; hence, the rejection of everything that contributes to plot is related to a negative view of being in time, to a view of historical change itself as some kind of gigantic entanglement that needs to be undone. On a more obvious level, the simple state of affairs at the beginning got twisted by the law: "The Lawyers have twisted it into such a state of bedevilment that the original merits of the case have long disappeared from the face of the earth" (*BH*, 72). From this initial moment of the twisting and corrupting of a pre-plot simplicity, everything follows according to an inexorable logic.

The "progress" of the plot in *Bleak House* is logical and fully motivated, since it always inheres in itself: since it is the business of the law to generate business for itself, everything that happens within the law is as it should be. And yet the plot also strikes one as arbitrary and illogical because it presents human agents as totally passive, unable to intervene in a process that continues to affect their lives: "we can't get out of the suit on any terms, for we are made parties to it, and *must be* parties to it, whether we like it or not" (*BH*, 73). This is a process that, once set in motion, follows an inevitable, logical course and hence is totally immune to human influence. It ends in a catastrophe that opens some space for human action, returning things to their original, human, state of affairs. The cobwebs are cleaned, and order is restored.

Dickens's overt critique of "precedent and usage" is thus not so simple: to the extent that precedent and usage mean inbreeding and self-perpetuation out of touch with human reality, they are condemned—condemned to follow their own course, their own internally determined end in combustion or entropy. But this end does not open the way for something new, from elsewhere. At the end of the novel Esther is the mistress of a new Bleak House. This new Bleak House is made of all the little plans and improvements Esther added to the old Bleak House, which itself has been changed into a cheerful house by Jarndyce after the death of his great uncle, who had made the house bleak through his involvement with the suit, changing it from its original state as a beautiful house called the Peaks. The changes that follow this initial act of misuse, then, are always in some sense restorations; they always erase a past in order to get back to a more remote past, to a pre-plot past. Though in *Bleak House* we do not have a "villain" such as Uriah Heep responsible for the plot, it is still the case that plot is here viewed negatively: the "good" characters— the ones through whose point of view we read and understand the story (Jarndyce is the prime example)—would rather not have anything to do with it. The plot is not viewed as the proper sphere of action for the characters; rather, they have to manage to free themselves of it in order to act. This "acting," however, is not in a new plot, but in the self-regulating order of a plotless, simple, and just life, as we know Woodcourt's and Esther's life is going to be.[7] As opposed to the corruption of the law is the everlasting power of justice, justice seen as legitimate continuity prevailing against any attempts—brought by time or by institutions corrupted in time—to change or corrupt it.

This is not the view of plot in *Our Mutual Friend*, where the organizing principle is transformation, not restoration. Harmon's main goal is not to regain his father's wealth from the hands of a usurper—to regain his legitimate rights—but to wash the taint and rust off this wealth, to purify it and make it different from what it was. As many critics have pointed out, the plot of *Our Mutual Friend* is different from that of most of Dickens's novels: unconcerned with the discovery of a past secret, it instead places great importance on the characters' will and ability to forge their own destinies, to create the plot of their life rather than simply to react and fight back.[8] This freedom is of course far from complete. John Harmon comes back to England and plans to disguise himself and meet Bella incognito. When Radfoot conspires to kill and impersonate him, what was a free choice becomes a fact imposed from outside, a plot generated by a villain: "It seemed as if the whole country were determined to have me dead. The Inquest declared me dead, the Government proclaimed me dead; I could not listen at my fireside for five minutes to the outer noises, but it was borne into my ears that I was dead" (*OMF*, 428). But Harmon does not merely assume, passively, the role imposed on him, nor does he automatically fight back against a plot generated by a villain to kill him. He chooses between these two possibilities: "John Harmon is dead. Should John Harmon come to life?" (*OMF*, 428) is a genuine question over which he deliberates. He reaches the conclusion that he should not come back to life, but again his decision is changed by the acts of others—by his discovery by the Boffins. Thus what characterizes the plot of *Our Mutual Friend*, especially when we look at it as a sequence of events—as a chronology rather than a teleology—is that characters, heroes and villains alike, make choices, act and react to the acts of others.

This process of choosing freely but always in relation to the choices and actions of others can never be as fully consistent or motivated as the process of internal development and passive reaction we have seen in *Bleak House*. Whereas, as I pointed out, in some sense there is nothing more logical than spontaneous combustion, inbreeding, and the entanglement of characters by the economic interests of the law, there is nothing at all logical about the plot of *Our Mutual Friend*. As Harmon, the chief plotter of the novel, realizes, acting generates wholly unanticipated consequences (the most obvious of which are the accusation against Lizzie's father and its effect on Lizzie herself). The flaw most critics find in the Harmon plot—that it runs out of all proportion to its presumed purpose of testing Bella—is one that Harmon is in his own way fully aware of himself; it is the result of the fact that his acts have consequences that he has not foreseen and that accordingly have little to do with his initial intention. The proliferation and expansion of the plot out of all proportion to an initial purpose that gave rise to it—the freedom of plot marked by a certain gratuitousness and illogic—is what Harmon's story is all about.

But lack of compelling logic is not the only distinctive characteristic of the plot of *Our Mutual Friend*. Since the plot is not generated by the villain alone or by some inner logic independent of human agency (a disembodied villain), but rather by the action and interaction of different characters, the distribution of activity and passivity between villains and heroes, respectively, cannot be maintained. The violence that characterizes the plot generated by the villain will have to be distributed among many characters, including the "good" ones. Hence the violence of transformation, of plot, cannot be seen as a mere regrettable evil; violence has somehow to become positive. This accounts for the curious mixture in this novel of education and positive change with gross manipulation and physical violence: it is totally within the "logic" of the plot that Harmon, its hero, will indulge in a gratuitous and rather cruel manipulation of Bella by stringing her along and delaying the revelation of the truth to her.

Though I will come back presently to the complexity, duality, and even ambiguity of *Our Mutual Friend*, it is important, at this stage, to emphasize its radical aspect; radical, that is, in comparison with the conservatism of *Bleak House*. It is a mistake, it seems to me, to dwell on the rainbow-colored nursery and on the general superfluous luxury surrounding Bella at the end of the novel, or on Lizzie's transformation into a conventional middle-class wife. There is no reason in the world why Dickens should not see the middle-class way of life, comfort and leisure, as highly desirable. What is interesting, however, is that he tries in this novel to show these middle-class privileges as having been achieved through a temporal, historical process of transformation— through the somewhat arbitrary, circumstantial, manipulative, and violent action of individuals reacting to each other—not as belonging to the main characters by legitimate right and restored to them after a painful digression into the world of time, narrative, and history. In other words, he tries through the plot of *Our Mutual Friend* to think of history as a process of transformation rather than as a process of preservation and restoration.

I have tried up to now to describe two narrative elements that are to some extent the result of one logic and yet are not entirely overlapping. The first element is thematic: the recyclability of matter in *Our Mutual Friend* as opposed to the hoarding and inbreeding of *Bleak House*. The second has to do with plot: the notion of transformation and education in *Our Mutual Friend* as against the notion of restoration, recovery, and erasure of plot in *Bleak House*. The link between the two elements can be expressed as follows: the lack of origin and the openness of the future, the dwelling in the middle, in process, that the notion of recyclability implies, is what on another level permits one to think seriously about genuine change—change brought about by the unexpected, conflicting actions of various agents. On the other hand, the inner logic of hoarding followed by combustion implies the erasure of temporality:

the end is a restoration of a state of affairs before the beginning, so that in a sense nothing "happens." The changes that do occur while one is in "plot"— in time, in history—are seen as internally determined and inevitable, inbred and logically produced; hence the possibility of real "events" (that is, unexpected ones) is again denied.

To this point, then, *Bleak House* and *Our Mutual Friend* prove to belong to two different plot models: one emphasizing classification or restoration (related to a conservative "culture of justice") and the other emphasizing transformation (and thus supporting a modern understanding of Bildung as constant change). My claim, however, is that texts never purely adhere to one formal model, never simply express one ideology. In what follows, I will attempt to show, by expanding on my reading of *Our Mutual Friend*, how it generates its specific choices as a response to the entire field of possibilities defined by the two opposed models.[9] I will argue, in other words, that the representation of history as a process of transformation does not occur in a void or in the abstract; it can be articulated only against other forms of plot, other conceptions of history. These other possibilities are not simply logical possibilities, nor are they purely extratextual; they exist in the text that performs the cultural task of thinking through their implications.

III

The best place to start analyzing the mixed form of *Our Mutual Friend* is its end. Using *Bleak House* for the last time as a foil to the later novel will help me make my point. At the end of *Bleak House*, the plot can be erased, effaced, forgotten; if Esther has indeed regained her beauty, as the end at least suggests, then even the material traces of time and plot are effaced. The end of *Our Mutual Friend* is much more complex. On the one hand, plot is seen as a mere unfortunate deviation, which can now be forgotten: "Mr and Mrs John Harmon's first delightful occupation was, to set all matters right that had strayed in any way wrong, or that might, could, would, or should, have strayed in any way wrong, while their name was in abeyance," owing to "John's fictitious death" (*OMF*, 874), that is, while the narrative was going on. On the other hand, Lizzie and Eugene have changed drastically, so that in their case, at least, plot has left indelible marks and cannot be erased as a mere aberration.[10]

But even if we leave aside for a moment the plot of Eugene and Lizzie and look at the Harmon plot alone, the duality of the end remains. The final resolution of the novel—whereby Harmon marries Bella and inherits his father's wealth, leaving Boffin the small mound—is in complete accord with the Harmon will that sets the entire plot in motion. From this perspective, the entire plot seems like a monstrous detour leading us back to the beginning; this meeting of beginning and end—this closure—together with the revelation of true identity and through it the right to inherit, is precisely the sign that the plot can now finally be erased. And yet the final distribution of wealth is effected not through legal obligations or "rights," but rather through the choices of and agreements between characters—choices and agreements they have reached through a process of thinking, acting, and reacting (that is, through the plot). The whole business of the different wills found in the mounds has precisely the function of making us hear at the end of the novel two distinct and opposed voices: the terms of the will that gave rise to the plot have been fulfilled, but the characters have freely chosen to bring their story to this particular end; Harmon inherits and marries Bella as his father's will decreed, and yet he does so not out of any legal obligation but out of choice and through a course of action.

Many novels that end with the restoration of rights to the hero and the exposure of the villain's "plot" include a final scene of "trial": someone (character or narrator) explains what has really taken place, shows what the true motivations and intentions of the characters were, and passes verdict accordingly.[11] This act of rendering justice has a narrative dimension: a true account of events, short, authoritative, usually following a precise chronological order, replaces the previous account of events, which has been the plot. This true account shows the plot to have been lies, error, distortion; it replaces the plot and thus erases it, banishes it as a mere aberration. Such a scene, which dramatizes the negative valuation of plot, terminates *Our Mutual Friend*. It starts when Harmon tells the police inspector the true account of the Harmon murder (which we do not hear, since it presumably repeats the reconstruction of events Harmon has given in an earlier chapter);[12] it continues when Mrs. Boffin gives Bella the true account of Harmon's identity and Boffin's miserliness; and it ends when Harmon, Boffin, Sloppy, and Venus tell Wegg the truth about the "friendly move." Thus testimony is given, truth manifests itself clearly, and justice is done: we can forget the plot, since it was merely error and lies.

But the last chapter of *Our Mutual Friend* is another scene of trial, whose function is quite the opposite. Mortimer goes to dinner at the Veneerings to find out the verdict of society concerning the marriage of Lizzie and Eugene. Lady Tippins informs Mortimer that "such a ridiculous affair is condemned by the voice of Society" and to prove this, she suggests that all the guests form themselves into a committee on the subject (*OMF*, 888). Since all the members of this committee have been ridiculed throughout the previous nine hundred pages, their verdict certainly cannot be taken as the "truth" about the affair. The story of Eugene and Lizzie cannot end with a scene in which an authoritative narrative replaces and thus effaces the actual plot. This in itself indicates that even though Lizzie ends up finding her proper place as the wife of a gentleman (for which her standard English, in spite of her illiteracy, has prepared her and us), this end (this "classification") is not as important as the process of transformation that brought it about.[13]

And yet the story of Eugene and Lizzie is the one that comes closest to having a plot generated by a villain. Lizzie and especially Eugene do change, but not through their own action. Headstone is the "mutual enemy" who brings about, in spite of his own intentions, the changes in Eugene and Lizzie, who remain more or less passive.

The passivity of the hero indicates a resistance to change, just as the linking of plot to the villain signifies that changes are illegitimate. Legitimacy here does not depend on the approximation of reality to a set of abstract ideals but depends rather on an uninterrupted, continuous chain between the present and a certain originating event in the past (the moment when rights, the "rights of our fathers," were granted). If every change is conceived of as an interruption of the chain and hence illegitimate, legitimization takes the shape of erasing or suppressing any marks of change. Thus, in order to be a gentleman, a legitimate bearer of rights, a man has to have had wealth and social position to begin with; if not, he has to acquire them passively; if in fact he had to engage actively in their acquisition, he has to erase or suppress all signs of that process of acquisition. In *Our Mutual Friend* it is Headstone and Charley who are most clearly engaged in this erasure. Both are intent on erasing all marks of transformation, intent on pretending that they, like "genteel" people, did not "get" to where they are but have always been there. In the case of Headstone, we see how this erasure of transformation is also a resistance to what I have called recyclability.

Headstone's profession as a teacher turns him into a conflicted man, torn between a desire to hoard and the need to recycle:

> From his early childhood up, his mind had been a place of mechanical stowage. The arrangement of his wholesale warehouse, so that it might be always ready to meet the demands of retail dealers—history here, geography there, astronomy to the right, political economy to the left...this care had imparted to his countenance a look of care. . . . There was a kind of settled trouble in the face. . . . He always seemed to be uneasy lest anything should be missing from his mental warehouse, and taking stock to assure himself. (*OMF*, 266–67)[14]

What maddens Headstone in Eugene is his "self-possession," and Headstone's own anxiety is manifested by his feeling that nothing he owns is fully and legitimately his, since, on the one hand, it was acquired (and acquired with pain, so that the process of acquiring it cannot be quite forgotten) and, on the other, it has to be given away for him to fulfill the duties of his profession. The way Headstone goes about solving this problem is self-contradictory and hence potentially dangerous: he chooses to instruct a young pupil of poor origin who will become like another self, so that the process of instruction, of recycling knowledge, will not involve any loss to his storehouse. But this young man is necessarily a reminder of his own origins, of his own past that he would rather not remember. In order not to lose anything, Headstone has to remember that he has a past, and in order to suppress the past, he has to agree to let go, to empty himself out with the danger of never being replenished.

The Dickens novel most squarely concerned with the attempt at self-legitimization is of course *Great Expectations*. It is interesting to note that *Our Mutual Friend* contains various scenes that are in one way or another reminiscent of the earlier novel. One is the scene in which Mortimer and Eugene sit late at night in their chambers. The wind is blowing hard, "as if we were keeping a lighthouse," says Eugene. After discussing the merits of keeping a lighthouse, Eugene tells Mortimer about his father's matrimonial designs for him and then relates to him his life story. When he finishes, "It had grown darker as they talked, and the wind was sawing and the sawdust was whirling outside paler windows. The underlying churchyard was already settling into deep dim shade, and the shade was creeping up to the housetops among which they sat. 'As if,' said Eugene, 'as if the churchyard ghosts were rising.' " At this point, a "ghost" appears: "Apparently one of the ghosts has lost its way, and dropped in to be directed. Look at this phantom!" Eugene exclaims (*OMF*, 194). A similar scene—with the dark stormy night, the thoughts of the past, and a ghostly apparition—takes place in *Great Expectations*: "It was a wretched weather; stormy and wet, stormy and wet; mud, mud, mud, deep in all the streets. . . . The wind rushing up the river shook the house that night, like dischargers of cannon or breakings of a sea. When the rain came with it and dashed against the windows, I thought, raising my eyes to them as they rocked, that I might have fancied myself in a storm-beaten lighthouse. . . . I heard a footstep on the stair. What nervous folly made me start, and awfully connect it with the footstep of my dead sister, matters not. It was past in a moment, and I listened again, and heard the footstep stumble in coming to."[15]

The ghost that comes to visit Pip on that stormy night is the ghost of the past, of his own past actions that he attempts to forget, to suppress, in order to believe that his present situation as a gentleman does not depend on his own (hence criminal) acts. But in *Our Mutual Friend*, in the same situation, including the allusions to living in a lighthouse, to being distant, isolated, protected from the world, that the apparition ironically negates in the next minute, the ghost has no relation whatsoever to Eugene's past or actions: it is Rogue Riderhood coming to give evidence against Gaffer Hexam. Whereas the point of the atmospheric description and the evocation of Eugene's background would seem to be to link the apparition to the past, to the psychosocial depth of the character, this is clearly not the case. The similarity to the scene in *Great Expectations* highlights the difference by indicating how Eugene is anything but another version of Pip having to face up to his suppressed past and to the actions that brought him to his present condition. Eugene's passivity is the mark of his legitimacy, of his being a real gentleman; it also means that when he changes—as he certainly does—this change has to be inflicted on him.

Whereas Eugene remains passive, Harmon, as we have seen, not only reacts but acts. And yet one can show that the active Harmon, engaged as he is with others, acting and reacting, does not undergo a genuine transformation. The lack of ease that characterizes him in his first appearances, and that makes Bella think he is a murderer, was merely a temporary reaction to the shock of the attempt on his life. The change of attitude toward Mr. Boffin, his acceptance of insults and rudeness, is revealed to have been only a role he has agreed to play. When Mrs. Boffin finally recognizes Harmon under the disguise of Rokesmith, it is by noticing his similarity to the dejected, sad child that he was years ago. In more general terms, Harmon's near drowning has very little to do with death and rebirth, with drastic transformation, and in this he is totally different from Eugene. Since this is not a universally shared interpretation of the Harmon plot, let me expand on the point.[16]

Eugene's near death obeys the logic of conversion: his old careless self dies, and out of his maimed body, a new man is reborn; this is the metaphysical equivalent of the economy of recycling. Accompanying the near literal death is a figurative death. Eugene here comes closest to Jenny's idea of the relation between life and death. As Jenny explains to Fledgby in the scene on Riah's rooftop, to be alive is to care about money (and one can add, though Jenny does not, that this means to be spiritually dead); to be dead means to be dead to the world of money and thus, at least by implication, to be reborn, spiritually, in the private space of the garden upstairs. Hence her plea to Riah, "Come up and be dead"; hence also her understanding of Fledgby when he says, "Instead of coming up and being dead, let's come out and look alive. It'll pay better" (*OMF*, 785). It is part of Jenny's double nature that she can alternate between being dead and being alive. But the main point in Jenny's distinction between death and life is that you have to die as someone in order to be reborn as someone else; that is, that the duality of life and death (when you are alive to something, you are dead to something else, and vice versa), when translated into a temporal sequence—of dying and being reborn— necessarily implies a radical change: you die to the world, to money, in order to be reborn as a person who cares nothing about money; or conversely you may die spiritually to the values of the rooftop and thus become alive to your interests and to the possibilities of earning money.

Now, if we look at the case of Harmon, we can see that his death and resurrection (unlike Eugene's) have nothing to do with Jenny's scheme. Harmon's death is obviously not a literal one; nor, however, can it be taken as a figurative death. We cannot say that having died as Harmon and been reborn as Rokesmith, he has died to the interests of the world. As Rokesmith, for example, he continues taking extraordinary care of the Harmon fortune: " 'He takes more care of my affairs, morning, noon, and night,' said Mr Boffin, 'than fifty other men put together either could or would' " (*OMF*, 362). The state of living death he experiences has nothing to do with the figurative death that certain living persons can assume when, for example, they go on Riah's rooftop. Instead of a conversion, there is a disguise—a role that can be dropped at any moment.

In fact, Harmon's story fits much better another view of the relation between death and life, a view expressed at the very beginning of the novel by Gaffer Hexam. Like Jenny, Gaffer defines the difference between life and death in terms of money; for both of them, being dead means being dead to money. Hence Hexam's rhetorical questions: "How can money be a corpse's? Can a corpse own it, want it, spend it, claim it, miss it?" (*OMF*, 47). On this definition, death is the moment in which money becomes free to circulate. According to Gaffer, death is not the moment of transformation but merely the occasion or the vehicle for money changing hands, for circulation (which is not recycling). One thing of which Gaffer is absolutely certain is that the dead are not going to come back to life or be in any sense reborn. And since the dead are categorically dead, their money is free to circulate—by theft, but also, as we know from Harmon's case, by wills. When one is "alive" (both literally, in Gaffer's sense, and figuratively, in Fledgby's and Jenny's sense), one owns money, or earns it, or steals it, or saves it; when one is dead, one either gives it up as unimportant (in the figurative sense of death: "Come up and be dead") or merely allows it to circulate (the literal meaning of death). Rather than being *figuratively* dead, Harmon merely *pretends* to be *literally* dead, and since this is merely a pretense, he can come back to the same life, to the same values, to the money. To come back to life, then, is not a betrayal of higher values (accepting the world of Fledgby as opposed to the world of Riah) but an act of just restitution, of getting money back to its rightful owner; it is the catching of thieves, as the final scene with Wegg is designed to demonstrate. The relation between Harmon's pretense of a literal death and the dialectics of figurative death and rebirth is analogous to the relation between the travesty of production in the economy of speculation and the economy of recycling.[17]

Whereas Eugene undergoes a genuine transformation but not through his activity, and Harmon, who is active and plotting, merely puts on and takes off a disguise, Boffin is a mixed and complex case. Immediately following Lightwood's communication that he has come into the possession "of upwards of one hundred thousand pounds" (*OMF*, 133), and long before he has started "playing the role" of a miser, Boffin is accosted on the street by Rokesmith: " 'Now,' thought Mr Boffin, 'if he proposes a game at skittles, or meets a country gentleman just come into property, or produces any article of jewellery he has found, I'll knock him down!' " (*OMF*, 140). Boffin in this scene is not childish, naive, or innocent, but wary and suspicious. This change in him, which has been brought about by the change in his circumstances, by his coming into money, is important to the story, for this suspicion or lack of innocence is what allows him to play an educational role later on. Boffin shows, in fact, that in order to change others—tempt, test, or educate them— one has to change oneself. His ability to improve Bella, test Venus, and tempt Wegg to his destruction is predicated on his moral integrity, on his having not been changed by his fortune, his having not been turned into a suspicious miser; yet at the same time it requires as a condition of possibility his having lost his innocence and become suspicious of people, as misers usually are. This is why it is impossible to decide whether Boffin has been playing a role or has really changed into a greedy miser; he is somewhere in between. Mrs. Boffin shows some understanding of this complexity when she gets genuinely alarmed about Boffin's behavior, even though she is fully aware that he is "merely" playing a role; she knows that one cannot merely play a role. Role playing and real change are here mingled, where Harmon and Eugene embody just one of these elements.

But at the end of the process, Boffin gives the money over to Harmon and thus returns to his status nine hundred pages earlier, innocence and all. The process of education is decidedly over, and the characters can settle for a life of no change. The end of the educational process and Boffin's surrendering of the money are one and the same event because as long as he has money, he is the suspicious, knowing (hence "miserly") character who tempts, tests, and educates.

Though Harmon is the beneficiary of Bella's education, and though he is asked by her to "try" and "test" her, it is Boffin who is the agent of her change. Bella changes by hearing her own words in Boffin's mouth, by seeing herself in another's behavior: she starts changing when her "mean tone . . . has been echoed in her ears by Mr Boffin" (*OMF*, 663). The process of education here is the one in which the teacher, by reflecting or repeating the pupil, becomes a mirror where she can see herself. But teaching by negative example is always a risk, since it involves identification and can produce the opposite of its desired effect. Its success here rests on the assumption that Bella's moral nature is fine—"she's the true golden gold at heart" (*OMF*, 843)—and that she just needs to find her own true nature, which has been hers all along but has been hidden under her willfulness and capriciousness. For Bella, then, it is not so much a matter of change as a recovery of her true nature.[18]

The same is true of Boffin's relation to Wegg. Certain as he is in his own mind that Wegg is a villain beyond cure, Boffin does not try to change him but again, as with Bella, holds up a mirror that reflects—though Wegg does not see it—his villainy. When Boffin pretends to be a miser and takes Bella along in his daily searches for books about misers, the purpose is, as we have seen, to hold a mirror in front of her mercenary face so she can discover her true, moral being. When he brings these books over to the bower for Wegg to read to him, in the company of Venus, his purpose is to excite Wegg into indulging in his own folly. Whereas Wegg is under the impression that, in reading about misers, he is exposing Boffin's miserliness to him, he is in fact reading about himself and is being read by Boffin, who watches him. Thus in the case of both Bella and Wegg, education is conceived of not as a formation of something new, unpredictable (hence also accidental, partial), but as the discovery or recovery of a nature that has always been there. Education here plays the same role that "justice" does in a novel like *Tom Jones*.

IV

I have tried in the first part of this chapter to give an account of two plot models as exemplified in *Bleak House* and *Our Mutual Friend*. These plot models were presented as opposed to each other, and the opposition involved a certain number of features, constituting what I have called the field of possibilities opened up by the two models. In the second part of the chapter, I have tried to show how each of the stories told in *Our Mutual Friend*—that of Eugene, Lizzie, Harmon, Bella, and Boffin—shows a different combination of these features, none of which fully conforms to one model or the other.

This does not mean that something like the culture of justice or the modern idea of Bildung does not exist as an ideological construct, or that it exists but does not impinge on literary works. It certainly does not mean that texts get generated by purely formal, logical constraints having nothing to do with their historical and cultural context. But what gets lost by seeing form as historically determined is the relative autonomy of form: formalization is not simply an expression; form does not simply perform an ideological task. From the moment something like the ideology of justice gets formalized—gets translated into a certain structure of plot with certain features (and it is not really important whether this process takes place in quite the perfect and complete way Moretti makes it appear or manifests itself as a certain formal virtuality), from that moment on, a certain space is opened up in which these features and elements can combine in many different ways. *Our Mutual Friend* may not be a subversive or a radical novel, demystifying this or that ideology, but it shows precisely this freedom of combination, this thinking through of a whole array of possibilities that impose themselves or become available once something like justice or Bildung is seen as congruent with a certain form of plot.

CHAPTER 8

Mortgaging Freedom: The Aesthetic and Its Limit in 'The Princess Casamassima'

❧

The Princess Casamassima (1886) is often regarded as the most Dickensian or Balzacian of James's novels. It is said to be his "most sociological novel," the one most turned outward, toward society, the world, the city, rather than being closed upon "vessels of consciousness" receiving their fine impressions in a kind of social vacuum.[1] The critical question then raised is to what extent James was successful in representing London, the working class, late-nineteenth-century social unrest.[2] Yet critics have also pointed out that the opposition implied in thus situating the novel within the James canon is not so much an opposition between *The Princess Casamassima* and other James novels as a division within the novel itself.[3] Indeed, even a cursory reading of *The Princess Casamassima* would suggest that the opposition between the external and the internal, between social reality and its contemplation, is in some sense the very subject matter of the novel.

There can be little critical disagreement that thematically *The Princess Casamassima* is concerned with the relation between social engagement in the form of revolutionary activity and aesthetic experience. But what exactly is the nature of this relation? Most critics (following the lead of the characters themselves) see Hyacinth as choosing, in the course of the novel, aesthetic experience over political engagement. The issue then becomes *Hyacinth's* failure in regard to the "social question," rather than James's failure or success in dealing with social reality. But could one not say that for Hyacinth, just as for James, the question is not simply choosing one alternative or the other (either "realistic" representation of the social world or representation of the intricacies of consciousness, either social engagement or aesthetic contemplation)? It is true that in the life of Hyacinth aesthetic experience and revolutionary activity are presented as opposites; but it is also true that he can neither combine them nor entirely give up either one of them. Though in the last chapters of the novel Hyacinth claims that he has found a "solution" to his problem, and though the novel is replete with references to "sacrifice," Hyacinth neither reaches a synthesis between the two currents that underlie his experience nor manages to discard one in favor of the other.

I would argue that this double impossibility results from the fact that, despite much of the rhetoric of the characters in the novel, the relation between the political and the aesthetic is not one of pure opposition because the two cannot be separated, clearly distinguished from each other. Indeed, as we shall see, the aesthetic is always in danger of "falling" into the political while at the same time a political act, such as Hyacinth's vow, becomes the condition of possibility for the aesthetic. This unstable relation between what seems to be a set of opposites ends up erasing differences without producing a coherent whole (a consistent way of life, a coherent or stable identity). If Hyacinth at the end of the novel commits suicide, it is not because his choice of the aesthetic brought him to betray the revolution but because he cannot institute such clear differences as to make choice, betrayal, sacrifice, synthesis, possible. This erasure of difference bears strong similarities to the "freedom" we find in Stendhal's novels or the "confusion" (of rank) we find in Austen's. But whereas Austen and the Stendhal of *L'Abbesse* show how differences can ultimately be redrawn, *The Princess Casamassima* does not provide such a solution. It is here that Hyacinth's and James's "failure" lies.

I

Hyacinth's life is often described in the novel as an oscillation, without resolution, between two opposing forces. His fate is "to be divided, to the point of torture, to be split open by sympathies that pulled him in different ways; for hadn't he an extraordinary mingled current in his blood" (165). His diminutive figure, his childlike appearance, may be taken as an indication that he has not grown up, has not advanced beyond an infantile need to reconcile or choose between his two parental figures. When asked whether he is French, Hyacinth cannot answer: "He really didn't know whether he were French or English, or which of the two he should prefer to be. His mother's blood, her suffering in an alien land . . . all this made him French; yet he was conscious at the same time of qualities that did not mix with it" (127). Hyacinth's identity, then, is composite, a mixture, a mingling of incompatible elements. English and French, aristocrat and plebeian, he feels with equal force his "debt" to both his father and his mother. To choose either one would be to repeat that parent's own guilty act: it would amount to "betraying" Florentine once more, as Lord Frederick has done, or to "killing" Lord Frederick all over again, as Florentine has done.

This impossible choice is sometimes presented in the novel as "treachery" ("To desert one of these presences for the other—that idea had a kind of shame in it, as an act of treachery would have had"; 479), and at other times as "sacrifice" ("Sometimes, in his imagination, he sacrificed one to the other, throwing over Lord Frederick much the oftener"; 480). But "sacrifice" proves to be as impossible as "treachery." Hyacinth's only ground for accepting either one of his parents is the belief that that parent has expiated his or her crime. Florentine has paid for her crimes through her suffering in prison; and the "sacrificial Lord Frederick" (167) "had suffered as well, and had fallen under a blow, and had paid with his life" (127; also 168). The death of each parent is an expiation, a suffering that pays, a sacrifice that redeems. To "sacrifice" either one again is to repeat not the initial violence of the crime but the quite as horrible violence of the punishment that should have redeemed it; it is to propose that the payment has not been enough, that the account has not been closed—that death was not a sufficient expiation.

But if sacrificing either parent implies that the initial crime has not been expiated, that the debt has not been paid, affirming that the parents did pay for their crimes does not close the account either, since by paying their debt to each other the parents incurred a new debt, this time toward Hyacinth himself. Hyacinth feels that his father has thrown over not only Florentine but also himself, and the reason for this second treachery is his having paid the penalty for the first one. Thus Hyacinth asserts that "his father would have done great things for him if he had lived" (480); and when Millicent tells him that women have "a great deal to make up to [him]" because of his mother, he replies, "Ah, *she* would have made it up, if they had let her" (529). Accepting either parent (on the grounds that he or she has paid for his or her deeds), just like the betrayal or sacrifice of either one, does not settle accounts but simply creates new debts.

Hyacinth's reluctance to choose, then, is the other side of his desire to stay out of the vicious circle of violence and revenge, of debt and restitution. And this is where the question of revolutionary activity becomes relevant, for Hyacinth's very participation in the revolution can be explained only by stating that he is "a child who has an account to settle. Oh, a thumping big one!" (216). By virtue of his parentage, "it was conceded to him that he had a larger account to settle even than most. He was *ab ovo* revolutionist" (282). The revolution is very often described in terms of redressing a balance: "We all have an account to settle," Muniment tells Hyacinth on their first meeting, and Hyacinth's thought is that Muniment "would be sure to be one of the first to be paid. He would make society bankrupt, but he would be paid" (127). Hyacinth's distance from revolutionary activity and ideals is precisely his resistance to a settling of accounts that involves further aggression, acts of spoliation, and violent possession. His inclination toward the world of art and culture does not express his having "chosen" his putative father over his mother (we have seen that he resists such a choice) but rather indicates his attempt to occupy a position outside the circuit of accounts, an "aesthetic" position defined as disinterested contemplation, free of desire for possession.

The initial problem for Hyacinth is that he needs to choose between his incompatible and incongruous parents if he wishes to fashion for himself some sort of coherent identity. The problem can be rephrased as that of a choice between revolutionary involvement and aesthetic engagement only when the mother—French and plebeian—and the presumed father—a British aristocrat—are cast as the representatives of revolutionary fervor and artistic sensibility, respectively. It is the thought of his French, "passionate, plebeian mother" that initially fills him "with the vague, clumsy, fermentation of his first impulses towards social criticism," whereas the thought of his "long-descended, supercivilised sire" is evoked when he has to account for "the fact that many things in the world as it was constituted grew intensely dear to him" (479). The "things in the world" that are dear to him are objects of beauty, products of culture; and they belong to "the world as it was con-stituted," since for Hyacinth any attempt to constitute the world differently will result in their destruction. The revolution as Hyacinth sees it involves not only a change in possession but the destruction of objects of value through their equal distribution among many. "You know how extraordinary I think our Hoffendahl (to speak only of him)," Hyacinth tells the Princess, "but if there is one thing that is more clear about him than another it is that he wouldn't have the least feeling for this incomparable, abominable old Venice. He would cut up the ceilings of the Veronese into strips, so that every one might have a little piece. I don't want every one to have a little piece of anything, and I have a great horror of that kind of invidious jealousy which is at the bottom of the idea of a redistribution" (396–97). Hence Hyacinth implicitly equates investment in aesthetic experience (disinterested con-templation, which refuses possession and leaves the object intact) with a conservative support of the social status quo, which he links to his presumed father.

But the simple equating of mother with revolution and father with the preservation of culture cannot be sustained. Hyacinth looks like a French-man, "and a large part of the time he felt like one—like one of those he had read about in Michelet and Carlyle" (102); this, together with his facility in picking up the language, makes him, in his mind, suitable for some clandestine revolutionary activity: "if it should become necessary in certain contingencies that he should pass for a foreigner he had an idea that he might do so triumphantly, once he could borrow a blouse" (102). But Hyacinth also looks like a "duke in disguise" (445), and when he is called upon to act for the revolution in a particular circumstance, it is because he would easily "pass" not for a French worker but for an English aristocrat: " 'Hyacinth is to receive a card of invitation to a certain big house,' [Muniment] went on, 'a card with the name left in blank, so that he may fill it out himself. It is to be good for each of two grand parties which are to be given at a few days' interval. That's why they gave him the job—because at a grand party he'll look in his place' " (581).

Revolutionary activity, then, is not exclusively related to the mother but can be linked also, paradoxically, to the father, who thus does not stand unequivocally for the social status quo and the preservation of culture. This double aspect of the father is expressed also in the double paternity read in Hyacinth's very name, Robinson being the name Lord Frederick used when visiting Florentine, and Hyacinth being the name of his maternal grandfather, a revolutionary who was killed on the barricades. But the inner division of the father does not end here. The grandfather, as one who died on the barricades, can stand for the tradition of the French revolution and thus for France as a symbol of the struggle for social justice. But as an artisan, a clockmaker, the grandfather can also symbolize France as the center of culture, Paris as "tremendously artistic and decorative" (382), an association that runs throughout the novel, as when Poupin's taste and excellence as a bookbinder are explained by his having "la main parisienne" (125). (Indeed, one can claim that as a clockmaker the grandfather can function as a metaphor for the novelist, since clockmaking involves attention to detail and an understanding of time.)

One can of course see the clockmaker-revolutionary not as an image of the inner division of the father but rather as a figure who has managed to successfully combine the two strands that for Hyacinth remain tragically separate and antagonistic. Such an interpretation can account for Hyacinth's emotional investment in his grandfather, his attempt to find in him a model for an undivided identity. When he is in Paris, Hyacinth imagines that he is accompanied by his grandfather who, in his double capacity of revolutionary and artist, can oversee his visit to a city that, like him, unites revolution and culture. But though Hyacinth can easily imagine his grandfather in his revolutionary activity—he can "reconstruct" the place of the barricade he died on, he can see him good-humoredly going with him to visit churches despite his status as a "republican martyr" (381)—he cannot bring him to life in his other, artistic capacity; and the grandfather fades away as Hyacinth is walking along the quays, looking at books, and disappears when he enters the Louvre. His insubstantiality in the cultural domain, as well as the fact that he ended up dying on a barricade, suggests that he too could not successfully combine the artistic and the revolutionary, that rather than reaching a synthesis, he either remained a divided figure, oscillating between the two ways of life, or ended up on the side of the revolution at the expense of artistic vocation.

We have seen that revolutionary activity cannot be represented exclusively by the figure of the mother, any more than the figure of the father can stand unambiguously for the world of culture. Revolutionary engagement, then, is not the result of the choice of one parent over the other, but rather an expression of the desire to settle accounts with both parents, whereas the inclination toward the world of culture, of artistic appreciation and production, represents an attempt to occupy a position outside this cycle of debt and violence. The involvement of the father figures (the grandfather but also Poupin and Vetch) in both revolutionary activity and the world of culture can now be read as the instability of the aesthetic position, as its liability to fall into its opposite, the political.

Indeed, the aesthetic ideal of disinterested contemplation free of desire for possession is, in this novel, hard to maintain. That position depends on a certain affinity with the world of beautiful objects, but it also requires that a certain distance from these objects be maintained. The "leisure class," those who are in possession, can function as *representations* of culture; thus, for example, Lady Aurora's perfect manners; Sholto's clothes; or the Princess's conversation, art objects, and music can all embody for Hyacinth culture and civilization, just as much as the pictures in the Louvre do. But one cannot really say that any one of them occupies the aesthetic position toward the culture they embody: Lady Aurora has no appreciation for Inglefield; Sholto's crudeness and vulgarity preclude any true appreciation of the culture he represents; and the Princess's interest in art may be just one fad among others,[4] or the *mise en scène* for her acting the role of a princess, so that when she decides to play the role of a *bourgeoise* instead, she gets rid of her art objects.

But if those in possession cannot occupy the aesthetic position, neither can one claim this position for the dispossessed, since they either lack taste altogether (for example, Millicent) or, as in the case of Poupin, their artistic position is vitiated by their resentful desire for possession; thus when Hyacinth praises the monuments of Paris, Poupin says: "Ah, yes, it's very fine, no doubt . . . but it will be finer when it's ours" (405). Hyacinth, by virtue of his double, contradictory inheritance, is situated between the dispossessed and those in possession (is neither or both), and this position determines his possibilities and impossibilities.[5]

Hyacinth's particular situation is described in the novel by the Princess (who echoes James's own description of Hyacinth in the Preface): "Fancy the strange, the bitter fate: to be constituted as you are constituted, to feel the capacity that you must feel, and yet to look at the good things of life only through the glass of the pastry-cook's window!" (337).[6] The "good things of life," especially when put in the context of a pastry-cook's shop, suggest objects of consumption; the glass of the window is what prevents possession; and according to the Princess, Hyacinth's predicament, "watching from behind the pastry-cook's window," is one of "ressentiment." And indeed Hyacinth often feels envy and a desire for "the good things of life": "He wanted to drive in every carriage, to mount on every horse, to feel on his arm every pretty woman" (164). But resentment leads to a desire for revenge, for restitution, for a settling of accounts, possession, and spoliation—in other words, precisely to the circuit of debt and violence Hyacinth, because of his double parentage, seeks to avoid. If the revolutionaries see Hyacinth as a person who, by virtue of the wrong done to his mother, has an account to settle with society, and if the Princess sees him as a claimant who, by virtue of his refinement and sensibility (which he presumably inherited from his father), has a better right to the good things of life than those in possession, Hyacinth himself refuses either to settle accounts or to press a claim for possession, since both lead to violence and destruction.[7] On the other hand, merely remaining at a distance, behind the glass, yields only a feeling of melancholy and sense of loss:

> He was liable to moods in which the sense of exclusion from all that he would have liked most to enjoy in life settled upon him like a pall. They had a bitterness, but they were not invidious—they were not moods of vengeance, of imaginary spoliation: they were simply states of paralysing melancholy, of infinite sad reflection, in which he felt that in this world of effort and suffering, life was endurable, the spirit able to expand, only in the best conditions, and that a sordid struggle, in which one should go down to the grave without having tasted them, was not worth the misery it would cost, the dull demoralisation it would entail. (163–64)

The problem Hyacinth faces is how to stay on the other side of the glass without feeling "paralysing melancholy," how to enjoy without taking possession. To the extent that the word "enjoy" connotes possession, it dramatizes the difficulty, if not the impossibility, of Hyacinth's desire. Hence the attempt to make a distinction: "It was not so much that he wished to enjoy as that he wished to know; his desire was not to be pampered, but to be initiated" (164). But it is not at all clear whether knowledge can be exercised at a distance (without being sheer fascination), whether it can be attained without "possession." Hyacinth's impasse remains the same: he can neither break the window nor simply stay on the other side.

II

Since political involvement is seen in the novel in terms of desire for spoliation and possession, it can function as a figure for, or be figured by, the sexual.[8] Thus Hyacinth's story can also be read in terms of his relation to sexual desire, his position within the Oedipal triangle he constitutes with his parents. But since the sexual is also seen as the opposite of the political (the revolutionaries, stereotypically misogynistic, do not trust women and see them as a threat to their revolutionary ardor), this figuration is not a sheer repetition or redundancy.

With his prostitute mother and noble father, Hyacinth acts out the typical "family romance" in its second, sexual stage (following the discovery of the difference between the sexes).[9] The certainty of maternity means that the figure of the mother remains anchored in reality, whereas the uncertainty that always surrounds the father means that he can be "worked" by the imagination, transformed and translated into a higher status. Hyacinth does not need to sympathize with the poor to prove that he is Florentine's son; if anything this is the oppressive reality (the prison, the "chain"; 160) from which he would like to free himself. But he can never have proof enough that he is a "natural gentleman"; since his doubts about his father's identity (which create, express, and double his sense of illegitimacy) preclude any certainty about his status as a "gentleman," this status has to be constantly earned anew by demonstrating a natural affinity with the world of the presumed father.[10] The world of the father is created and imagined rather than given, and the right to this world is never fully gained and possessed but needs always and over again to be reaffirmed, regained.[11] And it can always be given the lie by material reality.

Since Hyacinth can neither accept both his parents nor choose between them, he attempts to find surrogate parents who, as models for identification, will allow him a way out of his impasse. In various ways Pinnie and Mr. Vetch, M. and Mme. Poupin, Millicent and Sholto, the Princess and Paul Muniment all serve as parent figures. These surrogates, however, do not prove much different from the original pair. Like Florentine and Lord Frederick, Pinnie and Mr. Vetch have a lot "to make up" to Hyacinth because of the initial harm they (and he) feel they inflicted upon him by taking him to see his mother in prison. Pinnie feels that she has never paid enough for this crime, that despite her sickness, loss of livelihood, and general degeneration, she has not made full amends: at the moment of her death "what was most alive in Pinnie . . . was the passion of repentance, of still further expiation" (370). Vetch's giving Hyacinth money can also be interpreted as an attempt to pay a debt and thus expiate a crime—especially since Vetch's initial attitude to Hyacinth was one of curious contemplation ("The youngster is interesting. . . . I shall watch him with curiosity"), but with a definite lack of "investment" ("I shall always be glad that . . . I never invested in that class of goods"; 72). On the other hand, the other pairs of parents get involved in a cycle of betrayal and sacrifice. Hyacinth knows that the Princess will "sacrifice" him (Sholto tells him as much), and he presses Muniment quite forcefully to explain how he could have sacrificed him by bringing him to Hoffendahl. His spying on the Princess and Paul in the company of the Prince puts him explicitly in the position of the betrayed, a position he also occupies when he sees Millicent and Sholto in the shop toward the end of the novel. As the Princess puts it, Hyacinth's friends "have a curious way of being fond of [him]" (331)—they sacrifice or betray him. If Paul has sacrificed him by bringing him to Hoffendahl, the Princess (but also the Poupins and Mr. Vetch) are intent on betraying him by trying to prevent him from keeping his word. The cycle of treachery and sacrifice, of debt and payment, continues; the displacement of parental relations onto surrogate parents does not take Hyacinth out of this cycle but merely gives it a new form.

Pinnie and Vetch, M. and Mme. Poupin, function as surrogate parents in the most literal sense: Pinnie brings him up, and Poupin, when Hyacinth joins Crookenden's workshop, "was parental," "he took him in hand, made him a disciple" (120). The other two pairs—Millicent and Sholto, the Princess and Paul—are parental in a more figurative sense (only Millicent is ever explicitly described as a parent). What differentiates them from the other two pairs is that their betrayal is seen as explicitly sexual. The "literal" parents lack sexuality entirely. Millicent sardonically calls Vetch Pinnie's "young man" (109); Pinnie's adoption of Hyacinth is described as the only way for her to become a mother (57–58); and the marriage between the Poupins is a marriage only of minds and hearts (123). With Millicent and Sholto and the Princess and Paul, by contrast, we have parent figures whose sexuality is quite as explicit as that of the original parents. In both these cases, the scenes of betrayal have an Oedipal flavor; they are repetitions of the "primal scene."[12] The betrayal and the sacrifice become in these instances the sexual betrayal of the mother (her prostitution), her sacrifice of the child, her giving herself to the father.

But if the classical Oedipal scenario casts the discovery of sexual relations between the parents as the betrayal and prostitution of the mother, in Hyacinth's case the betrayal is on the part of both the mother and the father. Clearly Hyacinth has very little interest in his Oedipal rival, Sholto, whom he supplants with the Princess, just as Sholto "supplants" him with Millicent; it is Millicent's betrayal that hurts. But in his relation with Paul and the Princess, the reverse is true. With all his love for the Princess, Hyacinth takes his being "sacrificed" by her for granted. What comes unexpected is his betrayal by Paul: "The tears rose to his eyes, as they had done more than once in the past six months, and a question, low but poignant, broke from his lips, ending in nothing. . . . 'How could he—how *could* he—?' " (293). What hurts Hyacinth in this case is not the betrayal by the prostitute mother but that of the father who is ready and willing to abandon the child. Since Muniment's "sacrifice" of Hyacinth to Hoffendahl is followed closely by his betrayal of him with the Princess, it can be said that it is the father's *sexuality* that leads him to abandon the child in order to replace him in the mother's affections.

But the situation is even more complex: the betrayal is not simply on the part of mother and father but also on the part of the child. When Hyacinth reflects on the (inverted) "primal scene" in which his mother killed his father "with a long knife," we are told:

> He was conscious that he didn't hate the image of his father, as he might have been expected to do; and he supposed this was because Lord Frederick had paid so tremendous a penalty. It was in the exaction of that penalty that the moral proof, for Hyacinth, resided: his mother would not have armed herself on account of any injury less cruel than the episode of which her miserable baby was the living sign. She has avenged herself because she has been thrown over, and the bitterness of that wrong had been in the fact that he, Hyacinth, lay there in her lap. He was the one to have been killed; that remark our young man often made to himself. (168)

Thus Lord Frederick dies because Hyacinth has been born, he dies instead of him ("He was the one to have been killed"); more than his father betraying and abandoning him (and having to make up to him for this betrayal or sacrifice), it is Hyacinth who supplants his father, who owes a debt of life to the father who died because of him, instead of him.

It seems, then, that for Hyacinth Oedipal sexuality (like revolutionary activity) involves all participants in acts of violence, betrayal, and sacrifice. His attempt to stay out of the cycle of debt will thus depend on his ability to establish relations that bypass the Oedipal, to find a sexuality that will be the equivalent of the aesthetic. His relation to Hoffendahl is precisely such an attempt, though, as we shall see, a failed one.

Hoffendahl offers a particularly appealing fantasy of undivided parent-hood (hence, of undivided identity) since, not caring for women himself, he can be seen as a father whose relation to the child is not mediated by the mother, is, rather, specular or narcissistic: "when Hyacinth stood before him [Hoffendahl,] he recognized him as the sort of little chap that he had in his eye (one who could pass through a small orifice"; 334). Where the aside seems to suggest both a homosexual relation and a certain kind of sexual reproduction (cloacal birth), the main sentence evokes a narcissistic relation understood both as a specular relation (this specularity accounts for the ambiguity of "he recognized him," where the "recognition" starts out as Hyacinth's recogni-tion of Hoffendahl and changes into its specular opposite, Hoffendahl's rec-ognition of Hyacinth) and as artistic, asexual production.[13] Narcissistic or artistic creation, "through the eye," resists the urge for possession that always brings about destruction, and avoids Oedipal betrayal by remaining specular and dual.[14]

In *The Princess Casamassima*, then, vision stands for the possibility of imaginative creation. Vision is not presented as the tool of observation (hence of spying, surveillance, and discipline); rather, what the novel emphasizes about vision is its implausibility, the ability to "see" more than is really there, hence to create.[15] Thus, in the theater, where Hyacinth and Millicent are seated across the house from the Princess, Sholto, and Mme. Grandoni, Millicent can still "see" with impossible precision:

> Millicent Henning had a glance of such range and keenness that she was able to make out the details of his [Sholto's] evening dress, of which she appreciated the "form"; to observe the character of his large hands; and to note that he appeared to be perpetually smiling, that his eyes were extraordinarily light in colour, and that in spite of the dark, well-marked brows arching over them, his fine skin never had produced and never would produce, a beard. (180–81)

She also "observes" Mme. Grandoni's face and clothes, including the fact that "her rather soiled white gloves were too large for her" (182).

At any rate, the understanding of Hoffendahl as a narcissistic creator, a father who withholds himself from women, explains why this supreme revo-lutionary is also characterized as an artist. Moreover, he is an artist not only for Hyacinth, who speaks of him as "a great musician" and "composer" (334), but also for other characters, who refer to him as "the Master," "the real thing," "the genuine article" (332, 334, 295), terms that in James's writings are used to describe artists and artistic creation. Hoffendahl, then, embodies the impossible combination of the revolutionary and the artist; hence his hold on Hyacinth.

In Hyacinth's search for a non-Oedipal relation, Hoffendahl was preceded by Muniment. Hyacinth's understanding of Muniment is that though he is a revolutionary who talks of "settling accounts," he is neither bitter nor resentful, and Hyacinth implicitly links this lack of drive toward possession to Muniment's (presumed) sexual indifference:

> For a revolutionary, he was strangely good-natured. The sight of all the things he wanted to change had seemingly no power to irritate him, and if he joked about questions that lay very near his heart his pleasantry was not bitter nor invidious; the fault that Hyacinth sometimes found with it, rather, was that it was innocent to puerility. . . . Apparently he cared nothing for women. (205)

Muniment, then, can be seen as a figure for the artist, and we can interpret his rationalistic (rather than sentimental) way of looking at the revolution as indicative of aesthetic judgment. In his assessment of Hoffendahl's past exploits, Muniment insists on the "economy of material" (288); this concept is not simply a sign of a rational mind (of "too much arithmetic," as Poupin says); it can also be understood as a formal criterion one may use in evaluating a work of art (for example, a novel by Henry James). But Muniment cannot retain his "artistic" detachment: he becomes the Princess's lover (at least this is what Hyacinth and the Prince think), sacrifices the aesthetic, and betrays Hyacinth. Since his indifference to sexuality is what allowed him to successfully unite artistic detachment and revolutionary involvement, his "fall" into sexuality can also be read as his political downfall.

In describing characters who withhold themselves from sexuality, the novel represents, at least momentarily, this impossibility—the revolutionary or political artist. Sexuality seems to serve here as a mediating term, in Lévi-Strauss's sense: a term whose function it is to resolve a contradiction. It is as if characters can keep their "artistic" detachment while engaging in the political since—and to the extent that—they have refused the equivalent of the political, that is, the sexual. The key question, however, is to what extent this refusal is possible. In Muniment's case, it seems simply a matter of giving in to sexual desire. But in the case of Hyacinth's relation to Hoffendahl, the "Oedipal" involvement seems both a structural inevitability and independent of the characters' choice. The vow, the promise made to the father, the sign of the bond between them, is not simply outside the Oedipal triangle since, as we have seen, it represents Hyacinth's attempt to pay with his life for the life of the father who was killed instead of him, because of him. The mother reappears here in the figure of the Princess, who tries to come between Hyacinth and Hoffendahl, separate father and son, kill the Duke instead of him, be like Florentine all over again. Fulfilling the vow (killing a duke) is thus necessarily a repetition of the crime of the mother.[16] If, for a moment, it seemed that resistance to Oedipal sexuality would allow a synthesis between the political and the aesthetic, now, when such resistance is proved impossible, the two options between which it was supposed to mediate become impossible too: the revolutionary artist loses his aesthetic detachment (becomes involved in sexuality) and by the same stroke loses his political credibility and power.

III

A simple way to read the plot of *The Princess Casamassima* (and a common way for the characters themselves to read their story) is as a depiction of Hyacinth's gradual shift from social commitment to aesthetic engagement. Hyacinth is initially positioned on the side of the social revolution, with his involvement increasing through a series of mediators, each of whom is himself more involved, closer to the "center"—from Vetch, to Poupin, to Muniment, to Hoffendahl. The climax of this involvement is the moment in which he meets Hoffendahl and takes the vow to act at the call of the master-revolutionary. This encounter completes a movement, as Hyacinth himself notes when he tells the Princess, "I was hanging about outside, on the steps of the temple, among the loafers and the gossips, but now I have been in the innermost sanctuary—I have seen the holy of holies" (330). Having reached the innermost point at the moment of the vow, Hyacinth's social engagement starts declining, giving way to a growing knowledge, acquaintance, appreciation, commitment to its opposite: aesthetic contemplation and creation. This interest also undergoes development. If the intensification of the social commitment is described in terms of an approach to a center, the increasing acquaintance with the world of culture is described in terms of an extension of the periphery. This movement of expansion (of Hyacinth's world, hence of his impressions and aesthetic pleasure) starts with his first meeting with Rosy Muniment and her "double," Lady Aurora,[17] and grows from the initial acquaintance with the Princess and the visit to Medley up to the trip to Europe. It reaches its climax at the moment Hyacinth decides to go beyond binding books to writing them, and his letters from Europe to Vetch and the Princess are the first fruits of this artistic vocation.

Since there is no doubt that Hyacinth's entry into the world of culture follows his involvement with the revolutionaries, and since social engagement is repeatedly seen as the opposite of aesthetic activity, the usual reading of Hyacinth's life (by critics and characters alike) is that his social engagement, which for a while was in the ascendancy, declines *when and because* its opposite starts gaining hold on him. Hyacinth's tragedy, then, becomes one of bad timing (a kind of Hardyesque "anachronism"); the order to carry out the promise comes too late, when Hyacinth is no longer committed to the cause.

There are some indications, however, that this is not really the case. The first has to do with the most elaborate artistic effect in the novel—the ambiguity James generates at the beginning of Book III. The last chapter of Book II (Chapter 21) ends with Hyacinth riding in the carriage together with Paul, Poupin, and Schinkel to see Hoffendahl: "They all ended by sitting silent, as the cab jogged along murky miles, and by the time it stopped Hyacinth had wholly lost, in the drizzling gloom, a sense of their whereabouts" (296). Book III starts with the sentence, "Hyacinth got up early—an operation attended with very little effort, as he had scarcely closed his eyes all night" (299). In reading the novel for the first time, we assume that the morning is the one following the night of the visit to Hoffendahl, and that Hyacinth did not close his eyes all night because of what took place among the conspirators. This assumption can be maintained for a whole page; despite several indications that under normal circumstances would have led us to believe we are dealing with a different kind of scene, our tendency is to interpret these points to conform to our strongest assumption—that we are presented with Hyacinth's situation and state of mind after the meeting with Hoffendahl. For example, the indication that we are in the country, probably in a large country house, is not what we would have expected and yet we make it fit, especially since the last sentence of the previous chapter explicitly mentioned Hyacinth's loss of sense of his whereabouts, making it possible that he may have been taken to the country. The indication that "there entered through his open casement the breath of a world enchantingly new" seems at first incongruous, but since it is followed by "after his recent feverish hours, inexpressibly refreshing to him," and since the only "recent feverish hours" we know about are those of the scene in the Sun and Moon and what presumably happened afterward, we reinterpret even this indication (for example, by giving "the breath of a world enchantingly new" a symbolic, rather than literal, meaning). It is only on the next page that we receive an unambiguous indication that the scene we have been reading about does not take place on the day after the meeting with Hoffendahl: we are told that Hyacinth arrived at wherever he is at ten o'clock the night before, whereas we know from the previous chapter that he did not set out to Hoffendahl's place before midnight (296). Immediately afterward the Princess is mentioned, and gradually we find out that a considerable time has elapsed between the end of Book II and the beginning of Book III (three months, to be precise; 326), and that the night before, with its fever and excitement, is another night, involving another excitement.

This is a very explicit "trick" on the part of James, and a unique one in the novel. We have had other instances of temporal manipulation, to be sure. For example, there was an unannounced lapse of time in Book I, when

Millicent reappears in Lomax Place, and we find out only gradually that ten years have passed since, at the end of the previous chapter, we left Hyacinth and Pinnie in the carriage coming back from Millbank prison (98). Nor is this the first instance of an important scene told in flashback. The scene in which Hyacinth confronts Pinnie with questions about the woman he had visited in prison years ago and achieves complete clarification on the subject of his parents is also told in retrospect, out of sequence (166). What makes this episode unique (and sets it apart from the others) is the creation of a deliberate ambiguity, of a temporary confusion between Hoffendahl and the Princess, the Sun and Moon and Medley, the site of social revolution and the world of culture and privilege. The text, in other words, proposes that, opposed as these two possibilities are, they can be confused, read for each other, stand for each other.

Hyacinth himself suggests a way to understand the conflation of his vow and his stay in Medley. The visit to Medley is the result of a vow he made to the Princess ("wherever you should call for me, I would come"; 253); but it is also the result of his vow to Hoffendahl. Hyacinth hesitates to stay at Medley past the weekend because he sees the Princess as a threat to his liberty. This liberty has always been of a precarious nature: it is the "liberty he had managed to keep" in the face of economic constraints (he is not economically free), and it is a liberty that he has recently mortgaged to Hoffendahl (311). This freedom is clearly linked to the aesthetic position: culture for Hyacinth is always equated with economic privilege, and "expanding the spirit" depends on leisure, on being free from the "sordid struggle" for everyday subsistence (163). That is why the freedom to do whatever one wants is always for Hyacinth the freedom to enjoy aesthetic experience. But though Hyacinth gave Hoffendahl a mortgage on this freedom, and though he feels the Princess is curtailing it, he also gains a certain freedom. Hyacinth does succumb to the Princess—is in her service—but that allows him the luxury of staying at Medley, of enjoying its library and the conversation and music of the Princess, as opposed to the daily task of earning money (though not as opposed to bookbinding, which is an expression of artistic talent—he will bind books for the Princess). Similarly, Hyacinth does limit his freedom by the vow he makes to Hoffendahl, but that allows him, among other things, to go to Europe and see Paris and Venice. Hyacinth is ready to lose wages by staying at Medley and to spend all his money on going to Europe because, having taken the vow, he does not have to worry about the future, about his survival. The trip to Europe is an example of aesthetic experience not only because Hyacinth sees the monuments of culture, receives new impressions, and makes his entry into the world of art as a writer, but also (and primarily, since this is the condition of possibility of all that) because he lives a life of leisure without concern for economic survival: he has become one of the privileged (but without an act of violence or even the pressing of a claim).[18]

Thus instead of saying that Hyacinth lost interest in social struggle, symbolized by his vow, because he gained greater access to the world of culture and aesthetic production, we have to say quite the opposite: that it is because of his absolute commitment, which has made him take the vow, that he gains greater access to the world of culture, be it Medley or Europe. The relation between the vow and Medley is temporal and causal—Medley follows the vow, as a consequence—but the relation between them is not one of simple opposition and exclusion. The vow is not (or not only) in opposition to the life he leads in Medley and Europe; it is also its condition of possibility. Whereas the Princess thinks that if Hyacinth had come to Medley before he took the vow, he would not have taken it, and Vetch thinks that if Hyacinth sees Europe and discovers all the beauty of the existing world, he will give up wanting to change it (374–75), Hyacinth understands that Medley and Europe have become a possibility only because he has taken the vow (327–28). Whereas Poupin, the Princess, and even Paul see Hyacinth as having deserted the cause because of his growing commitment to the world of culture, Hyacinth knows that if it were not for the vow he has taken, he would have never gained access to this world. The vow, we can say, allows Hyacinth to overcome his "paralysing melancholy" by making the world of culture accessible to him without engaging him in acts of spoliation and possession. This "solution," however, is only of short duration.

IV

Though the vow was taken in a moment of revolutionary zeal, it does not really stand for social commitment (though it manifests itself in acts that may be considered revolutionary). The vow is in a certain sense empty of all content; it is, as Hyacinth says, not a vow to believe in something but a vow to obey. In its semantic emptiness, the vow can thus function to at once limit Hyacinth's freedom and leave him free to do whatever he wants, that is, to give him the necessary grounds for aesthetic experience.

The vow is a promise given at a certain moment to act in the future. But under what circumstances can one make such a promise? Hyacinth tells Vetch, "We don't know what we may be when the time comes" (173), and in general thinks "that there was no knowing what might happen" (161). Mme. Grandoni, all too aware of the unpredictability of the Princess, declines to promise the Prince that she will always stay with her (238). Since we do not know what we or others may be or do in the future, the promises we make cannot engage our feelings, moral standards, or beliefs; they can only be promises of blind obedience or word of honor (Vetch thinks that if Hyacinth made a promise, he will keep it, as a gentleman, no matter how he feels; 469). The promise engages only actions that are seen, from this perspective, as separate from sentiments and beliefs. As opposed to the romantic and sentimental notion of the Poupins that our actions are outward manifestations of our inner nature, temperament, feelings, and beliefs (they object to Hyacinth's acting, since he does not believe any more), Hyacinth's vow assumes action in possible disjunction with inner belief. Indeed, it is precisely because of the impossibility of engaging one's beliefs and feelings in the future that a promise to act in a certain way is necessary in the first place. Thus the very promise to act in a certain way is predicated on the possibility of disjunction between feelings and actions, a disjunction that the promise in fact entails. As Hyacinth puts it, once he has committed himself through his vow, he is "free" to feel and believe whatever he wishes: " 'Isn't it enough, now, to give my life to the beastly cause,' the young man broke out, 'without giving my sympathy?' " (336). We can say that from the moment of the vow, Hyacinth becomes a different person; he is now free to feel and believe whatever he wishes; he is no longer the creature of his reality and conditions, and this difference and freedom depend precisely on his having taken the vow. The vow as a disjunction between inside feelings and outside action functions as a limit to freedom that enables freedom.

The vow Hyacinth takes is that if called, he will obey, but there is no certainty that he will be called. In narrative terms an event such as the vow opens up two possible sequences: Hyacinth will either be called to act or not be called (with the first possibility again opening up two possible sequences: Hyacinth will either obey the call or not obey the call).[19] We expect one of the sequences to be realized—become the actual story—whereas the other, the road not taken, remains a virtual road, not actualized because excluded ("sacrificed").

This narrative bifurcation into the actual and the virtual manifests itself in James's texts through the theme of the ghost. In a ghost story ("The Jolly Corner," for example), a self compares its life to a "ghost," to the self one might have been had one made another choice, considers the life one could have lived had one taken a different turn. But for Hyacinth, as for other James characters, the "virtual" or "ghostly" is not substantively different from the "actual" or "lived." Hyacinth claims that once he has made the vow, it does not really matter whether he will be called or not (and we shall see in a minute that, in a certain sense, one can assert the same about the subsequent choice—

it does not matter if he obeys the call or not). When the Princess suggests that if Hoffendahl's call never comes, "he would wait all the while, *sur les dents*, in a false suspense," he admits "that this would be a sell, but declared that either way he would be sold, though differently" (335). A true difference between the virtual and the actual would mean that each would lead to a different outcome. But the vow, rather than creating a true bifurcation between two distinct possibilities, between an actual and a virtual sequence, abolishes the distinction, since the outcome of both is the same. The vow changes the present (the actual) into a virtual present, which one can express only as a future perfect: "The Princess appeared to consider this fact with an extreme intellectual curiosity. 'If, after all, then, you are not called, you will have been positively happy.' 'I shall have had some fine moments. Perhaps Hoffendahl's plot is simply for that' " (336).

This is why the space opened up by actions such as the vow is both free and determined (virtual and actual). One can say that the equivalent to the vow (which closes the action of the novel) is the visit of Mrs. Bowerbank (which opens up the novel). From the moment the visit takes place, it does not matter what Pinnie does, since the consequences will be the same (as Vetch points out to her, Hyacinth will curse her whatever she does; 72). Whereas for Hyacinth this indifference toward the outcome (because the end is independently determined rather than produced by the actions that precede it) opens up a space of freedom and happiness, for Pinnie it has the opposite effect.

As in Stendhal, where prediction (or another narrative) functions to sever middle from both beginning and end, thus turning the middle into a realm of freedom (which can also be understood as futility, since it cannot change the end, cannot generate its own end), so in *The Princess Casamassima* the middle is a space of freedom and futility. When all bifurcations from a certain initial act (the visit of Mrs. Bowerbank, the vow) lead to the same end, the difference between apparently distinct possibilities or different stories is abolished; they can thus be conflated, taken one for the other. If from a certain initial beginning, all possible roads lead to the same end, then the middle that separates them loses all significance, and beginning collapses into end. This may explain the curious conflation in the novel between the secret of Hyacinth's parentage (his birth, his beginning) and the secret of the vow (which is what seals his end, his death: "I gave my life away"; 327). Not only does Hyacinth reveal both these secrets to the Princess as if in the same breath, but after Pinnie's death he observes the following about Millicent:

> Something in her behavior at this period had even made Hyacinth wonder whether there were not some mystical sign in his appearance, some subtle

betrayal in the very expression of his face, of the predicament in which he had been placed by Diedrich Hoffendahl; he began to suspect afresh the operation of that "beastly *attendrissement*" he had detected of old in people who had the benefit of Miss Pynsent's innuendoes. (386)

Pinnie's innuendoes clearly concern the story of his birth, and here somehow a revelation of this secret is collapsed into his feeling of involuntarily betraying his other secret, the secret of the vow, of his impending death. The same is true about his conversation with Lady Aurora: "The way Lady Aurora spoke proved to him, later, that she now definitely did know his secret, or one of them, rather. . . . She knew the smaller—not, of course, the greater; she had, decidedly, been illuminated by Pinnie's divagations" (357). This "confusion" between the two secrets is thematically a confusion between his link to the aristocracy (what Pinnie's innuendoes and divagations refer to is his noble descent) and his link to the revolutionaries (the same confusion we have seen in the "equation" of Medley and the Sun and Moon). Narratively, it is the collapse of beginning and end that results from the impossibility of the middle's making a difference.

We can say that throughout his life, Hyacinth's impossible task was to differentiate between courses of action, make them different enough so that they can yield different sequences. He most explicitly tries to see his life as the actualization of one sequence, significantly different from other possible ones, when he speculates on what would have happened to him had Pinnie not adopted him:

He had followed, with an imagination that went further in that direction than ever before, the probable consequences of his not having been adopted in his babyhood by the dressmaker. The workhouse and the gutter, ignorance and cold, filth and tatters, nights of huddling under bridges and in doorways, vermin, starvation and blows, possibly even the vigorous efflorescence of an inherited disposition to crime—these things, which he saw with unprecedented vividness, suggested themselves as his natural portion. Intimacies with a princess, visits to fine old country-houses, intelligent consideration, even, of the best means of inflicting a scare on the classes of privilege, would in that case not have been within his compass. (371)

Had Pinnie not adopted him he would have committed a crime, like his mother, either because of his heredity or because of the similarity in their social conditions. Scaring the rich by killing a duke seems to him a totally different matter, continuous with such things as intimacy with a princess and visits to country houses. At the end, however, Hyacinth realizes that these two possibilities are not at all different, that in killing a duke, he will only be repeating his mother's act:

> He had a sense of his mind, which had been made up, falling to pieces again; but that sense in turn lost itself in a shudder which was already familiar—the horror of the public reappearance, on his part, of the imbrued hands of his mother. This loathing of the idea of a *repetition* had not been sharp, strangely enough, till his summons came. . . . Yet now the idea of the personal stain made him horribly sick. . . . It rose before him like a kind of backward accusation of his mother; to suffer it to start out in the life of her son was in a manner to place her own forgotten, redeemed pollution again in the eye of the world. (582–83)

What causes the collapse of difference between apparently different sequences, between actual and virtual, between beginning and end, is repetition, the middle as repetition (hence, the inability of the middle to effect a meaningful change).

If for Hyacinth the aesthetic realm (predicated on a life of leisure and privilege) seemed to have the merit of keeping him out of the cycle of violence and sacrifice that characterizes the political (and the sexual), he has found out that political-revolutionary activity is continuous with the life of privilege (scaring the rich by killing a duke is continuous with intimacy with a princess), is indeed the condition of possibility of the aesthetic position (the vow allows him freedom). The difference between the two supposed opposites that structure his life is abolished—but not by his sacrifice of one or a synthesizing of the two. Thus his killing himself "instead" of the Duke is not a matter of choosing one way of life over another but a matter of abolishing the difference between supposedly different courses of action. As we have seen, Hyacinth feels that his father, who according to Pinnie at least was a duke, died because of him, instead of him. Since his father is dead, he himself is a duke in disguise: his true nature is that of a duke but his circumstances hide it. As such, he can go to the house of a duke unobserved and kill him—that is, kill a father who (by dying) failed to recognize him (make him a real duke). Instead of killing the Duke—or in order to do that—he kills himself, since he is a duke; he kills himself, since he should have died long ago instead of the Duke, his father. At this point, the difference between supposedly distinct and even contradictory options has been abolished. The coming of the call is no different from its not coming; to obey the call is no different from not obeying it; to kill oneself is the same as killing the Duke; to have been adopted by Pinnie has the same results as not having been adopted by her; and so on. This abolition of all differences can explain how Hyacinth, presumably in good faith, makes Vetch another promise, which on its face blatantly contradicts his vow: "I shall never do any of their work" (565).

The visit of Mrs. Bowerbank, just like the vow later on, opens up a temporality where actions are either totally free or totally irrelevant. Thus if

Hyacinth's aim has been to differentiate between various possible stories or courses of action, and more specifically, between the "political" or "sexual" drive for possession and spoliation and the "aesthetic" contemplation that does not destroy through possession, then he has found the condition of possibility for the aesthetic position—the vow—but the vow, and the freedom it makes possible, also entail, necessarily and contradictorily, the abolition of all differences between the two courses.

If, by the end of the novel, differences have been abolished, what, if anything, has been gained? Hyacinth gives us a clue when, after realizing that in killing the Duke he will be repeating his mother's crime, "the thought that was most of all with him was that he had time—he had time. . . . He had another day, he had two days, he might take three" (583). All that has been gained, then, is time—but time not as the possibility of doing any particular thing, since the possibility of any doing, of doing something that will make a difference, has been abolished. In this respect, Hyacinth has his double in the Princess: while he, having gained his freedom through his vow, has gained "empty" time (rather than the time necessary to "make a difference"), the Princess, whose freedom is expressed as capriciousness (as Mme. Grandoni says, one never knows what she will do), repeatedly asks, or is said to be asking, simply for time (and her capriciousness suggests that she does not ask for it so she can do one thing rather than another): "I want you to give me time! That's all I ask of my friends, in general" (321); " 'Give her time, my dear, give her time,' said Paul" (490); " 'Give her time—give her time,' replied Madame Grandoni" (511).[20]

V

We have seen that the vow implies a view of action divorced from feelings and beliefs. Such a view sees action as "theatrical," as "representation" in the sense of playing a role, and can be opposed to another view (exemplified by the Poupins) that sees action as the true manifestation of inner feelings and beliefs. But the novel in its insistence on the theme of theatricality makes clear that "playing a role" cannot be simply opposed to authentic action.[21] The novel shows that the naive, sincere, or simple characters are just as much engaged in playing a role. Thus Poupin is an enthusiast, a romantic, utopian dreamer who wants to stop Hyacinth from fulfilling his vow in the name of authenticity of action. And yet Poupin can also be said to be playing the role of the revolutionary: Poupin "owed his position at the 'Sun and Moon' to the brilliancy with which he represented the political exile" (284). Similarly, Millicent, simple and spontaneous as she may be, works as a model, displaying herself in front of an audience as an actress playing a role.

But the point is more often made that role playing, even in the most "unauthentic" characters, cannot be opposed to some genuine behavior that is not role playing. Of course Sholto is a "radical" only in costume; he has a costume for each role he plays, and just as he dresses one way for the opera and another way for a visit to a country house, so he dresses in yet another way when he goes to the Sun and Moon. If this shows Sholto to be a fake radical (we know that he has no interest at all in the social question), it also suggests that the "fakeness" is not to be opposed to some genuine behavior since Sholto is only a collection of costumes. The Princess too is seen primarily as an actress, a performer;[22] but if her revolutionary interest is a "pose," it is not because it is opposed to some genuine self; it is different only from other roles she plays (for example, the role of a princess). Though Hyacinth suspects that she may only be playing a role, he does not think that this really makes any difference: "Hyacinth was lost in adoration of the Princess's housewifely ways and of the exquisite figure that she made as a little *bourgeoise*; judging that if her attempt to combine plain living with high thinking were all a comedy, at least it was the most finished entertainment she had yet offered him" (424). He knows from the start that his own desire "to go through life in his own character" (109) is naive: Hyacinth is seen (and sees himself) as an actor, in disguise, as much as the Princess, and on this count one cannot oppose them (as "sincere" vs. "phony," or "transparent" vs. "enigmatic").[23] The similarity between these two characters on this score is another reason why, when Christina Light "has been looking for a situation" (44), she was placed in a novel having Hyacinth for its hero.[24]

Acting, then, is and is not a sham; as role playing that cannot be opposed to authentic behavior, it is a "representation" without a "present" prior to and different from it. This explains the way in which the revolution—the novel's most extended instance of action—is characterized. In the sense that the revolution is the making visible of forces that lie under the surface, it is a "representation." And since it is a "representation," it is necessarily both genuine and a sham—it is both a manifestation of the force of the people and a theatrical performance, a make-believe: "In silence, in darkness, but under the feet of each one of us, the revolution lives and works. It is a wonderful, immeasurable trap, on the lid of which society performs its antics. When once the machinery is complete, there will be a great rehearsal" (330), Hyacinth tells the Princess, following his illumination by Hoffendahl. The theatricality, the falseness of performance, does not characterize only a society that "performs its antics" on top of an abyss; it also characterizes the revolution itself ("trap," "rehearsal"). Similarly, like that society, which "seem[s] to know nothing and suspect nothing and think of nothing" (330), the revolutionaries do not understand the nature of the revolution of which they are the agents any better than society does. Hence, revolutionary activity is a certain kind of make-believe. As Muniment explains, the leaders'

> game must be now to frighten society, and frighten it effectually; to make it believe that the swindled classes were at last fairly in league—had really grasped the idea that, closely combined, they would be irresistible. They were not in league, and they hadn't in their totality grasped any idea at all. . . . All the same, society was scareable, and every great scare was a gain for the people. (292)

This "cynical" view of the revolution is not peculiar to Muniment; it is shared also by Hyacinth, and indeed it remains unchallenged in the novel. Thinking of the day of action, the day on which Muniment as a leader may choose to exercise his influence, "Hyacinth only wished that day would come; it would not be till then, he was sure, that they would all know where they were, and that the good they were striving for, blindly, obstructedly, in a kind of eternal dirty intellectual fog, would pass from the stage of crude discussion and mere sharp, tantalizing desirableness into that of irresistible reality" (281). The revolutionaries do not know what they are and what they are capable of until they act, that is, until the revolution comes. The revolution cannot follow an understanding by the people (cannot be the representation, the making visible, of a preexisting but hidden understanding on their part). Instead, that understanding follows the revolution, an action that is hence always somewhat illegitimate, a fraud, a sham, a pretense. The view of the revolution presented in the novel depends, then (or entails), a view of action as force that can be retroactively infused with "meaning" rather than as an expression (or representation) of a preexisting understanding.

Such a view of revolutionary action accounts for the way in which revolutionary characters are represented in the novel: no character can be both a "true revolutionary" and a fully embodied character. The one character viewed as a genuine revolutionary is Hoffendahl—the "incarnation of a programme," the "genuine article"—the man who convinces Hyacinth (who can then convince the Princess) of the solidity of the revolution. But no matter how solid the revolution, incarnated in Hoffendahl, is for Hyacinth and the Princess, its solidity cannot be represented through him to the reader. Hoffendahl remains a mere name to us: we do not meet him (*we* do not gain access to the "holy of holies"), we do not hear him talk, we do not see him act, we do not read any of his letters, though all of these are subjects for report and speculation. As the figure representing the revolution in all its solidity,

Hoffendahl remains vague and insubstantial (he is just a "hope," not a reality). By contrast, all the "real," fully embodied revolutionaries he leads are far from being "the genuine article" or "first rate," are, in fact, but a sham. The revolutionaries we see and hear, the "real" revolutionaries, are the insipid visitors to the Sun and Moon, the inconsistent Hyacinth, the capricious Princess, the sentimental and anachronistic Poupin; and we do not and cannot see or know the man who stands for the true revolutionary idea. Thus no character within the novel can be seen as a "true representation" of the revolution, and this, I have argued, is related to the revolution's own status as representation. If "true" representation (as opposed to sheer role playing, false representation or pretense) means a coincidence between inside meaning and outside action, between what is hidden and what reveals it and gives it form, then the revolution cannot be represented; it can be represented only as what it is—an "empty" or "pure" representation (with nothing "present" prior to "representation" that authenticates representation), action not predicated on understanding (since understanding follows rather than determines action).

In this respect, Muniment is an intermediary figure: represented and embodied, he is still inscrutable; his possible meaning and future action remain vague. As Hyacinth recognizes, Muniment's influence depends precisely on his inscrutability and vagueness. Muniment may be a Monument of the revolution, as Hoffendahl is an "incarnation of a programme," and his large and solid body, his happy brutality, his blunt and unruffled manner, can be seen as part of this purely representative function, pure monumentality that has nothing to do with the concrete, human, and contingent and so remains incomprehensible. By the end of the novel, however, Muniment's engagement with the Princess changes him from an inhuman, unfeeling monument, the pure but incomprehensible representation of an idea, into a feeling human being. When Rosy is surprised that he should care for the Princess, his response is to insist on his human nature: "Ain't I soft, ain't I susceptible?" (491). From that moment on, he is no longer the "real thing," Hoffendahl's double and surrogate (he is not trusted anymore at headquarters); he is simply a bumbling revolutionary like the rest of the crowd at the Sun and Moon.

The impossibility of representing the revolution (or of the revolution itself being a representation) in the sense of making visible a prior but hidden meaning manifests itself in a split. On the one hand, we have the meaning or the "real thing," but it remains vague or unknown; the genuineness of Hoffendahl remains abstract, the monumentality of Muniment inscrutable. On the other hand, when it comes to the concrete and the known, we have only inauthenticity or mediocrity. The visitors to the Sun and Moon, Hyacinth, and Poupin all merely "play the role" of revolutionaries—all they do is mere talk; it is not the "real thing." But this sham is not opposed to any known genuine revolutionary behavior (only to its abstract idea), since action is always theatrical, does not express a prior meaning. Action as representation or as a "sign" does not reveal the nature of a thing but rather points toward a thing that is not known beforehand. Representation here has the status of a performative act; it generates meaning rhetorically.[25]

This is why the most appropriate representation of the revolution and of the people with their potential to act is Millicent Henning. Daughter of the people, a product of the streets of London, consuming beer and buns and dropping her h's, Millicent stands for the spirit and force of the revolution without knowing it, indeed without giving it any sympathy:

> She was bold, and free, and generous, and if she was coarse she was neither false nor cruel. She laughed with the laugh of the people, and if you hit her hard enough she would cry with its tears. . . . She had no theories about redeeming or uplifting the people; she simply loathed them, because they were so dirty, with the outspoken violence of one who had known poverty. . . . Millicent, to hear her talk, only wanted to keep her skirts clear and marry some respectable tea-merchant. But for our hero she was magnificently plebeian, in the sense that implied a kind of loud recklessness of danger and the qualities that shine forth in a row. She summed up the sociable, humorous, ignorant chatter of the masses, their capacity for offensive and defensive passion, their instinctive perception of their strength on the day they should really exercise it; and as much as any of this, their ideal of something smug and prosperous, where washed hands, and plates in rows on dressers, and stuffed birds under glass, and family photographs, would symbolise success. She was none the less plucky for being at bottom a shameless Philistine, ambitious of a front-garden with rockwork; and she presented the plebeian character in none the less plastic a form. Having the history of the French Revolution at his fingers' ends, Hyacinth could easily see her (if there should ever be barricades in the streets of London), with a red cap of liberty on her head and her white throat bared so that she should be able to shout the louder the Marseillaise of that hour, whatever it might be. (160–61)

Millicent can represent liberty because she does not care about it; she can stand for the people because she does not sympathize with them or worry about their plight. Hyacinth's ideas about the people are most vivid in Millicent's company though "she had no such ideas about herself; they were almost the only ideas she didn't have" (160). Indeed, it is her complete detachment from and unawareness of what she represents that makes Millicent an allegory of the revolution. And it is also what makes her a true member of the people in their capacity to act, since what characterizes the people is not their understanding of their nature and predicament but rather their force, their "instinctive perception" of their strength *as they exercise it.* As force, they may impose themselves in an action that posits a meaning—revolution for the sake of social equality and liberty.

Yet if Millicent's vulgarity, philistinism, and middle-class aspirations make her one of the people she so loathes, these properties are not sufficient for making her the most suitable figure to represent either the people or the spirit of the revolution. What makes her suitable is her beauty: she presents the plebeian character in a "plastic form." This means both that she *is* like a sculpture, well formed, and that she *can be* modeled and formed into one by an artist. But Hyacinth's appreciation of her beauty, of the "plastic form" that makes her the suitable medium for representing the people, does not square with her own ideas about herself. For though Millicent undoubtedly thinks of her attractions in the highest possible terms, it is not because she has the taste to appreciate real beauty. On the contrary, she is repeatedly depicted as vulgar and lacking in taste. In that sense she is unable to appreciate her beauty—what makes her a suitable medium of representation—just as she is unaware of the qualities she represents.

Thus Millicent has both the qualities of the people she represents and the plastic form necessary for such representation. In the figure of Millicent as an allegorical representation of the revolution, we find a coming together of the aesthetic and the political, the work of art and the revolution. This coming together is possible only because Millicent herself is totally unaware—she does not understand—that she is either the epitome of the people or a "plastic form" that can be used to represent the revolution.[26] Such a lack of awareness would have been the "solution" to Hyacinth's predicament, as he himself "realizes" (but this precisely indicates the ironic impossibility of his situation) when he tells Millicent toward the end of the novel: "I mean to think no more—I mean to give it up. Avoid it yourself, my dear Millicent—avoid it as you would a baleful vice. It confers no happiness. Let us live in the world of irreflective contemplation—let us live in the present hour" (526). Though the vow has enabled him to live in the present moment—"to live each hour as if it were to be one's last" (335)—"irreflective contemplation" remains impossible, since it is self-contradictory. If action is "irreflective," contemplation is not; if contemplation allows for the distance that safeguards from aggressive possession, action does not. By "choosing" irreflective contemplation, Hyacinth shows the impasse that structures his life story.

The three strands the novel follows—the formation of a personal identity, the search for a vocation, the transformation of the social world—are all "plots" that are normally understood in terms of a "becoming." This becoming depends on the ability to transcend contradictions, to use the contradictions with which one is faced as a means for defining a higher concept, goal, or realm where these contradictions are resolved. Hyacinth cannot resolve the contradictions of his initial predicament; he cannot define a goal or a realm that would transcend them. In the figure of Hyacinth, then, James is as far as possible from describing the artist who sacrifices social engagement, or even an interest in social issues, for the sake of constituting a separate aesthetic realm—the common view of James the artist himself. Rather, through the figure of Hyacinth, James thinks through the urgency and impossibility of separating the aesthetic from the political, of clearly demarcating reflection (as mental or artistic representation) and action.

CHAPTER 9

'The Awkward Age': Modern Consciousness and the
Sense of the Past

∿

In a famous passage in the Preface to "The Spoils of Poynton," James writes: "Life . . . is capable, luckily for us, of nothing but a splendid waste. Hence the opportunity for the sublime economy of art, which rescues, which saves, and hoards and 'banks,' investing and reinvesting these fruits of toil in wondrous useful 'works' and thus making up for us, desperate spendthrifts that we all naturally are, the most princely of incomes."[1] On the one hand, this passage articulates as clearly as possible the redemptive view of art: the fact that life is but a "waste" is what requires and makes possible the superior realm of art; it is not so much a flaw as an "opportunity." On the other hand, in his deliberate, almost aggressive use of the monetary metaphor, James suggests that if art "saves" life, it is not by transcending it but by doing something analogous to the most mundane activities of this very life: art saves by hoarding and banking, investing and reinvesting. I would like to suggest that the use of this analogy is strategic. By presenting art as a superior form of investment, James can avoid talking about the way art is bought and sold in the market for (literal) investments; by suggesting that it makes for us, but only figuratively, "the most princely of incomes," he avoids reflecting on the way the production and appreciation of art becomes a profession that provides an income (princely or not).[2] The analogy, then, can be read as a compromise formation, mediating between two views of art's relation to life—that of transcendence and that of entanglement.

I have quoted this passage because James here articulates and relates with "sublime economy" the different views of art's relation to life one finds in his work. Though *The Awkward Age* is not about "art" in any obvious way, it touches on issues related to our understanding of the aesthetic realm and the different ways (transcendence, analogy, entanglement) its relation to mundane life may be conceived. In what follows I will trace some of these issues. I will argue, first, that the novel's preoccupation with historical determination undermines the possibility of a sphere outside social reality, the sphere of the aesthetic. I will then show how the specific way in which artistic form and representation (pictorial or theatrical) function in the novel undermines some of the common ways in which the relation between art and life are conceived (in James and elsewhere). Finally, I will show how in the figure of Mrs. Brook, James takes a critical distance from the figure of the "intelligent observer"— who in most of his texts is understood to be a figure for the artist.

I

The Awkward Age (1899) is generally seen as centering on the moral question of the influence a corrupt adult world has on the young. Like *What Maisie Knew* (published two years earlier), with which it is often compared, it is read as the story of the loss of innocence brought about by a growing knowledge of sexuality.[3] According to this reading, having been exposed to the social world of her mother, Nanda is, on the one hand, marked by it, is "damaged" (which explains why Van, the fastidious man she loves, will not marry her), and on the other hand, led to resist or refuse that corrupt world. "Saved" by Longdon, "the fairy godmother" (143), she renounces the world of her mother, a world of shady transactions (erotic and monetary), and leaves London for Longdon's world. This world reflects Longdon's moral integrity, "the beauty of his life," and is marked as different from the world of trade and exchange: "Everything, on every side, had dropped straight from heaven, with nowhere a bargaining thumb-mark, a single sign of the shop" (253). The main drama of the novel would then be in the relation between Nanda and the world around her, and the end will offer a resolution to the drama in her finding a haven, a world separate from the social world. Depending on the way we valorize the social world (and James's art), we would define this other world either positively, as a refuge where one can heal, or negatively, as a world of sterility and death.

But such a reading of the novel, centering on the moral question and offering resolution through utopian (or dystopian) space, leaves out a crucial aspect of the text. True, the way Nanda is shaped and marked by the adult social world around her is an important issue. But as important is the issue of her relation to, and determination by, a past (embodied in the figure of her grandmother). Thus, the novel poses not only the "moral" question—to what extent does Nanda resemble her mother, is she shaped by the world around her? It also asks a "historical" question—does she "hark back" and resemble her maternal grandmother, Lady Julia, or does she take after her own mother, is she the "modern" daughter?

Asking whether Nanda resembles her grandmother or her mother suggests that Nanda's identity is determined in terms of her relation to two different points in time (that is, in historical terms), rather than in relation to two different forces in her present situation (as was the case, for example, with Hyacinth, who saw his identity as determined by two opposed forces: mother vs. father, French vs. English, working class vs. aristocracy). The temporal emphasis of *The Awkward Age* is highlighted by its depiction of filiation as simple derivation (that is, determined by one term rather than by two, heterogeneous terms). This is true both in the case of Nanda and in the case of her mother. We do not even know who Mrs. Brook's father was (all we know is that Lady Julia did not marry Mr. Longdon), and Mrs. Brook is entirely defined by her relation to—and difference from—her own mother. Similarly, Mr. Brookenham is on the whole overshadowed by his wife, and no one in the novel seems to worry whether Nanda, or even Harold, takes after him or not.

The question of Nanda's relation to the past is raised by Longdon's arrival in London, and this event has a special status in the novel. If we start from the "germ" of the story as James describes it in the Preface, we find that *The Awkward Age* deals with one of the "minor 'social phenomena'" of modern London—"the difference made in certain friendly houses and for certain flourishing mothers by the sometimes dreaded, often delayed, but never fully arrested coming to the forefront of some vague slip of a daughter" (8). But if this "phenomenon" is common in a certain society, defined both historically (modern) and geographically (English, as opposed to French or American), the novel, as a story, deals by necessity not with the general or even the typical, but with the particular—"the manner in which [this situation] came to be in a particular instance dealt with" (11). What gives *this* instance its particularity is that Nanda's coming of age, her dreaded and delayed coming "downstairs" to mix with the adult social world, coincides with another event—the arrival in London of Mr. Longdon who, as his name suggests, has been long gone from London and who, Rip van Winkle–like, returns to a world he left thirty years ago.

Longdon is not just a perspective on the world of Mrs. Brook, "a fresh eye, an outside mind" (107), a witness who, by virtue of his detachment, can observe and judge the situation and the roles the various participants play in it, but a significant actor himself. His offer to provide a handsome dowry if Van will marry Nanda is probably the most important event in the novel—it takes place at its dead center—forcing decision and resolution to a situation that might otherwise have remained the same forever. Longdon's offer forces the ambivalent, irresolute Van to act, to decide, to give an answer, so that his failure to do so is now itself an act and leads to the dénouement. In a way quite characteristic of James, Longdon's action or intervention makes it impossible for Van to do what Longdon wants him to, and yet without this intervention, he would not have done anything at all.

Thus it is Longdon's return to London that turns a situation into a story both in the sense that a story involves a particular "handling" ("Handlung"—plot) of a common situation and in the sense that it involves at least minimal action, leading to some kind of transformation. Though at the end of the novel Nanda is back upstairs, this by no means indicates that nothing has changed, or that things have gone back to their pre-story state. The difference between Book I (Lady Julia) and Book X (Nanda) is clear in spite of, or rather because of, their apparent similarity.[4] The similarity and difference between generations, between grandmother and granddaughter—historical time—that Longdon's return makes visible constitute the "plot" of the novel. And since it is Longdon who makes the complex relation between present and past visible, Nanda's leaving London with him at the end of the novel cannot be seen as an escape from her historical predicament, as an outgrowing of her "awkward age."

For the James of the Preface, as for most critics, Nanda's "awkward age" is a period of transition—the "interval" that has "to be bridged" (11) between a girl's coming to adulthood and her marriage. What makes this interval "awkward," a period of "tension or apprehension" (11), is that as part of the adult world, the girl stands the risk of being exposed to adult knowledge, whereas as an unmarried woman she is supposed to retain her innocence. To the extent that the novel describes Nanda's "exposure" to the adult world, it deals with the general issue of the shaping of consciousness by the surrounding world, be it Nanda's family, her mother's circle of friends, or modern London. But Longdon's return introduces another dimension into this situation—the dimension of time. The moral problem of "exposure"—of the determination of consciousness by what surrounds it—is always the problem of being of one's time. Defined as "one's mind and what one sees and feels and the sort of thing one notices" (175), consciousness is always "modern." But Longdon, who comes back to London from "a long sleep," who is being "disinterred," "literally dug up" (31), is someone of a different era, lingering out of his time. This "*revenant*," this ghost, brings with him the past, brings to modern consciousness a sense of the past. We can say that it is the intrusion of the past into modern consciousness that makes Nanda's (and everyone else's) age awkward, an awkwardness that cannot be overcome or evaded.

II

As its title clearly indicates, *The Awkward Age* is concerned with the question of time. Nanda's growing up involves a process of development in time that is both continuous, made in small, almost imperceptible steps, and inevitably unidirectional: her mother can dread and delay the process, but she can neither arrest nor reverse it. The same is true of Nanda's growing knowledge. There is nothing catastrophic or even punctual about Nanda's acquisition of knowledge because, as she says, "there was never a time when I didn't know *something* or other" (372); her knowledge has simply increased gradually as she has grown older, until it reached an endpoint.[5] When Nanda says that she knows "everything" (e.g., 258, 369), she is also saying that she will not grow anymore: "I shall never change—I shall be always just the same" (164).

Longdon's return brings a different notion of temporality into this process of development. To begin with, whereas Nanda's growing up and coming downstairs are determined by clear biological and social laws, Longdon's return is defined only in terms of its own necessity, the "doom of coming back" (28). Neither he nor anyone else tells us exactly why or for what purpose he decided at a certain point to leave Beccles and come back to London.[6] But as a person who is "literally dug up," Longdon is a ghost, and the figure of the ghost is common enough in James's novels and tales to allow us to speculate on the reasons behind his return. In general the ghost is a person who (for whatever reason) did not live in his or her own time and comes back in order to have what the hero of "The Middle Years" calls "a second age, an extension"—another try, a "second go."[7] Longdon's return, in other words, suggests that time is in some sense reversible, that one can continue beyond the end, go back to the beginning, start all over again—though whether the outcome would be the same or not remains to be seen.

There is enough in the novel to explain Longdon's return in terms of the ghost's claim for a "second go." This would mean that his relation to the living—and especially to Nanda and Van—is an attempt to live vicariously, through surrogate figures, what he failed to live directly, in his own time, in his relation to Lady Julia. Thus when Nanda tells Longdon that she will be "one of those who haven't" lived, he says: " 'No, my child . . . you shall never be anything so sad.' 'Why not—if you've been?' He looked at her a little, quietly; then, putting out his hand, passed her own into his arm. 'Exactly because I have' " (177). The "beautiful loyalty" to Lady Julia is here redefined as a failure to live and is seen as "sad"; its counterpart is forging a different fate for Nanda. This vicarious living explains Longdon's love for Nanda—the reincarnation of Lady Julia—as well as his (probably greater) love for Van, who is not only the son of another woman he loved and failed to marry but also a younger, more beautiful, better, version of himself—that is, himself as loved by Nanda/Lady Julia. In a way, the marriage between Nanda and Van would be a "sacrifice to Lady Julia's memory more exquisite than any other" (190): "sacrifice," since it will show that loyalty to her was finally "sad," a failure to live, but "exquisite" since it would be "by the same token, such a piece of poetic justice" (190). Longdon's intervention, his attempt to induce Van to propose to Nanda by the offer of a considerable dowry, represents an attempt to relive the past vicariously, Longdon's hope to make happen now, for his surrogates, what did not happen in his own life in the past.

This plan does not materialize, and Longdon, we can say, fails in his vicarious second go. But that failure allows for an even more literal success on the part of Longdon: taking Nanda back to Beccles himself, "this time . . . never to leave [him] again—or to be left" (380). The terms of their future relation remain unclear to the reader at the end of the novel, but adoption is not the only possibility: when Mrs. Brook asks Nanda in Book VI if she would marry Longdon, Nanda says "yes," though her answer is qualified as "ironic" (237); she tells Longdon that they are one of the "couples" who are invited together, like the Duchess and Petherton (174); and she does not contradict Mitchy when he describes her departure to Beccles with Longdon as a lovers' elopement, "with [a] post-chaise and . . . pistols" (369).[8] One can argue, then, that Longdon, going back to Beccles, has gained what he had failed to gain in his first go. But this gain also entails a certain loss: Longdon wins in his second go by giving up his initial desire to repeat the past; he wins the "duplicate" of Lady Julia at the price of realizing and accepting Nanda's difference from Lady Julia and his own difference from the idealized image of himself represented by Van.

Moreover, there is no way to read Longdon's gain but as Nanda's loss— loss of Van, of love—so that, in the end, it is she who repeats Longdon and becomes in turn "one of those who haven't." At the close of the novel, she retires to Beccles not only *with* Longdon but also *like* him—to live the rest of her life in the shadow of her one beautiful attachment. (As Mitchy says of Nanda's love for Van, "Any passion so great, so complete . . . is—satisfied or not—a life"; 341). Thus by his ghostly return, Longdon not only relives the past himself but also makes apparent that other characters are ghosts in the sense that they too relive a past. Nanda is more than just a "revival" of Lady Julia—a dead person or a picture (on the mantelpiece, in one's memory) coming back to life. She is also a replication of Longdon, of his ghostly existence, his failure to have lived. If Nanda's coming of age raises the question of her exposure—her inevitable determination by the present, by the world in which she lives—Longdon's reappearance in this world brings to life the dimension of her determination (and the determination of others) by the past.

Longdon's return makes clear that the past is not simply past and gone but inhabits the present, as a ghost. A ghost himself, he makes manifest that the others are ghosts too; rather than being "modern," they too, in different ways, do not fit or belong in their time. This lack of fit can be read first of all in the curious insistence in the novel that characters do not quite look their right age. Though twenty years old at the end of the novel,[9] Nanda has the air of being older even than Longdon (382). But she can be passed off by her mother in Book I as only sixteen (38) and is later said by the Duchess to be "any age you like" (187). Mrs. Brook appears to Longdon to be "fresh" because, at age forty-one, she looks only thirty, but the Duchess says that "she looks about three. She simply looks a baby" (187–88). Harold, whom his mother calls "a mere baby" (57), has, in his first appearance, the voice, air, and clothes of a forty-year-old (52), but at the end of the novel, he is clearly the representative of the younger generation, the one that replaces not only Van's but also Nanda's (so that, as Nanda says, her mother "has transferred to him all the scruples that she felt . . . in *my* time, about what we might pick up among you that wouldn't be good for us"; 278). And Aggie "who the other day was about six is now [after her marriage] practically about forty" (314).

Longdon's return brings consciousness of time as difference: he is the one who knew (and loved) the mothers ("I am an old boy who remembers the mothers"; 33) and who can see and show others how the children differ from them. Time has passed, and time brings about changes, and the proof is that a daughter does not resemble her mother. Mrs. Brook tries to neutralize this idea of change in time by declaring a complete separation between her and her mother ("I am disconnected altogether"; 150): since she does not resemble her mother in either physical appearance or manner, there is nothing that can bring them together to a common ground where they can be compared and she found different and wanting. Mrs. Brook claims that she is totally modern: "the modern has always been my own note—I've gone in, I mean, frankly for my very own Time" (133)—a claim that can be understood as the necessary correlative of her equating her life with the life of the mind, with her consciousness and her talk as an expression of this consciousness ("I happen to be so constituted that my life has something to do with my mind and my mind something to do with my talk"; 210). By declaring herself of her "very own Time," Mrs. Brook refuses to see herself as in any way defined by the past. But she cannot maintain this position, since if she is totally separated from the past and from Lady Julia, she has no grounds for any claim on Longdon, for making him "the *oncle d'Amérique*, the eccentric benefactor, the fairy godmother" (143), who is going to set them all up. Mrs. Brook cannot separate herself entirely from the past and live simply in the present for the very same reason that she cannot simply live in her mind and talk, as pure consciousness: she depends on Longdon as much as she depends on her friends to provide the material base of her existence, of her "life" (as Nanda explicitly puts it, "We [her family] seem to be all living more or less on other people, all immensely 'beholden' "; 252). This is why Mrs. Brook has also to claim that no matter how different they all are from Longdon's generation, they still have in them something of that past: "however much we may disappoint you, some little spark of the past can't help being in us" (150).

Longdon himself seems to have remained at a fixed point in time: his thirty years in the totally static Beccles have preserved him, so that, to Van, "though . . . he could not look young, he came near—strikingly and amusingly—looking new" (29). But if at first Longdon functions simply as a ghost who makes the difference between past and present apparent, once he is out of Beccles and in London—back from the dead—he himself is a subject in time (in his talks with Nanda, he comes back again and again to "the growth of his actual understanding"; 168), so that the yardstick itself, so to speak, changes. He is no longer a fixed point in the past by which change can be easily measured. Indeed, with Longdon's return, it becomes clear that neither he nor Lady Julia (that is, no "past") can be seen as a fixed point in time. When Nanda's resemblance to her grandmother is first discussed by Longdon and Van, Van attributes it to Nanda's anachronistic form: "I have always positively found in it [Nanda's face] a recall of the type of the period you must be thinking of. It isn't a bit modern. It's a face of Sir Thomas Lawrence" (120–21). But Longdon is quick to correct him, noting that Lady Julia herself was not of her time:

> "It's a face of Gainsborough!" Mr Longdon returned with spirit. "Lady Julia herself harked back."
> Vanderbank, clearly, was equally touched and amused. "Let us say at once that it's a face of Raphael."
> His old friend's hand was instantly on his arm. "That's exactly what I often said to myself of Lady Julia." (121)

Just as Lady Julia herself, in her own time, "harked back," so Longdon's old-fashioned standards are not simply the result of his having slept, Rip van Winkle–like, for thirty years. As he puts it, "he had finally been brought to believe that even in his slow-paced prime he must have hung back behind his contemporaries" (167). This "anachronism" in relation to his own time is something Longdon was not aware of in the past: "He had not supposed at the moment—in the forties and the fifties—that he passed for old-fashioned" (167). It is his encounter with the present that makes him realize what he (like Mrs. Brook or like Van) did not realize before: that he too did not exactly fit his time. Rather than belonging to a past radically different from the present, he was a ghost in his own time; rather than being different from the present—for example, from Van—the two are similar in their anachronism. By the end of the novel, we see that Van too is old-fashioned, adhering to principles that are already almost obsolete. Nanda tells him that "very often, in London now, you must pass some bad moments" (250). Now it is Harold who is the *enfant terrible*, and Van comments, "I feel as if I must figure to him [Harold], you know, very much as Mr Longdon figures to me" (283). If characters are not simply of their time—if they "hark back" or are "old-fashioned" in their own time, if they appear "new" or "fresh" or younger than they really are—there is no stable point from which the passage of time, the difference between past and present, can be measured. Thus what Longdon makes apparent is not simply the *difference* between past and present but also the fact that the past inhabits the present, so that one is never quite of one's own time. This lack of "synchronization" does not characterize only modern society, since, as we have seen, it afflicts the past as much as the present.

What complicates the simple passage of time, time as development and change, is the existence of patterns of repetition. Van repeats Longdon— repeats the past—not only in being old-fashioned in his own time but also in his "loyalty" to Mrs. Brook, who explains that "he *is* as loyal to me as Mr Longdon to mamma" (75). Nanda repeats her grandmother not only because of her physical resemblance but also because the only man she can love is Van, the old-fashioned person who in a sense belongs to her grand-mother's time. At the end of the novel, when she treats her own mother "maternally" (she tells Mitchy, "When I think of her [Mrs. Brook] down-stairs there so often nowadays practically alone, I feel as if I could scarcely bear it. She's so fearfully young"; 356), she becomes "literally" her own grandmother.

But if this were all, then time would be simply repetitive rather than developing, the changes brought by time would be merely superficial ones— of words and gestures—while deep patterns of life would remain the same and repeat themselves, so that Lady Julia, Longdon, Van, Mrs. Brook, and Nanda would all finally be seen as belonging to the same world. The contradiction between Nanda's "form" (which "harks back") and her consciousness (which is modern: "Girls understand now"; 249) would be merely illusory, since she repeats Lady Julia in more than mere form. But the situation the novel presents is more complex, for Nanda, who "reproduces . . . so vividly Lady Julia" (42), who repeats Longdon, is also like her mother. Their sharing the same name (her mother's name is Fernanda; 33) is the most obvious indication of their similarity, but her understanding, her knowledge, her talk, are all at various times mentioned as indications of her resemblance to her mother (e.g., 244, 252, 265). Nanda's similarity to her mother is a mark of her difference from Lady Julia. Time does bring change, and for all her resemblance to Lady Julia, Nanda is also "the modern daughter" (133), her mother's daughter, the mother who is so different.

Longdon claims that Nanda is "*all* Lady Julia. There isn't a touch of her mother. It's unique—an absolute revival. I see nothing of her father, either—I see nothing of any one else" (120). But "absolute revival," the exact reproduction of the past in the present, is impossible. It is not that one cannot bring back the past—we have seen that with the ghost one does precisely that. It is simply that no point in time is purely past or purely present. Every moment in time is both "modern" and inhabited by the past, and this makes absolute revival impossible and every age awkward. If the impossibility of being fully of one's time is that the past does not "die," that, as Mrs. Brook has to admit, Lady Julia is "with her" (75), then the fact that Nanda cannot help being like her own mother is an indication that the past cannot simply live in the present (or be revived). This historical consciousness, the intrusion of the past as an alterity within the present, means that one cannot escape from/into the past or present. If Beccles may be read as an alternative world to which Nanda can escape from the bruising of the real one, it cannot offer refuge from the "awkwardness" of her age (any age); it cannot be seen as a space of the past, "outside" the present, to which one escapes from the present, since the past cannot be localized (in the past).

Whereas Nanda's resemblance to her mother is a matter of being of one's time, and as such, a matter of consciousness, her resemblance to Lady Julia is a matter of "form," which is anachronistic. That their similarity is a matter of form should not be taken to mean that it is purely external: after all, if they resemble each other in their physical, facial features, they differ from each other in "manner" and "talk" (125). Rather, it is a matter of form because it cannot be defined except in terms of modes of representation, of artistic styles of portraiture. Nanda's awkward position is that, in her case, the form monstrously clashes with the consciousness it shapes.

But if Nanda, monstrously, both "harks back" and lives the life of the modern daughter, what of Lady Julia herself? The idealization of Lady Julia ("Lady Julia had everything"; 41) means that though she, just like Nanda, "harked back," in her case there was no monstrous disjunction between past and present, between history and modernity, between form and consciousness. If the illusion of absolute modernity (Mrs. Brook) means negating the persistence of the past in the present, the idealization of the past, of which Longdon is the main agent, means erasing the necessary modernity of consciousness.[10] In both cases what is complex and heterogeneous is made simple. The sacrifice of Lady Julia that allows Longdon to leave for Beccles together with Nanda may mean not simply his acceptance of Nanda's *difference* from her grandmother but also his acceptance of Lady Julia's *similarity* to her, a realization that in Lady Julia's case too there must have been a discrepancy between outside and inside, between, on the one hand, a form that was not of her time, an inherited form, and, on the other hand, a consciousness that was necessarily modern. The only other way to understand Lady Julia would be to say that she was like Aggie, whose consciousness is (or is made to appear) a blank. In either case, the idealization of the past as a perfect fit between form and consciousness would be destroyed (for the reader, if not for the characters); the result of Longdon's "revival" is that the ideal is killed rather than (or by) being brought back to life.

The intrusion of the past—of the form of the past—into modern consciousness creates a divided self, whose relation to its other is that of sameness and difference. As such, the historical relation is different from specular relations, which construct the other as an idealized mirror image, symmetrically opposite to the self. Such idealized mirror images are Aggie for Nanda and Van for Mitchy. Thus Nanda's omniscience is "mirrored" in Aggie's absolute ignorance (which may be, after all, only an illusion). Aggie is clearly Nanda's idealized self: Aggie, says Nanda is "the real old thing"; she is "a miracle. If one could be her exactly, absolutely, without the least little mite of change, one would probably do the best thing to close with it" (250). Aggie is what Nanda would have liked to be (228), just as Van is what Mitchy would have liked to be: "He's the man," Mrs. Brook tells Mitchy, "with no fortune, and just as he is, to the smallest particular—whom you would have liked to be" (85). Van is Mitchy's specular opposite: "I'm everything dreadful that he isn't" (107).[11] In a somewhat different fashion, we can see the Duchess as an idealized image of Mrs. Brook, not only through the association of the one with Aggie and the other with Nanda, but also in Mrs. Brook's phantasmatic aggrandizing of the Duchess. For Mrs. Brook, the Duchess is (as Nanda puts it) not a mere woman but "a standard" (232)—someone who has always done whatever she wanted (Mrs. Brook just knows that there "has always been some man"; 70) but "has never had to pay for anything!" (233).[12]

To idealize the other is to conceive the other as specularly opposite rather than as same-and-different. When Aggie is seen as the ideal girl ("It *is* the way we ought to be!" says Nanda; 259), she is also seen as an ideal that was possible only in the past, in the idealized past. "*She* ought to have been mamma's grandchild," Mrs. Brook tells Longdon, idealizing both Lady Julia and Aggie. Idealizing the past means conceiving the past as identical to itself (simply in the past) and simply different from the present. Aggie as an "absolute revival" of Lady Julia would be the absolute reproduction in the present of the complete otherness of the past. This, as we have seen, is impossible, and it is this impossibility that shows Aggie's innocence to be a sham.

III

We have seen that in *The Awkward Age* form "harks back," and is thus in disjunction with consciousness, to which it ostensibly gives shape. Form is thus an "alterity within" rather than a limit, as James often claims. For example, in his Preface, James explains the "growth" of the novel by invoking "the fact that, though the relations of a human figure or a social occurrence are what make such objects interesting, they also make them, to the same tune, difficult to isolate, to surround with the sharp black line, to frame in the square, the circle, the charming oval, that helps any arrangement of objects to become a picture" (10). "Growth," in other words, is not the result of change and development in time (and of the author's inability to control this development) but the result of the impossibility of framing—of isolating an object, surrounding it by a limit or a frame. This impossibility of isolating an object from the relations that constitute it explains why a small subject, a minor idea, refuses to remain contained within a small canvass.

James's insistence on the inability to frame and to limit "a human figure or a social occurrence" can be, and very often is, taken to imply that any limit, any frame—hence any "form" ("the square, the circle, the charming oval")— is an arbitrary imposition by the artist. "Relations stop nowhere," as James put it in the Preface to *Roderick Hudson*, but novels do stop, and the limit imposed on them—which gives them identity and meaning—is but the result of an act on the part of the artist.[13] In *The Awkward Age* this understanding of form as an arbitrary limit imposed on a limitless subject is undermined in various ways through the representation within the novel of acts of artistic forming.

The most obvious of these acts is the "production" of Aggie. Here is the "impression" she makes on London:

> From the point of view under which she had been formed, she was a remarkable, a rare success. Since to create a particular little rounded and tinted innocence had been aimed at, the fruit had been grown to the perfection of a peach

on a sheltered wall, and this quality of the object resulting from a process might well make him feel himself in contact with something wholly new. Little Aggie differed from any young person he had ever met in that she had been deliberately prepared for consumption and in that, furthermore, the gentleness of her spirit had immensely helped the preparation. (181)

Aggie is the product of a process of artistic creation and can be called a success on the aesthetic grounds of her perfect form ("rounded and tinted"). The metaphor of the "peach on a sheltered wall" should not mislead us into thinking that Aggie is the product of a natural rather than artistic process; James frequently uses organic metaphors to talk of his works, as, for example, in the Preface to *The Awkward Age* where, speaking of the initial "germ" for the novel, he says, "It was not, no doubt, a fine purple peach, but it might pass for a round ripe plum" (8).

However, nowhere in the description of the "production" of Aggie are we invited to see the process of "forming" as the imposing of a limit or a frame or a form on an otherwise endless or formless material. Aggie clearly has form—she is, indeed, nothing but a form, "a particular little rounded and tinted innocence." The form is all, and it is imposed literally on a blank (innocence). About Aggie's face we read that it was "one of the most expressive little faces that even her expressive race had ever shown him [Longdon]. Formed to express everything, it scarce expressed, as yet, even a consciousness. All the elements of play were in it, but they had nothing to play with" (182). The form of Aggie's face is that of pure expressiveness, not the expression—the outward form—of some particular content. As a face with the potential of expressing everything, it is pure form.

In the case of Nanda, form also cannot be seen as a limit. On the one hand, as we have seen, form in her case intrudes from the past and clashes monstrously with consciousness; on the other hand, this consciousness is far from limitless, since it is shaped and determined by the world around her. This shaping or determination is described, again, not as the imposing of a limit but as a process of marking, the writing of "figures on the slate" (181), even violent marking by the "London world," which, as the Duchess says, "so fearfully batters and bruises" women (187).

By making "form" what harks back, a form of the past, the novel brings together the question of history and the question of art or, more specifically, of artistic representation. Representation always posits the temporal priority of the original, and the status of the original as prior and hence superior can be maintained only through its absence from the scene of representation. Longdon's ghostly return brings back the past and thus brings into the present of representation the past original. When the past is shown to inhabit the present, the status of the original and the hierarchy of representation are undermined.

This convergence of issues is made evident from the start, in the opening scene between Longdon and Vanderbank. Here we meet not only the "revenant" Longdon but every other major character as well, each of whom is somehow in a state of limbo, neither fully present nor entirely absent: Mr. Longdon talks about Lady Julia and Van's mother, who are now dead but alive in his memory; he and Van discuss the members of the Brookenham family and the Duchess, whom they have just left and who, absent from the scene, are present in their memory; and finally they look at the pictures of the two characters Longdon has not yet met, Nanda and Aggie. All these characters, then, are for the moment absent/present, present only through some kind of representation, be it in memory or in pictures on the mantelpiece. That the novel opens with the discussion of *portraits* (of Van's mother, Aggie, Nanda) suggests an investment in mimetic representation. And yet, at the same time, the fact that we (and Longdon) *start* with the portraits, rather than with the "models," destabilizes the relation of mimetic representation by suggesting the primacy of the representation.

Longdon and Van center their attention primarily on Nanda and Aggie, discussing which is the prettier and whether Nanda is pretty at all. Like Aggie's picture, Nanda's is, as Vanderbank remarks, "a present from the original," and also like Aggie's, it presumably represents the original. But to Mr. Longdon's eye, it does something else—it "reproduces" not Nanda but her grandmother Lady Julia (42). Nanda's picture is a representation but Nanda herself is not an original, and one can say of her picture, what Longdon says of her, that it/she is "much more like the dead than like the living" (42).

In Book III Longdon sees Nanda in person for the first time. The discussion is again aesthetic: the subject is Nanda's beauty. But though the face has come out of the picture, it is judged as a picture—a portrait or a painting. The fact that Nanda (just like Nanda's picture) represents her grandmother means not only that she brings Lady Julia back to life, but also that her face can be described only in terms of styles of painting, of old masters; accordingly, Nanda's face is "a face of Sir Thomas Lawrence," "a face of Gainsborough," "a face of Raphael" (121). Nanda, who "reproduces" her grandmother, represents her as a portrait does a model, hence resembles her only in her form.

Initially, as we saw, both Van and Longdon have their doubts whether Nanda is beautiful at all. In Van's estimate she is not as pretty as Aggie (who, mistakenly taken for a pure revival of the pure past, is idealized). In Longdon's eyes too she does not measure up, though the comparison is not with Aggie—

whom he has not yet seen—but with Aggie's picture and with Lady Julia. Lady Julia was "exquisite," but Nanda, who is "exactly like her," is not "so pretty" (41). This seeming contradiction can be resolved in terms of the relation between original and copy: all Longdon sees of Nanda is her picture, and though a picture resembles the model, it also, as a picture, falls short of the real. Hence when faced with the "real" Nanda, rather than with her picture, Longdon may revise his judgment. But Nanda herself, and not simply her picture, is a copy of Lady Julia, and so, by definition, though she is similar, she is also inferior, and this condition will not change when Longdon is faced with the "real" Nanda. And indeed when Longdon sees Nanda for the first time, he does not compare her to her own picture; he sees the real Nanda only as a copy of Lady Julia and yet as a copy that is in no sense or degree different from its model: "She's *all* lady Julia . . . an absolute revival" (120). But this equating of original and reproduction necessarily undermines the status of the original. The Lady Julia with whom Nanda is equated is not the "real" Lady Julia; she is only an image in Longdon's memory, a portrait; and the absolute identity between the two, which turns Nanda beautiful (Longdon asks Van, "Why did you tell me . . . that she isn't beautiful?"; 120), raises the question of whether Lady Julia was indeed "so exquisite," had "everything" (41). By being brought back from the past into the present (of representation), the original loses its privileged status as an original that has "everything." But if the introduction of the past into the present undermines the status of Lady Julia, it also makes Nanda's status "awkward." She is not a copy (whose value can be determined in relation to an original), but neither is she the "real thing" (in the sense of idealized origin, whose value is absolute). Her value is indeterminate.[14]

Nanda's beauty, as Van puts it, "isn't a bit modern" (120), by which he means, as we soon find out, that it is not the kind of beauty appreciated—or fetching a price—in modern London. "Beauty, in London," Van tells Longdon,

> staring, glaring, obvious, knock-down, beauty, as plain as a poster on a wall, an advertisement of soap or whiskey, something that speaks to the crowd and crosses the foot-light, fetches such a price in the market that the absence of it, for a woman with a girl to marry, inspires endless terrors and constitutes for the wretched pair—to speak of mother and daughter alone—a sort of social bankruptcy. London doesn't love the latent and the lurking, has neither time, nor taste, nor sense for anything less discernible than the red flag in front of the steam-roller. It wants cash over the counter and letters ten feet high. Therefore, you see, it's all, as yet, rather a dark question for poor Nanda. (42–43)

If Nanda's prospects of marriage are grim, it is not because she is too modern in her consciousness but because her anachronistic form does not conform to the image of the age. The beauty that is appreciated, Van suggests, is the beauty that gives the age an "aestheticized" image of itself: it is a beauty that is as vulgar, commercial, materialist, as the age, and yet as beauty it can "beautify" these features. As an aesthetic analogue, it reassures the age about its own interests and values by giving a "beautiful" image of "cash over the counter." That this is the case is made manifest by Longdon's failure to increase the value of Nanda's beauty by offering, literally, cash over the counter. Longdon fails because he literalizes Nanda's value as a specimen of beauty, as a work of art, whereas what makes beauty or art valuable is precisely that it is not crude cash over the counter but an aestheticized version of it. At the same time, the novel as a whole valorizes beauty as what comes from the past, as a (disturbing) otherness; it thus can argue that "true art" does not function as the legitimization (assertion and obfuscation) of the age's materialist interests. Such an art does not belong in the market (even when it is bought and sold) because as "true art" it does not "reflect" (give a specular image of) the age.

IV

I have been arguing that by centering exclusively on the question of Nanda's moral exposure, critics have neglected another aspect of the novel— that of the intrusion of the past. I have linked this aspect both to the novel's properly narrative aspect and to its understanding of artistic form and beauty. But concentrating on Nanda's exposure to a corrupt society that contaminates her also obfuscates another aspect of the novel, another sense of "exposure": the process by which Nanda, as well as Nanda's knowledge, is exposed to others—revealed, made visible, "laid bare." The paradigmatic opposition between Aggie and Nanda ("Nanda," says Mrs. Brook, "of course, is exposed . . . fearfully. . . . But Aggie isn't exposed to anything—never has been and never is to be"; 153) can be given a different inflection if one bears in mind this other meaning of exposure. Following the passage describing the impression Aggie has made on Longdon, we find the inevitable comparison: "Nanda, besides her, was a northern savage, and the reason was partly that the elements of that young lady's nature were already, were publicly, were almost indecorously, active" (181). Rather than defining Nanda in terms of her exposure to the corrupting influence of the world around her, the passage suggests that "the elements of her nature," by being "active," are exposed to others, laid bare, "publicly, almost indecorously." What is indecorous, one can argue, is not her nature or her knowledge, but the act of making (or the activity that makes) it publicly known.

The difference between Aggie and Nanda, then, would not be simply that Nanda "knows everything," whereas Aggie "knows nothing—but absolutely, utterly: not the least little tittle of anything" (259), but also that whereas Nanda's nature is visible, ex-pressed or ex-posed, out there for everyone to see, Aggie's external form expresses nothing. Aggie's "coming out" would then mean more than a simple loss of innocence through sexual knowledge. It would also mean that, as with Nanda, the elements of her nature become visible—she is now not sheltered but exposed, her nature made visible publicly, "almost indecorously."

Nanda's knowledge is revealed, made visible to others, through "exposure"—a process of representation. And this representation or "exposure" occurs both in the represented "life" and through the novel. The novel as representation is not the limitation by a form of what in life is endless and unlimited, nor is it a copy of an original present to itself. Rather, the act of novelistic representation is a repetition of an act of exposure, of making visible.

This aspect of the novel as exposure is related to its dramatic form, its approximation in novelistic form of a theatrical play, something that James achieves both by creating his own version of "roman dialogué" and by making each of the ten books abide by the "unities" of time and place with the rigor of classical drama. The sense of moral exposure that most critics dwell on is taken for granted rather than dramatized: there is no scene in the novel in which we see Nanda being exposed to the immoral talk of her mother (the two appear together in only two scenes in the novel) or her mother's circle; nor could there be. As Nanda repeatedly makes clear (and as discussed above), her exposure and its result, her knowledge, have always been there. What is dramatic, on the other hand, and subject to dramatic representation, is her other exposure, the making visible to others of who or what she is.[15]

The scene at Tishy's in Book VIII is the clearest example of this exposure: it is not a scene where Nanda is shown exposed to the bad influence of the immoral French novels the adults around her read but rather a dramatic representation, a "wonderful performance" (313), almost a play within the large play that is the novel, where an entire circle watches Nanda (the "stage directions" are most explicit), where Nanda is publicly exposed.

But if the novel emphasizes exposure as making publicly visible over exposure as contamination, it does not follow that it merely displaces the question of knowledge from Nanda (who, by being exposed, "picks up" forbidden knowledge) to the audience—the other characters in the novel or us, the readers, who, through the exposure/representation, "learn" the truth (about Nanda, about the other represented characters). In the conversation between Van and Nanda that precedes her exposure, she tells him that the "danger of picking up" (278) forbidden knowledge is over for her (since she knows "everything"); and Van, for his part, is already aware that she has read the French novel in question, knows, in other words, that what Nanda reads or hears at this point can make no further difference in her (she is "about as good as [she] can be—and about as bad"; 165) or for him. She has already lost too much of her innocence—she is already "spoiled" for him (344), and he knows it. Thus if the effect of the scene on Van is such that it leaves him "more or less bruised and buried" (313), it is not because the representation in which he assisted revealed something new and shattering to him; the scene, as a representation, did not produce new knowledge, and its force is independent of its cognitive value.[16]

In the Preface to the novel, James makes explicit the way in which its theatrical aspect limits knowledge. The choice of a "roman dialogué" was dictated, he says, by a desire to avoid using the convention of the narrator who "goes behind" the characters, who knows what lies beneath or behind the surfaces (18). Though James does not get rid of the narrator altogether, the "observer" he introduces with some frequency is not a narrator who "knows."[17] And the result of this technique is that we, the readers, are also left in the dark. Having assisted in the performance and "seen" everything, we still do not know many things, indeed most of the important things. Whether or not we feel as Van does, "bruised and buried," it is still clear that the novel's ability to produce a violent effect (or effect of violence) does not diminish because of this ignorance. The novel, then, does not only leave unrepresented the process of Nanda's acquisition of knowledge. As representation it does not produce knowledge out of the (violence of) experience (a knowledge that would then redeem it, make its violence "fortunate"). It reproduces an experience of violent representation/exposure in which what is exposed is the violent marking of consciousness ("battered and bruised" by the world of London) and whose effect is violent (Van being "bruised and buried").

The analogic relation between the novel and the life it represents accounts for the fact that the whole "smash" at Tishy's has to do with the reading of a book. If we emphasize, as critics tend to, the issue of Nanda's contamination by the world around her, then the book in question is an emblem of the knowledge she picked up from others around her. It thus stands to reason that everyone "knows" the book: Van owns it; Mrs. Brook read it; Nanda borrowed it with the idea of lending it to Tishy; it is the "bone of contention" in the flirtatious play between Aggie (who wants to read it) and Petherton (whose knowledge of the author makes him think it unsuitable); it is passed on to Harold; and even Cashmore, "hilarious and turning the leaves," reads enough of it to be mildly shocked ("Oh, I say!"; 312).[18] The book, then, is an emblem of a shared knowledge, and Nanda's admission that she has read it is an admission that she knows what they all know, all they know, that she knows "everything."

If all the characters in the novel know the book, then the analogy between them and us, the readers, breaks down, since we certainly do not; for us the book, like all the other books mentioned in the novel, remains closed.[19] We are then like Aggie before her marriage, before she "came out" and became visible, since all the "horrors" have been left out of our book, excised, just as from hers, in order to keep us, even while we are reading, from "picking up" any knowledge that may be bad for us.

Though James's avoidance of representing "horrors" in any explicit way is well established, we may want to see what, besides prudishness, may motivate it.[20] For a start, we do know one thing that is written "in" the book—Van's name, written by Nanda—and it is precisely this writing on the cover of the book, so to speak, rather than any horror written within it, that allows Mrs. Brook to carry out her performance with all its hoped-for results.[21]

At the same time, Nanda's knowledge of the book in the sense of her knowledge of all they all know, her "omniscience," should not be taken for granted. She and others keep repeating that she "knows everything," and this "everything," just like the "everything" used to describe Lady Julia, is the mark of a specular projection, of idealization. As a "subject presumed to know," Nanda is a phantasm, an imaginary projection; she is a "dummy" or a cipher who, by transference, is constructed as the one who knows—knows what the others keep back, what is not said, what indeed is not in any objective way "known." Mrs. Brook says, "It's as if the dear thing *knew*, don't you see? what we must keep back" (133). Rather than "picking up" what is said in her presence, Nanda knows what must be kept back from her. It is what is left unsaid, not what is said (or written), that Nanda is presumed to know.[22]

Nor is Nanda unique in this respect. As Tzvetan Todorov has shown in his analysis of the language of the *The Awkward Age*, dialogue among the characters proceeds on the uncertain grounds of inference and implication; it can take, for example, the form of one character interpreting another's remark in a way that nothing in the context authorizes, thus sending the first speaker in search of what it was in his or her remark that would justify such an interpretation. Todorov concludes that the "indirect language" James employs in the novel (unlike that used by Proust or Joyce) does not lead to truth: "the deceptive surface leads into something else (it is in this sense that the language is indirect), but that something else is yet another surface, itself subject to interpretation. It is not a deeper interior."[23] In giving up "going behind" characters, James gives up not only the convention of the omniscient narrator but, more broadly, the claim that the novel as a representation reveals or produces knowledge that is behind or beyond experience. No one in the novel "knows"—neither characters nor narrator nor reader. The characters' knowledge, like Nanda's and like ours, is either limited to the surface (to the cover of the book) behind which they cannot go or consists of acts of projection, where meaning is tentatively proposed but can never be grounded. It is in the context of such "asceticism" of knowledge that we should understand the ambiguous figure of Mrs. Brook.

V

Critics of *The Awkward Age* are sharply divided over whether Mrs. Brook is a heroine or a villainess. The ambiguity, I would argue, stems from Mrs. Brook's status as "intelligent observer" and the critical distance James takes here from this crucial feature of his fiction.[24] The intelligent observer in James's fiction is a figure for the artist, since she or he possesses "the art of seeing," reproduces reality (in consciousness), and is detached—above or outside—the world of monetary and erotic transactions. The superiority of the observer's consciousness or vision over the things seen is made clear, for example, in the Preface to "The Spoils of Poynton" with which I began, where Fleda's understanding is contrasted with the "stupidity" of the "things" of Poynton.

There is no doubt that Mrs. Brook is such an intelligent observer. She is famous for taking up an object and studying it until she finally "understands" it (367). The "temple of analysis" (253) in Buckingham Crescent is "a place in which at all times, before interesting objects, the unanimous occupants, almost more concerned for each other's vibrations than for anything else, were apt rather more to exchange sharp and silent searchings than to fix their eyes on the object itself" (96). For Mrs. Brook and her circle, the "object" of analysis is far less important than the "vibrations" it produces in those who observe and analyze it; the object is interesting only to the extent that it occasions these "vibrations." Mrs. Brook's "watching" of Lady Fanny turns Lady Fanny's insipid life into a play one watches out of curiosity about its dénouement: "She's the ornament of our circle," says Mrs. Brook. "She will, she won't—she won't, she will [elope]! It's the excitement, every day, of plucking the daisy over" (141). It also turns Lady Fanny into an "ornament," "a great calm silver statue" (134)—an inert object, a work of art.[25] One can argue that Mrs. Brook's "understanding" of Lady Fanny renders her stupid and inarticulate by objectifying her. Or one can argue that Fanny is made "beautiful" by Mrs. Brook's "treatment" of her, that Mrs. Brook is here the artist who transforms and redeems "stupid" reality. In this case her stupidity is "fortunate," since it allows (requires and makes possible) her transformation.

Mrs. Brook then, as an observer and artist, is an ambivalent figure, since she can be seen both as producing knowledge and beauty that transform reality and as parasitically "living off" other people (in the sense that the others serve her as objects upon which she "vibrates"). This parasitic or exploitative aspect is made explicit in the parallel between Mrs. Brook's "living off" other people and her son Harold's borrowing money from family friends. At the end of the novel Harold keeps Lady Fanny from eloping, as his mother did before, and he gets paid for it—is "run" by Lady Fanny, just as his mother "lived" off Lady Fanny in the sense that Lady Fanny provided her with the necessary material for her conversation (on which she lives).

But Mrs. Brook's "vision" (132) and "watching" (153) are not only analogous to the monetary transactions that pervade the novel; her "exploitation" of others through her exercise of understanding is not simply parallel to Harold's borrowing or Petherton's monetary exploitation of Mitchy. Rather, the two issues are interwoven. Thus much as Mrs. Brook and her circle may take pleasure in observing Longdon, who is for them a kind of curiosity (150), they, and especially the Brooks, also have every intention of "working" him, of deriving monetary gain from their association with him. The circle is made of friends who discuss each other constantly, analyzing and better understanding each other (125), but they also, as Van says, keep giving each other away (39), not only in the sense of betraying each other's secrets, but also in the sense of trading in each other (as the Duchess and Mrs. Brook "trade" Mitchy); and most of Mrs. Brook's acts of manipulation are predicated on "exchanging" one person for another.[26] Mrs. Brook lives in her consciousness, nourished by her understanding of others, but she also has, as the Duchess says, a commerce, a business "in husbands and wives," where, though she "makes no charge whatever" for her advice, she is not "free" with it either (or else her advice will have no value); though "she doesn't take a guinea at the time, you still get your account" (94–95). And if there may be some doubt about how much knowledge Nanda gained to compensate her for the loss of Van, there is no doubt about the money that has been settled on her at the end. The issue for Mrs. Brook has not been so much Nanda's knowledge (and even less a knowledge of Nanda) as her trading value.[27] Thus Mrs. Brook shows the observer-artist to be not only figuratively exploitative (commodifying human beings by "knowing" them, or positing their "stupidity" in order to self-servingly justify the need for "transforming" them), but also literally engaged in trading, selling, and exchanging.[28] From this perspective, any attempt to "save" something (or someone) out of the circle of exchange is to be understood as an attempt to control exchange.

The world of London is a world of exchange to which everyone is drawn. Even Longdon cannot stand outside it, not only because he is immediately seen as an instrument for increasing Nanda's value (211) but also because he comes to see himself as an object in an exchange: when the Duchess tells him that Mrs. Brook "has put down her money, as it were, without a return. She has given Mitchy up and got nothing instead," Longdon surprisingly answers, "Do you call *me* nothing?" (291). Nanda is, of course, within this circle of exchange since the plot of the novel revolves around her chances in the marriage market, but also because she too inevitably gets involved in acts of trading (witness the role she plays in arranging Mitchy's and Aggie's marriage). Everyone gets drawn into the circuit of exchange, and yet the ability to control the exchange depends on being outside it. The master of the exchange is precisely the person who "doesn't pay," who does not have to give anything in exchange for what he/she receives; and we have seen how Mrs. Brook's idealization of the Duchess is expressed precisely as the Duchess's presumed ability to get whatever she wants without paying. Mrs. Brook's own desire to "save" or "hoard," keep something out of circulation, keep Van "to herself," would then be motivated by the desire to control the exchange.[29]

It is in light of this logic of exchange that we should come back to the smash at Tishy's orchestrated by Mrs. Brook. That the scene was put on to effect a certain exchange—where Nanda will pass out of the keep of her mother (who clearly does not want to keep her to herself) to the keep of Longdon—has been made clear by Mrs. Brook herself in her retrospective analysis of the episode. But beyond that, Mrs. Brook is trying to avoid another exchange, one in which Van, in order to get something from Longdon, will have to pay—by sacrificing Mrs. Brook herself (145). Mrs. Brook, then, tries in at least two ways to stay outside the circuit of exchange.

Van too tries to stay outside this circuit. Declining Longdon's offer is a way to avoid sacrificing Mrs. Brook, but also, and more importantly, a way to preserve his idealized image of himself as someone above exchange (who cannot be "bought"). But Nanda's writing of his name on the book, whose itinerary comes to symbolize all the exchanges in the novel, destroys this idealized image that he has of himself and would like to present to the others,[30] showing him instead as an object in exchanges over which he has no control. This is why, in the discussion between Van and Nanda preceding the scene of "exposure," Van's primary concern is not the fact that Nanda has read the novel but the fact that she wrote his name on the cover of a book he lent to her mother. Nanda explains that she has brought the book for Tishy:

> "And I wrote your name on it so that we might know—"
> "That I hadn't lent it to either of you? It didn't occur to you to write your own?" Vanderbank went on.
> "Well, but if it isn't mine? It isn't mine, I'm sure."
> "Therefore, also, if it can't be Tishy's—"
> "It's simple enough—it's mother's." (285)

The dialogue does not make much sense, though the fact that the two complete each other's sentences may mean that they make perfect sense to each other. Nanda wrote Van's name so that she and Tishy may know—what? presumably that Van is the owner of the book. In his elliptic retort, Van does not deny owning the book but is distressed at the implication that he lent the book to Nanda, or to Tishy. What he objects to is the circulation of the book, of his name, out of his control. Both Van's surprise that it did not occur to Nanda to write her own name in the book and Nanda's acquiescing conclusion that the book is her mother's serve the purpose of "saving" Van, keeping him out of the circuit of exchange (and thus keeping intact the "sacred terror" he inspires). But since Nanda has written Van's name on the book, Mrs. Brook cannot point to Nanda's involvement in the circuit of exchange (which would rid her of Nanda and allow her to keep Van to herself) without pointing to Van's involvement too; she cannot save herself—from being sacrificed by Van—without sacrificing Van himself. Van understands this, and that is why he feels particularly "bruised and buried." Mrs. Brook can "keep him to herself," outside the system of exchange, only by showing that he is well within it, thus, Samson-like, destroying not only Nanda and Van but also herself.

We saw at the beginning of this chapter how Longdon's return introduces a historical dimension that destroys the idealization of both the past as totally other and the present as identical to itself. We have seen now that, with his return to London and reinsertion in a system of exchange (his offer to Van), Longdon destroys another kind of idealization, namely, that one can stay outside the system of exchange, be the one who "saves" or "doesn't pay." The "doom of coming back" (28) would mean the impossibility of constituting a separate realm, outside change and exchange.

The ambiguity of Mrs. Brook suggests an awareness that the vision of the detached observer-artist may in fact be an act of exploitation, that it is motivated by a search for power. The narrator's refusal to "go behind," the sacrifice of knowledge that this refusal entails, may then be a protective measure, a last-ditch effort to "save" vision and art from such an entanglement with the world. As such, the critique only reproduces its object; the "asceticism" of knowledge is merely another attempt at transcendence. But the return of Longdon also opens up another perspective. If form as the form of the past is an otherness within, if art has a ghostly status, then it is involved in the present, in the world, and yet cannot be reduced to it. Always in entanglement with "life," it retains an otherness that is neither a transcendence of the world nor a figurative analogy to its other practices.

Reference Material

Notes

For complete authors' names, titles, and publication data on the works cited in short form in the Notes, see the Bibliography, pp. 243–48.

Introduction

1. Barthes, *S/Z*, 3.
2. Brooks, *Reading*, xiii.
3. Ibid., xii.
4. Ibid., 96.
5. Ibid., 101. For a feminist critique of this model in Brooks and others, see Winnett, "Coming Unstrung." See also de Lauretis's seminal essay "Desire in Narrative," in *Alice Doesn't*, 103–57.
6. Chambers, *Room for Maneuver*, 253.
7. *Essays on the Sociology of Literary Forms* is the subtitle of Moretti's collection *Signs Taken for Wonders*.
8. On this point, see especially Moretti's essay "On Literary Evolution" in ibid., 262–78.
9. Ibid., 263–64.
10. Moretti, *Way of the World*, 181.
11. Ibid., 75, 181.
12. The concept of "open" text comes from Umberto Eco's *Opera aperta* (Milan; 1962; English tr. 1989). The discussion of closure in narrative is drawn in part from Barbara Hernstein Smith's *Poetic Closure* (Chicago, 1968). The most important discussion of the necessity of closure remains Kermode's *Sense of an Ending*. Among the works extolling "open" texts and aligning them with modernist writing, one should mention Friedman, *Turn of the Novel*. Both Bakhtin's distinction between dialogical and monological and Barthes's distinction between *scriptible* and *lisible* lent themselves to a similar periodization and value judgment. In the case of Bakhtin, see, for example, Julia Kristeva, "Une Poétique ruinée," especially 15–16; in the case of Barthes,

see *S/Z*, especially 9–12. Richter, *Fable's End*, is intended in part as a critique of Friedman but in a way avoids the issue by not discussing 19th-century narrative, which is the most obvious term of opposition for modernist writing. D. A. Miller, *Narrative and Its Discontents*, is undoubtedly the best discussion of the ways in which the 19th-century novel resists closure or testifies to its impossibility. For other studies in this vein, see Welsh's collection *Narrative Endings*. D. A. Miller later distanced himself from this position in his essay "Balzac's Illusions," where he argues that "the failure of closure," giving evidence "of a process which is, on the one hand, inherent in textuality and, on the other, radically outside and subversive of all that a given text mundanely 'wants to say,' " contributes to the "myth" of literature as different from all other social practices. I will address the issues this essay raises in Chap. 3.

13. D. A. Miller, *Novel and Police*, 65.

14. Ibid., x.

15. On the relation between the symbolic and the real, see Žižek, *Sublime Object*, especially 87–99.

16. Brooks, *Reading*, xi.

17. In *Narrative and Its Discontents*, D. A. Miller proposed "to identify and account for a central tension in the traditional novelistic enterprise: namely, a discomfort with the processes and implications of narrative itself." Austen, Stendhal, and George Eliot, he argues, though in other respects very dissimilar novelists, "orient their texts towards a 'utopic' state that is radically at odds with the narrative means used to reach it." *Narrative*, x. I will have occasion to come back to Miller's specific readings in my chapter on *Mansfield Park*, but for the moment, I would like to acknowledge the similarity between his view of the traditional novel and my view of the common interpretation of novels. Whether interpretations of the traditional novel "respond" to or echo a discomfort with the processes of narrative already present in the novels or impose on those novels their own discomfort with narrative, their own desire for a "utopic" state of meaning, is less important than to note—and then question—the common assumption about the "odd" relation between narrative and meaning.

18. Consider, for example, Greimas's statement in *Du sens*, 104: "Toute saisie de signification a pour effet de transformer les histoires en permanences: qu'il s'agisse de l'interrogation sur le sens d'une vie ou sur le sens d'une histoire (ou de l'histoire), l'interrogation, c'est-à-dire le fait qu'on se place devant une manifestation linguistique dans l'attitude du destinataire des messages, a pour conséquence ceci: que les algorithmes historiques se présentent comme des états, autrement dit, comme des structures statiques."

19. Lévi-Strauss, "The Structural Study of Myth," in *Structural Anthropology*, 206–31.

20. In the words of Tzvetan Todorov, sequence is the syntagmatic projection of a set of paradigmatic relations. *Littérature et signification*, 55.

21. Critics are far from being of one mind on what a thematic reading of narrative is. If all accept that "themes" have to do with what a text is "about," there is much disagreement on whether themes are explicit or implicit, are on the surface of the text or on a "deeper" level, are individual and idiomatic to a certain text or common to several texts, and so on. In my understanding of thematic reading, which is arguably more in line with the French tradition than with the Anglo-American one, the important point is that, as Shlomith Rimmon-Kenan puts it, a "theme" is a con-

struction elaborated from discontinuous, that is, nonlinear, elements of the text. As such it is distinct from the level of plot. Since the elements that constitute themes are discontinuous in the text, the principle that pulls them together must be something other than succession, namely, the principle of recurrence, of similarity and differ-ence. Thus every thematic reading implies a move away from the syntagmatic to the paradigmatic, a transformation of the narrative flow into a spatial design or paradig-matic structure that is its meaning. For some recent debates about thematic reading, see Alleton et al., *Du thème* (which contains, among others, Rimmon-Kenan's essay "Qu'est-ce qu'un thème?"); Bremond and Pavel, *Variations sur le thème*; and Sollors, *Return of Thematic Criticism*.

22. For the concept of "spatial form," see Joseph Frank's seminal essay "Spatial Form in Modern Literature." In his follow-up essay, Frank convincingly demonstrates that the concept of spatial form is relevant not only to modern literature. As he notes in connection with Kermode's *Sense of an Ending*, "Plots . . . exhibit a tendency to counteract time by spatializing its flow—that is, to create relations of meaning de-tached from pure succession." "Spatial Form: Thirty Years After," 220.

23. Bersani, *Culture of Redemption*, 1.

24. Ibid., 18.

Chapter 1

1. As I indicated in the Introduction, the prime example for such a translation is Lévi-Strauss, but as Barthes notes, "All contemporary researchers (Lévi-Strauss, Greimas, Bremond, Todorov) . . . could subscribe to Lévi-Strauss's proposition that 'the order of chronological succession is absorbed in atemporal matrix structure.' Analysis today tends to 'dechronologize' the narrative continuum and to 'relogicize' it." Barthes, "Introduction," 98–99. Culler, *Structuralist Poetics*, 212–17, documents this shift in the work of specific "narratologists."

2. Propp, *Morphology of the Folktale*; Greimas, *Sémantique structurale*, especially 192–221.

3. On the question of the body in the novel, see Roland Le Huenen, "La Sémio-tique du corps dans *La Peau de chagrin*: Le Tout et le fragment," in Le Huenen, *Le Roman de Balzac*, 51–64.

4. In the following pages, I use "paradigmatic" and "spatial" relations interchange-ably, though the words are of course not synonymous. But paradigmatic relations, or relations of similarity and difference, emphasize the coexistence of the two terms rather than their sequentiality and hence can be said to be "spatial."

5. For a thematic reading of the relation among the three tableaux that constitute the first part of the novel, see Bilodeau, "Espace et temps romanesques," 47–55.

6. Emile's statement "la phrase est usée" participates also in the economy of loss and gain ("usure" being both "wear and tear" and "interest"), of the shrinking and increase that characterize, as we shall see, the entire dialogue between him and Raphaël. See Weber, *Unwrapping Balzac*, 60. I am much indebted, despite my various disagreements, to Weber's study throughout this chapter.

7. The lack of verisimilitude of the personal narrative is one of the things *La Peau* has in common with *Le Lys dans la vallée*, discussed in the next chapter. The use in

both novels of a first-person narrative in spite of a glaring lack of verisimilitude is all the more noteworthy because of Balzac's clear preference for third-person narration. On the point of view in these two novels, see Lastinger, "Narration."

8. This privileging of the temporality of narration over the temporality of experience is signaled by the very first words of the text. Rather than anchoring the *story* in a point in time (as does, for example, the first sentence of "Le Chef-d'œuvre inconnu": "Vers la fin de l'année 1612"), the opening words of *La Peau* situate it in relation to the act of narration: "Vers la fin du mois d'octobre dernier" (59). See Claude Duchet, "La Mise en texte du social," in Duchet, *Balzac*, 81–82. As Duchet points out, and as other critics have observed, this creates serious problems for the chronology of the novel. The novel contains the lived experience within the highly circumscribed scene of narration and yet fails to do precisely that.

9. Duchet points out how the very first sentence of the novel already evokes the end. Ibid., 81.

10. Verrier, "Récit réfléchi," 67–68.

11. José-Luis Diaz has commented on the "economy" that underlies the antique dealer's theories, but he sees it primarily in terms of saving or hoarding, not in terms of a loss that brings about a gain: "Mesurée à l'aune de la sagesse du vieillard, théoricien improvisé du romanesque selon la 'vision intérieure', l'activité littéraire n'en est pas moins donnée pour une *opération d'économie et d'épargne*, qui consiste à la fois à changer la matière périssable des événements passionnels en idées et expressions impérissables, et à *concentrer* sous forme *d'extrait mis à l'écart* le résultat spirituel de cette transmutation. Selon cette interprétation, le livre ou la pensée seraient un peu comme une banque où l'on viendrait mettre à l'abri, suspendre, sous forme monétaire réduite, les trésors ammassés." Diaz, "L'Economie: La Dépense et l'oxymore," in Duchet, *Balzac*, 162.

12. For a more detailed discussion of some of these oppositions, see Haig, *Madame Bovary Blues*, 12–14.

13. Another economy is exemplified by the dialogue between Raphaël and Emile before Rapahël starts his narration: there the discussion of this shrinking movement generates not (or not only) knowledge, but more text, more words. According to the first economy (in which "shrinking" leads to "increase" because knowledge is superior to the experience that was sacrificed in order to gain it), words produce meaning; according to the second, they produce other words. I elaborate on the difference between these two economies in my discussion of two understandings of reading and of translation present in the novel.

14. The skin, however, is not a clock or an hourglass: the decrease of time, the shrinking of the skin, is not independent of the subject's experience (his desire), though that experience itself is not autonomous (Raphaël cannot *not* desire, cannot *not* read the skin). I discuss the relation between the skin and desire later in this chapter.

15. Brooks draws the parallel between Raphaël's experience and the experience of reading, but, like most other critics, he does not distinguish between reading as sense making and the literal act of reading that is Raphaël's reading of the skin: "The paradox of the self becomes explicitly the paradox of narrative plot as the reader consumes it: diminishing as it realizes itself, leading to an end that is the consummation (as well as the consumption) of its sense-making." *Reading for the Plot*, 51–52.

16. Most critics fail to make this distinction and see the novel as governed by one economy. Weber, for example, says: "Raphaël's past shrinks in the phrases he utters to conjure it up just as the *peau de chagrin* will shrink his present and future with every desire he utters." *Unwrapping Balzac*, 61.

17. Raphaël shows a similar "confusion" between life and death during his visit to the antique store: "N'était-il pas ivre de la *vie* ou peut-être de la *mort*" (70–71); "il souhaita plus *vivement* que jamais de *mourir*" (79; my emphasis).

18. On Raphaël's relation to his father and to the Law of the Father, see Roland Le Huenen, "Le Personnage et son désir," in Duchet, *Balzac*, 93–113.

19. What defines Rastignac is that he does not subscribe to the antiquarian's idea of loss turning into gain. Dissipation, then, can be described as sheer loss, with no gain, but it can also, and with equal justice, be described as sheer gain, with no loss. Thus Rastignac, in explaining the dissipational system to Raphaël, describes himself as a person who only spends and does not have to pay: "Je me répands, je me pousse, l'on me fait place; je me vante, l'on me croit, je fais des dettes, on les paie!" ("I get everything I want. I jump the queue, and people make room for me. I brag, and they believe me. I run up debts and it's they who pay"; 153; *118*). Dissipation is precisely either a system of living or a system of dying; what it is not is a theory of life regained through death.

20. We cannot quite say that the skin is a material object *on* which a text is inscribed; that is, we cannot quite separate its materiality from its textuality. Balzac insists that the inscription is part of the skin, not on it: the characters encrusted in the skin look "comme s'ils eussent été produits par l'animal auquel elle [la peau] avait jadis appartenu" ("as if they had been part of the animal whose skin it had once been"; 86; *49*).

21. See, for example, Brooks, *Reading for the Plot*, 48–61.

22. Claude Bernard contests this point and argues that "nous ignorons si Raphaël a servi d'interprète auprès du marchand." Since, as he rightly observes, the sentence that serves as a transition between the "Arabic" and French texts reads, "Ce qui voulait dire en français," he holds that the interpretation has to be attributed to the narrator. "A propos de la *Peau de chagrin*," 256. But following the French text, we read, "Ah! vous lisez couramment le sanscrit, dit le vieillard" ("'Ah! so you can read Sanskrit with ease,' the old man said"; 88; *51*), which may mean either that Raphaël simply read the text in "Sanskrit" without translating or that he showed his knowledge of the language by translating the text into French. It all depends on whether we take "reading" ("vous lisez") as the actual uttering of sounds (reading in Sanskrit) or as an act of understanding (translating the "letter" into its meaning). It is the presence in the novel of both these "views" of reading that I am seeking to highlight. This does not discredit Bernard's observation that the narrator is also responsible for the act of translation, which I see as the way the reader gets introduced into the text, reading with and at the same time as Raphaël.

23. Not many critics have found this discrepancy worthy of attention. That is perhaps because they see the Arabic text as an afterthought, one of the changes Balzac introduced in later editions. Pierre Citron, editor of the Garnier-Flammarion edition I use, states that Balzac wanted to include an "original" Sanskrit text in the 1835 edition and asked Baron Hammer-Purgstall to provide him with one; the baron, says

Citron, maybe as a joke, gave him an Arabic inscription instead (27). M. Allem, in his notes to the Classiques Garnier edition (1967), points out that the 1831 and 1835 editions did not include either the Arabic inscription or the line, "Ce qui voulait dire en français." He then comments on the antiquarian's mention of "sanscrit": " 'Le sanscrit', dit Balzac dès la première édition, qui ne contenait que la version française de l'inscription, mais quand Balzac en a donné le texte original il l'a donné en caractères arabes." *Peau de chagrin* (1967 ed.), 336. Weber comments: "The 'original' is thus not simply,—be it through 'error' or 'design'—obscured: the problem of its *representation*, of the text as representation, is thereby made manifest." *Unwrapping Balzac*, 46.

24. The only way Raphaël can escape desire and fulfillment is by vegetating in drugged sleep. But this "death in life" is without any promise of regaining the life that is denied either on another level or at a later moment. It is an artificial stopping of the clock, creating an interval where Raphaël neither lives nor dies; and when this interval is over, nothing has changed—he is precisely in the same predicament, in the same point in time, as before.

25. The natural, in a novel, is the novelistically conventional. Hence, as Françoise Gaillard points out, Raphaël's desires are fulfilled in the way that events most conventionally occur in fiction (the long lost heir) and especially in the novels of Balzac (by coincidence). "L'Effet peau de chagrin," in Le Huenen, *Roman de Balzac*, 217. On the relation in Balzac between quotidian coincidences and the "strange," see Moretti, *Signs*, 109–29.

26. Weber's insistence that what "activates" the skin is Raphaël's wording, the uttering of his desire, seems misleading to me: it suggests that the desires are in fact Raphaël's and depend on his acts (of uttering), even if these acts can be seen as not entirely voluntary (on the order of slips of the tongue). It is important to stress in this context that in both examples, the agents involved in the chains of events that accomplish Raphaël's desires are seeking him—the action is on the part of others, so it is Raphaël's desires that seek him. For another discussion of the role of words in the novel, see Kanes, *Balzac's Comedy of Words*, 73ff.

27. We can argue, then, that even Raphaël's desire to possess the skin is not "his" desire—the skin "possesses" him long before he beholds it.

28. Especially since one can claim that the mother foretells not only Pauline's prosperity but also Raphaël's, though it is not clear whether the latter depends on the former or not: "Ce soir, j'ai lu l'Évangile de saint Jean pendant que Pauline tenait suspendue entre ses doigts notre clef attachée dans une Bible, la clef a tourné. Ce présage annonce que Gaudin se porte bien et prospère. Pauline a recommencé pour vous et pour le jeune homme du numéro sept; mais la clef n'a tourné que pour vous. Nous serons tous riches, Gaudin reviendra millionnaire" ("This evening I read the gospel of Saint John whilst Pauline held our door-key suspended from a Bible, and the key turned. It is a sign that Gaudin is well and prospering. Pauline did the same for you and for the young man in No. 7, but the key turned for you alone. We shall all be rich. Gaudin will come home a millionaire"; 173; *139*).

29. This idea that the strange, or the fantastic, in Balzac is the result of pushing a concept to the limit is Lukács's. As he puts it, "The fantastic element in Balzac derives merely from the fact that he radically thinks through to the end the necessities of

social reality, beyond their normal limits, beyond even their feasibility." *Studies in European Realism*, 60.

Chapter 2

1. For a discussion of *Le Lys* as an epistolary novel, on the one hand, and a "confession," on the other, see Lachet, *Thématique*, especially 45–48.

2. Brombert dwells on the "intention aphrodisiaque" of the bouquets. "Natalie," 185. For Perrone-Moisés, the description of the flowers does not constitute an interval where "nothing happens." She stresses the productive role of the description and analyzes the effect of the bouquets on both Henriette and the reader. "Balzac et les fleurs," 306–10, 312.

3. Perrone-Moisés, "Balzac et les fleurs," 323. Though Brombert does not argue explicitly against a referential reading of the bouquets, he does emphasize that they are always described in terms of another art. "Natalie," 184. Thus if the bouquets, as Félix says, constitute a language, the signs of this language are described not in relation to objects in the world but rather in relation to other signs, in other systems (such as musical phrases or words).

4. This is J. Hillis Miller's formulation of the "prosopopeia," which he sees as inaugural to all narrative. See *Versions of Pygmalion*.

5. My discussion of fixation and displacement is indebted to Leo Bersani's essay "Erotic Assumptions: Narcissism and Sublimation in Freud," in *Culture of Redemption*, 29–46. Analyzing Freud's essay "Character and Anal Eroticism," Bersani shows that "even a sexual drive as fixated as anal eroticism is comparatively indifferent to the objects and activities by which it can be satisfied." Bersani, 30. Fixation in the anal stage does not in the least mean fixation on the anal erotogenic zone. On the contrary, this fixation manifests itself precisely in the ability of an excitation that has originated in the anal zone to cathect any number of objects or activities, from stinginess to scrupulous scholarship. The result of this conjunction is not simply a loosening of a "referential" link ("orderliness can no longer be defined merely as the love of order"; 31), but the creation of what I have termed a "rhetorical" system of representation, where any character trait, intellectual activity, or object can be cathected and hence serve as a symbol (sign or symptom).

6. What I have called a "rhetorical system" can be linked to Lacan's notion of the metonymic chain of signifiers, where the differential interplay of the signifiers and the metonymic slide of the signified are arrested by a master signifier, the "point de capiton." This chain of signifiers also represents desire, since its metonymical displacement presupposes and produces an object-cause, the "objet petit a." I will come back to Lacan's theory at the end of the chapter.

7. Toward the end of his long letter, Félix tells Natalie how, consequent to Henriette's death, he made a resolution to never pay attention to any woman—it seems as if he has learned something from his past experience. But he immediately adds the obvious—that his resolutions came to naught—and it is this breaking of a resolution, or the inability to truly learn from the past, that accounts not only for his relation with Natalie but for the writing of the letter.

8. The relation with Lady Dudley seems at first to contradict this logic or to show

that Félix has found a way out of his fixation; but this is not the case. Lady Dudley, more than his mother, more than any other woman in his life, merely gets him to the brink of fulfillment. After all, she seduces him, brings him to her feet, only, like his mother, to reject him and deny that she has ever loved him.

9. The Mortsauf males are not the only ones to escape death in spite of, or because of, weakness and sickness. The King is another obvious example. Both the King and the Comte come back from exile—a living death that, in the case of the Comte, is explicitly described in terms recalling Félix's predicament. We read of the Comte in exile that he does not quite live, since "ses espérances toujours appointées au lende-main . . . des espoirs toujours déçus" ("his hopes always pinned to the morrow . . . hopes perpetually dashed"; 81; *39*) compromise his health and livelihood. His exile can be further glossed as a rejection by the mother: when he comes back to France, the Comte cries " 'Voilà la France!' . . . comme un enfant crie: Ma mère!" (82; *40*).

10. If we feel a certain inappropriateness in moving from Henriette's romantic love to her social and economical theories, it is because we have all too easily subscribed to Arabelle's view that a woman who loves gives herself entirely to the man she loves, has no business having theories of any kind. She tells Félix: "Elle [Henriette] sait cultiver les terres, dis-tu? Moi je laisse cette science aux fermiers, j'aime mieux cultiver ton coeur" ("She knows how to cultivate land, you say? I'll leave that knowledge to farmers; I would rather cultivate your heart"; 248; *206*).

11. See, for example, Niess, "Saint-Beuve," 124.

12. Barthes argues that Balzac even anticipates the society of the Second Empire. "Vouloir nous brûle," 90–93.

13. Henriette sees mothering as an act of reason rather than as a "natural" act. Though this may seem to us an important step forward, going against the stereotypi-cal identification of motherhood with nature, it is not enough to separate her from the social world she opposes. Henriette may have reversed the conventional view (which links the father with reason and makes the mother sheer matter), but in so doing she reproduces, as we shall see, the reason/matter opposition and thus remains, despite herself, complicit with the social order she attempts to reform.

14. Saussure, *Course in General Linguistics*, 110. For a discussion of this passage, see Goux, *Symbolic Economies*, 59–61.

15. The same thing can be said about Félix's neutralizing of the Comte in the backgammon game. Félix here follows Henriette's philosophy and attempts to reduce conflict: as a better player he could have always won, but this would have merely aggravated the competition between him and the Comte. He opts (in his own inter-est) to forgo the gains he could thus achieve (winning the game, becoming in-creasingly strong in relation to the Comte) and to manipulate the game in such a way that gains and losses will almost balance out. The fluctuations of loss and gain, as well as the conflict between strong and weak, are eliminated; a rational system is con-structed from which both are the modest beneficiaries. But the Comte, the element that threatened this system, is in fact eliminated from the game, since, unbeknownst to him, he is not a player anymore.

16. The text does not answer the question of what would take place in the next generation. On the one hand, Félix's perception toward the end of the novel is that Madeleine is healthy and strong—indeed, quite like her mother—whereas Jacques's

health is only apparent and delusive; Jacques himself (hypochondriac like his father?) affirms that he will soon follow his mother to the grave. But we know that Henriette's health does not prevent her from dying, whereas men survive in spite (because) of their weakness. Should this not apply also to Jacques? After all, Henriette (who reads the future of her children) is sure of Jacques's health, whereas Felix's ability to read and interpret correctly has been put in doubt many times before. It is possible, then, that the next generation will merely repeat the first. This possibility may explain a curious phrase in a passage toward the end of the novel. Following Henriette's death and Madeleine's rejection of his advances, Félix feels that he is totally different from the man he was when he first came to Clochegourde. And yet, in rejecting him, Madeleine behaved just as her mother did, so nothing has changed, everything can start over again, in the same way. Hence his emotion in seeing Madeleine standing on the terrace, as her mother did when he first saw her: "Quand Madeleine eut disparu par la porte du perron, je revins, le cœur brisé, dire adieu à mes hôtes, et je partis pour Paris en suivant la rive droite de l'Indre, par laquelle j'étais venu dans cette vallée pour la première fois. . . . Cependant j'étais riche, la vie politique me souriait, je n'étais plus le piéton fatigué de 1814. Dans ce temps-là, mon cœur était plein de désirs, au-jourd'hui mes yeux étaient pleins de larmes; autrefois j'avais ma vie à remplir, au-jourd'hui je la sentais déserte. J'étais bien jeune, j'avais vingt-neuf ans, mon cœur était déjà flétri. Quelques années avaient suffi pour dépouiller ce paysage de sa pre-mière magnificence et pour me dégoûter de la vie. Vous pouvez maintenant com-prendre quelle fut mon émotion, lorsqu'en me retournant je vis Madeleine sur la terasse" ("When Madeleine had disappeared through the French windows, I went back, sick at heart, to say my farewells to my hosts, and left for Paris, following the right bank of the Indre, the way I had come on my first visit to the valley. . . . Yet I was rich now; the world of politics smiled on me; I was no longer the weary pedestrian I had been in 1814. Then, my heart had been full of desire; now, my eyes were full of tears. Before, I wanted to fulfill my life; now, I felt it empty as a desert. I was young enough, I was twenty-nine, but my heart was already withered. A few years had sufficed to strip that landscape of its first splendour, and me of my taste for living. You will readily understand now, the emotion I felt when, on turning around, I saw Madeleine on the terrace"; 290; *250*).

17. This substitution appears also in the Comte's imaginary disease. Félix, com-pletely unaware of his own resemblance to the Comte, mocks him for his diagnosis, commenting that according to the Comte, "les gens de cœur périssent par l'estomac" (223). Nancy Miller, in her excellent reading of the novel and its "intertext," suggests that Henriette's illness "might be diagnosed more interestingly as a form of conver-sion hysteria, specifically as anorexia nervosa, than as generally interpreted: cancer of the pylorus." "Tristes Triangles," 74. I am less interested in diagnosing Henriette's "real" illness than in showing how it functions as a literalization of the Comte's and Félix's disease; from this perspective, both the question of taking nourishment and the malfunctioning of the stomach (read euphemistically) are equally important.

18. We can call this gesture assuming castration: as Brooks points out, cutting off "le membre du coupable" can be read as cutting off "le membre coupable." "Virtue-Tripping," 161. But it should be emphasized that if Félix here invites us to literalize the phallus (equate it with "le membre coupable"), it is only because he has identified

"castration" with the loss of all vital powers (not with the loss of the penis). As we shall see, the result of such equivocation is that castration can afflict both males and females, whereas phallic potency is available only to males. As Goux has put it in another context, this double logic, which has as its function to buttress the masculine position, asserts at one and the same time that "the loss of the penis is not *really* the loss of the penis" and that "the phallus is *really* the penis." *Symbolic Economies*, 119. Bowie spells out another version of this equivocation, or contradiction, in his discussion of Lacan's thinking of the phallus and desire: "For the phallus, and the entire 'masculinist' discourse that it unleashes . . . are at odds not with one but with two models of perpetual mobility and incompletion, neither of which has any particular bias on matters of gender. 'The subject,' divided in and by language, is genuinely neutral in Lacan's analysis. . . . Desire, born of the impossible confluence of need and demand, is genderless in the same way. But the agent that is called upon to tie the two views together, to give the subject 'his' desire by signifying it for him, is the male genital, transcendentalized." *Lacan*, 141–42.

19. Henriette's death is overdetermined: she dies because, as the doctor says, her stomach lost its "jeu"—that is, its regular functioning, as of the heart, depending on the alternation between two opposite states. By losing this "jeu," she achieved a state of inertia—of no oscillation. This has been Henriette's ideal: to so regulate the social, material, and sentimental existence of herself and those around her as to avoid alternations at any cost, to approximate inertia. But when this system is "translated" to the concrete, material reality of the body, the result is death. We see again how much Henriette's theory, rather than being "natural" or merely an expression of conformity to social ideas, rests on the principle of rational regulation.

20. Félix's discourse on the double nature of man appears as a justification for his love for Arabelle: "L'homme est composé de matière et d'esprit; l'animalité vient aboutir en lui, et l'ange commence à lui. De là cette lutte que nous éprouvons tous" ("Man is made up of mind and matter; in him the animal kingdom ends and the angel begins. Hence the struggle we all feel"; 217; *174*).

21. I thank Peter Fenves for comments that brought me to reconsider this question. He is, of course, not responsible for the conclusions I have drawn from his remarks.

22. Žižek, *Sublime Object*, 99. Žižek calls this "error" "Ideological Anamorphosis."

23. The question of what Lacan himself understands by the "real" is not easily answered. Bowie is right, however, to emphasize that Lacan's most substantial discussion of the "real" (in *Le Séminaire, livre XI: Les Quatres concepts fondamentaux de la psychanalyse*; 53–62) centers around the notions of "chance" and "trauma." As chance and trauma, the "real" is the arbitrary and violent limit to our systems of representation (or interpretation). See Bowie, *Lacan*, 94–95, 102–7.) For the fullest and most sustained discussion of the real in Lacan, see Žižek, *Sublime Object*; and Žižek, *Looking Awry*.

Chapter 3

1. For the two best examples of such a critique used for an analysis of the 19th-century novel, see D. A. Miller, *Novel*; and Gallagher, "Duplicity of Doubling."

2. D. A. Miller, *Novel*, 99n.

3. Ibid., 65.

4. Thus in his brilliant reading of *Bleak House*, Miller argues that the novel resembles both Chancery and the police in form and uses its similarity with one to differentiate itself from the other.

5. Miller makes this argument also in his essay "Balzac's Illusions."

6. D. A. Miller, *Narrative*, xiv–xv.

7. For a study of the relation between Stendhal's text and its sources, see Dédéyan, *Stendhal chroniqueur*, 43–52.

8. For a discussion of this topic, see Ginsburg, "Stendhal's Exemplary Stories."

9. This tendency is hard to resist. Even Michel Guérin, in his otherwise excellent discussion of *L'Abbesse*, tends to idealize the republic. *Politique de Stendhal*, 160–70.

10. Béatrice Didier rightly remarks that the existence of the "bravi" means "que le pouvoir n'est pas un, que toute famille, tout individu suffisament puissant peut avoir à son service des 'bravi' "; but she still draws a line between the "bravi" and the brigands—"les brigands relèvent de la force spontanée, populaire, désintéressée, les bravi au contraire sont des mercenaires au services des puissants"—thus failing to note how the opposition between "bravi" and "brigands" is constantly undermined. "Pouvoirs et énergie dans 'L'Abbesse de Castro'," in Berthier, *Stendhal*, 249.

11. Guérin, *Politique de Stendhal*, 167.

12. Here, and in the following discussion, I use narrative (*récit*), story (*histoire*), and narration (*narration*) in Genette's sense of these terms. See *Narrative Discourse*.

13. Didier, "Stendhal chroniqueur," 23.

14. *Chartreuse*, 403. For a discussion of Stendhal's plots in terms of a tension between scenario and improvisation, see Brombert, *Prison romantique*, 88–89.

15. I have been emphasizing here the dependence of the *end* on external intervention, the fact that left to themselves, the characters act interminably, that their self-generated plot cannot bring about its own end. Of course, one has to add that the same applies to the beginning: the "first step" also comes from outside, and left to themselves, the characters will never start acting. The external determination of the beginning is less obvious only because a narrative cannot present it except as already part of the story. If we go back, however, to *La Chartreuse*, we will see there a good dramatization of the dependence of both beginning and end on an external force. Gina is organizing a performance of *commedia dell'arte* for the young Prince's pleasure. But the Prince is shy and unable to act. Gina promises to prompt him—she acts as a personification of the predetermined plot, which is not only posted on the walls of the theater but also whispered in his ear. Once started by this external propelling, the Prince continues speaking his lines—interminably—and Gina must intervene again to bring his speeches to an end.

16. My analysis of the mother's "plot" is indebted to D. A. Miller's discussion of a similar structure in *Lucien Lewen*. *Narrative*, 235–59.

17. This of course does not mean that the narrative-limit cannot become thematized within the text—for example, as the theme of the happy prison.

18. *Le Rouge* contains the most explicit presentation of the narrative of destiny as sheer limit, the delineation of beginning and end. On the piece of paper Julien finds in the church of Verrière, he reads, on one side, the end of his namesake (his execution)

and, on the other, the words "The first step . . . " This piece of paper has an ambiguous status: since it comes from a newspaper, it presumably refers to an event that has happened; yet it presents itself as almost pure form, as empty of content as possible: on one side, a beginning, on the other, the end. The events that will create the space between beginning and end, the pages that will "separate" the two sides of the paper and give the form some kind of semantic content, are those of the novel we are going to read. The purely formal relation between the narrative-limit and the story can be seen also in the fact that Julien's life is shaped by the destiny of someone of whom he knows nothing. In contrast to the role playing involved in imitating Napoleon or Tartuffe or in being made to relive Danton or Boniface de la Mole, in the case of Louis Jenrel and Julien Sorel, intersubjective mirroring is replaced by a purely formal mirroring—their names are anagrams—a formal resemblance Julien does not even fully grasp. This determination by a form without content is thematized in the novel in the influence that Julien's ability to memorize texts without regard to their content has on his life.

19. The fact that all of Stendhal's heroes die in their youth results, then, not from their inability to grow up, become adults, but rather from the fact that they cannot die a natural death.

Chapter 4

1. Of the other *Chroniques italiennes*, four are set in the sixteenth century: "Vittoria Accoramboni," "Les Cenci," "La Duchesse de Palliano," and "Trop de faveur tue." Three are set at a later period: "San Francesco a Ripa," in 1720; "Suora Scolastica," in the 1740's; and "Vanina Vanini," in the 1820's. "Vanina Vanini," however, is not based on an old chronicle. My general remarks about the *Chroniques* go especially to the ones set in the 16th century and do not address the problems posed by "Vanina Vanini."

2. Fabrice mentions going to America as the logical step for him (115; *130*), but he of course does not go there. Ferrante Palla, who belongs either with the brigands of *L'Abbesse* or on the barricades of the French Revolution, intends to go to America, but the last we hear from him is in France (407; *418*).

3. Like most English translators, Shaw "italianizes" Fabrice's name into Fabrizio. But given the importance of the opposition French/Italian in Stendhal's system of values, one cannot simply transform a French Fabrice into an Italian Fabrizio. For this reason, I will stick with the French form and I have substituted it everywhere in the English quotes. Fabrice's "Frenchness" is conveyed not only through his name. For example, when he is in prison, and Gina communicates with him by way of light flashes, Stendhal gives her words in Italian—"Ina pensa a te" (which are then translated into French, the language of the text, to convey Fabrice's understanding of them: "Evidemment: *Gina pense à toi!*"), whereas Fabrice's words appear only in French—"Fabrice t'aime" (324); the English translation erases this difference by giving both Gina's and Fabrice's words—in Italian (*337*).

4. Stradella's story is told in *La Vie de Haydn* and repeated in *La Vie de Rossini*; the story of Pietro Buonaventuri's love for Bianca Capello is told in *Histoire de la peinture en Italie*.

5. See, for example: "Deux fois, en traversant la France, [Fabrice] fut arrêté; mais il sut se dégager; il dut ces désagréments à son passeport italien et à cette étrange qualité de marchand de baromètres, qui n'était guère d'accord avec sa figure jeune et son bras en écharpe" ("Twice on his journey across France [Fabrice] was arrested, and each time managed to get away. He owed these disagreeable experiences to his Italian passport, and that odd description of him as a 'dealer in barometers,' which hardly seemed to tally with his youthful face and his arm in a sling"; 73; *89*).

6. Compare *L'Abbesse*, "Chacun de ces tyrans connaissait personnellement chacun de républicains dont il savait être exécré" ("Each of these tyrants was personally acquainted with each of the Republicans by whom he knew himself to be execrated"; 561; *11*) with *La Chartreuse*, where Gina thinks, "Quelle funeste étourderie! venir habiter la cour d'un prince absolu! un tyran qui connaît toutes ses victimes!" ("What a fatal act of stupidity! To come and live at the court of an absolute prince! A tyrant who knows every one of his victims!"; 264; *278*).

7. Mosca tells Gina that "dans un moment d'ennui et de colère, et aussi un peu pour imiter Louis XIV faisant couper la tête à je ne sais quel héros de la Fronde que l'on découvrit vivant tranquillement et insolemment dans une terre à côté de Versailles, cinquante ans après la Fronde, Ernest IV a fait pendre un jour deux libéraux. Il paraît que ces imprudents se réunissaient à jour fixe pour dire du mal du prince et adresser au ciel des vœux ardents afin que la peste pût venir à Parme, et les délivrer du tyran. Le mot *tyran* a été prouvé. Rassi appela cela conspirer" ("in a moment of boredom and anger, and also a little in imitation of Louis XIV, who cut off the head of some hero or other of the Fronde, who was discovered, fifty years after the Fronde, living peacefully and insolently on an estate near Versailles, one fine day Ernest IV had two liberals hanged. It appears that these rash fellows used to meet on a certain day to speak ill of the Prince and address earnest prayers to heaven that the plague might visit Parma and rid them of the tyrant. The word *tyrant* was proved. Rassi called this a conspiracy"; 106; *121*).

8. The analogy between the Farnese tower and the Bastille is made explicit when, on the day of the insurrection, the people of Parma plan to go to the citadel to free the prisoners. But they never quite get there: "Le peuple se rassemblait pour massacrer le fiscal général Rassi: on voulait aussi aller mettre le feu aux portes de la citadelle, pour tâcher de faire sauver les prisonniers. Mais on prétendait que Fabio Conti tirerait ses canons" ("The people were gathering together to go and slaughter Chief Justice Rassi; they also wanted to set fire to the gates of the citadel, to enable the prisoners to escape. But some declared that Fabio Conti would fire his guns"; 390; *401–2*).

9. Clélia, on the other hand, sees Fabrice's imprisonment and impending death as the attempt of tyranny to destroy freedom. She thinks of Fabrice, "il allait périr! et pour la cause de la liberté! car il était trop absurde de mettre à mort un del Dongo pour un coup d'épée d'un histrion" (304). Clélia, however, is often deluded in her interpretation of the events around her.

10. The active participation of the people of Parma in this fiction-making is clear, since it is not only the Prince and Rassi who fabricate a "reality," but also Mosca, Gina, Raversi, and others. In the world described in *La Chartreuse*, everyone vies for power—the power to impose on others their own version of reality. These competing versions of reality (just like the different "versions" of identity, the disguises) are all

produced by special interests, as means to certain ends, and they are clearly seen as fictions—we are in a world of lies, pretenses, forgeries. Nevertheless, those fictions have powerful effects: Ascagne's false accusation against Fabrice sets the police after him, the forged letter produced by la Raversi takes Fabrice to prison, and so on. What the novel insists on again and again is the power of fictions.

11. For a discussion of social reality as constructed and supported by "as if," see Žižek, *Sublime Object*, especially 36–43. I am indebted to Žižek's analysis throughout this chapter.

12. Pascal, *Pensées* (for example, nos. 233, 250, 252; Brunschvicg edition). Žižek, in his Lacanian-Althusserian reading of this kind of conduct, refers to Pascal, as Althusser himself does in "Ideology and Ideological State Apparatuses," in *Lenin and Philosophy*, tr. Brewster (New York, 1971), 127–86.

13. Žižek, *Sublime Object*, 80–81.

14. That Fabrice's "ancestor" and role model is a Farnese generates a certain amount of confusion between Fabrice and the Prince (who is a Farnese). Alexandre Farnese of the chronicle can thus be seen as the "ancestor" of both the Prince and Fabrice (and their antagonism would then be that of "enemy brothers"). But since the novel is a transposition of the chronicle to the present, Alexandre Farnese is (also) Fabrice, and his story is Fabrice's story. Moreover, as I have indicated before, the chronicle relating the origins of the Farnese family is represented in the novel in the genealogy of the del Dongo family. The genealogy mostly tells the story of rulers and their exploits, and this allows it to be "confused" with another origin of both the novel and its hero—the stories of the Napoleonic wars. We see this confusion, for example, when Fabrice is said to have learned to read both from the genealogy given him by his father (12; *28*) and from the Napoleonic battle stories given him by Count Pietranera (84–85; *100*), the surrogate for both the real father, Robert, and the symbolic father, Napoleon. But the genealogy also has an appendix, a "supplement" that is the story of the bishops and archbishops of Parma, that is, the story Fabrice himself continues in his own life when he becomes a man of the church. But what is a supplement in the genealogy—the life of the archbishop—is in fact in the chronicle, which is its model, the origin: the chronicle, telling the story of which the novel is an imitation, does not put the archbishop in supplementary relation to the rulers and soldiers but places him as their origin, beginning, and source. The "modernization" of the chronicle puts it in the position of the origin of the story, a supplement to the story, and the story itself.

15. We read in the "Origins of the Farnese Family" that Alexandre, "Parvenu dans les dernières années de son âge mûr, . . . changea de vie et des mœurs, ou du moins feignit d'en changer; il devint un homme de grande sagesse, affable, libéral, plein d'un esprit sublime" ("Having reached his last years, he changed his way of life and his customs, or at least pretended to; he became a man of great wisdom, affable, liberal, full of sublimity"; 482–83; translation mine).

16. This helps explain why he keeps his love for Clélia a secret from Gina. By following Gina's and Mosca's advice, Fabrice becomes the kind of person they would like him to be: he becomes, as Mosca puts it, "worthy" of Gina (113; *128*); he becomes "singular," "adorable," lovable. Hence the great importance he attaches to recounting his various experiences to Gina and Mosca—in some sense, he lives in front of, even

for, this audience; he has an identity only as long as they consider him "worthy." That Fabrice cannot tell Gina about his love for Clélia means that this love is not part of his identity as "lovable."

17. Žižek, *Sublime Object*, 165–69.

18. Thus Clélia is imprisoned by a tyrannical jailkeeper, and Fabrice's passion for her is in defiance of this tyrannical power. Clélia indeed understands their love as a transgression of the Law of the Father, suspects that Fabrice has attempted to kill Fabio in order to "rescue" her and himself, for the sake of "freedom." But the poisoning of Fabio is only a faked one and is only very indirectly related to Fabrice (mediated as it is by Gina and her servants). Just as this faked poisoning suggests that we are not dealing with the Renaissance world (this is no Cesare Borgia), so the diffusion of power suggests that we are well in the modern world. There is no direct confrontation between Fabio and Fabrice, since Fabio is not the "real" tyrant: on the one hand, various other figures mediate his "tyranny" (for example, Barbone); on the other, Fabio himself can be seen as mediating the "tyranny" of the Prince who wants Fabrice dead.

19. Too fascinated by the transparency of Oedipal sentiments in *La Vie de Henry Brulard*, critics tend to read all of Stendhal's heroes as fixated on the Oedipal scenario of transgressive love for the mother and aggression toward the father. I think Michel Guérin, however, is right in making distinctions: "Lucien, œdipien, valorise son père; Julien, anti-œdipien, valorise la haine de son père, la constitue même comme son devoir-être: il sera, il se fera le non-père (le Fils 'hermétique' et suffisant), il sera en tant qu'homme le meurtre-du-père. Fabrice lui, est parfaitement anœdipien." *Politique de Stendhal*, 188n.

Chapter 5

1. Trilling, *Sincerity and Authenticity*, 76–77.

2. Many critics insist on *Mansfield Park*'s difference from *Pride and Prejudice*. See, for example, Julia Prewitt Brown, *Jane Austen's Novels*, 83–84 (she also dwells on the failed dialectic of *Mansfield Park*; 91–92). Though Duckworth does not find *Mansfield Park* an anomaly because he sees it as dealing with the same issues as Austen's other novels, he still holds that it is markedly different from *Pride and Prejudice* because it cannot end dialectically, as *Pride and Prejudice* does. *Improvement of the Estate*, 37–38. Litz, *Jane Austen*, 112, goes farther, seeing *Mansfield Park* as the antithesis of *Pride and Prejudice*, and, like Mudrick before him, he locates the difference in the later novel's lack of irony. The same thesis is advanced by Mansell, *Novels of Jane Austen*. On the other hand, Morgan argues against the privileging of *Pride and Prejudice*, and of Elizabeth Bennet as the standard by which the rest of Austen's corpus should be judged. *In the Meantime*, 133.

3. Edmund thinks that a marriage between Fanny and Henry would be highly desirable precisely because it would constitute such a coming together of opposites. Speaking to Fanny about Henry Crawford, he says: "there is a decided difference in your tempers, I allow. He is lively, you are serious; but so much the better; his spirits will support yours. It is your disposition to be easily dejected, and to fancy difficulties greater than they are. His cheerfulness will counteract this. He sees difficulties no-

where; and his pleasantness and gaiety will be a constant support to you. Your being so far unlike, Fanny, does not in the smallest degree make against the probability of your happiness together: do not imagine it. I am myself convinced that it is rather a favourable circumstance. I am perfectly persuaded that the tempers had better be unlike" (264). Fanny not only disagrees with Edmund on the subject of her own marriage but also sees his marriage to Mary—that other coming together of opposites—as leading to the destruction of one of the poles rather than to a synthesis. Having just received Edmund's letter, she says to herself: "He will marry her [Mary], and be poor and miserable. God grant that her influence do not make him cease to be respectable!" (322).

4. Trilling, *Sincerity and Authenticity*, 76.

5. Ibid., 79.

6. See, for example, Franco Moretti's discussion of Austen in *Way of the World*.

7. D. A. Miller, *Narrative*, x.

8. Yeazell, using an anthropological perspective, observes the novel's "anxiety of boundaries" and of confusion: "Anxiety about transitional states and ambiguous social relations is repeatedly countered in *Mansfield Park* by [a] categorical sorting of things into the clean and the dirty, the sacred and the profane." "Boundaries of *Mansfield Park*," 135.

9. Other critics have analyzed the concept of "action" in the novel but in terms different from my own. Brodsky, *Imposition of Form*, 148–63, discusses Fanny's inability or refusal to act in terms of the relation between practical and theoretical knowledge. In Marshall's view, Fanny "seems to believe for much of the novel that playacting means nothing seriously. . . . Henry and Mary could not be serious, they could not intend or mean anything in earnest, because everything they say and do takes place for Fanny under the sign of play. . . . They force Fanny to confront the possibility that theater might not signify nothing." He concludes, then, that Fanny's encounter with the Crawfords, her involvement in their "action," means that she too must act; that acting for her is not impossible but in fact inevitable. "True Acting," 99, 101.

10. As Thomas R. Edwards rightly points out, Mary "seeks to exploit the scene's obvious symbolic possibilities": in her description of the walk she and Edmund took, she attempts to cast the wilderness as a Forest of Love. Maria and Henry, on the other hand, infuse their remarks about the landscape with figurative meaning but insist that their conversation is literal, thus refusing to take any responsibility for their insinuations. "The Difficult Beauty of *Mansfield Park*," in Bloom, *Jane Austen's 'Mansfield Park*,' 8–10. If the Sotherton scene is the most explicitly emblematic in the novel, it is by no means the only such scene; the theatricals, for obvious reasons, have the same status of duplicating the action and foreshadowing subsequent events; and P. J. M. Scott sees the card-playing scene, during the dinner party at the Grants, too as "emblematic." *Jane Austen*, 143–44.

11. Mary Poovey is one of the few critics who consider the relation between Fanny and Mrs. Norris worthy of analysis. Following her main theme of the tension between female desire and the social code of propriety, she sees Mrs. Norris as the one sister whose "hopes have been thwarted by society's inability to satisfy the expectations romance has generated. . . . Mrs Norris is a typical victim of the discrepancy between romantic expectations and social possibilities." Her "activity" is useless because it is "a woman's imaginative energy misdirected by her dependence and social

uselessness." Her relation to Fanny is dictated by her sense of her own worthlessness, which she tries to project onto Fanny in order to deny it in herself. *Proper Lady*, 216.

12. The latter point is made by Scott, *Jane Austen*, 159, but for a different purpose: his main thesis is that Fanny's character is shaped by years of dependence on others, and that this dependence is not over at the end of the novel, since as the occupant of the parsonage, she is still dependent on the favor of the Manor.

13. Thus it is wrong, it seems to me, to read Mrs. Norris as vicariously enjoying motherhood or, later on, erotic desire through her "assistance" to Lady Bertram or the Bertram girls. Whatever erotic desires Mrs. Norris may have had, she seems to have buried with her husband, and her concern for her financial security and comfort has taken the place of any maternal instinct she may have had. Unlike Aunt Penniman in James's *Washington Square*, for example, Mrs. Norris is not the aunt who lives vicariously the repressed or frustrated desires of her youth; the fact that she finally joins Maria in her exile should not be understood to mean that the two receive the same punishment because they lived the same forbidden desires. Mrs. Norris leaves Mansfield Park because once Fanny's nature becomes known, Mrs. Norris's activity is shown all too clearly to be a simulacrum.

14. Much has been made recently of Antigua. There is no doubt that Sir Thomas's sojourn in Antigua is not simply an expedient to remove him from the scene but a way to indicate the dependence of the class he represents not only on labor at home but also on labor in the colonies. But the reference to Antigua is revealing mostly to the extent that it shows Austen's inability to represent this dependence (whereas the gentry's dependence on other classes is fully thought through, as my analysis of *Emma* will demonstrate). Though I agree with Edward Said that "there is nothing . . . in *Mansfield Park* that would contradict us were we to assume that Sir Thomas does exactly the same things—on a larger scale—in Antigua" that he does at home ("Jane Austen and Empire," 104), there is also nothing in the novel that supports this claim, since unlike relations at home, relations in or to the colony are one of the things the novel cannot represent. Since this inability is in itself meaningful, marking as it does the novel's historical and ideological specificity, to "fill in" what Austen could not seems to me to miss the point. This is, however, what most critics concerned with the topic do, often less honestly than Said, without even indicating that their remarks rest wholly on suppositions. For example, Moira Ferguson writes, "Sadistic overseers, with whom Sir Thomas may have been content in the past, provided returns were satisfactory, would no longer do"; and having discussed sexual exploitation in the Caribbean, she "establishes" that this is also Sir Thomas's conduct: "Does Sir Thomas banish his daughter, Maria, and censure Henry Crawford because their sexual indulgence mirrors his Antiguan conduct?" "*Mansfield Park*," 120, 128.

15. Henry Crawford expresses most explicitly the fact that Fanny is a mystery: "I do not quite know what to make of Miss Fanny. I do not understand her. . . . What is her character?—Is she solemn?—Is she queer?—Is she prudish? Why did she draw back and look so grave at me? I could hardy get her to speak" (174). Critics have often seen their task as answering these questions: yes, Fanny is prudish; no, she isn't. I have tried to suggest why all such descriptions are wrong. Yeazell has rightly remarked that "events do not compel the heroine to grow; they simply drive others to recognize what she has always been." "Boundaries of *Mansfield Park*," 142. This is also my

argument, except that it needs to be made clear that "events" are not some impersonal happenings but the concrete action of other characters, of those who act.

16. Ann Banfield has discussed the relation between "notice" and "neglect" in the novel. But she simplifies the issue by claiming a purely linear progression from a "neglect" of Fanny to "notice." Thus, she says, the theatricals episode is one where Fanny is "repeatedly ignored." But as noted below, this is one of the episodes that show most explicitly how pained Fanny also is by being noticed. Banfield's insistence on reading the novel in terms of chronological progression (which echoes the changes in place) requires that she see Fanny as changing and developing in time, though she also rightly points out that Fanny is "a fixed point against which the conflict of values in the novel is measured." "Moral Landscape," 19, 24.

17. Various critics have made a different, though related, point: that it is Fanny who has memory, whereas Mary and Henry lack all historical sense, live purely in the present, and literally do not remember. See, among others, Morgan, *In the Meantime*, 146; and Tave, *Some Words*, 195ff.

18. Not all critics agree on this point. Trilling, for example, sees the objection to the theatricals in the novel as "Rousseauist"—impersonation may lead to loss of the self (*Sincerity and Authenticity*, 75)—or as "Platonic"—"the impersonation of any other self will diminish the integrity of the real self" ("Mansfield Park," 132). This idea is echoed by many critics, for example, Mansell, *Novels of Jane Austen*, 127. To my mind the text does not support this view; I agree, rather, with critics like Stuart Tave who emphasize that the objection to the amateur theatricals is that they are not in fact play-acting, that they fail to separate life from role playing. *Some Words*, 191–92. Hardy elaborates on this lack of separation by showing that Edmund and Mary cannot talk to each other until they rehearse their "roles," and it is in these rehearsals that their "courtship" takes place. *Jane Austen's Heroines*, 61. Marshall's detailed analysis of the relation in the novel between "true acting" and "real feeling" is congruent with this line of thought.

19. This kind of objection explains why the prohibition against acting should affect primarily women. But I cannot agree with Claudia Johnson who, in her otherwise excellent reading of the novel, claims that the objection to the theatricals is "restricted" to women. *Jane Austen*, 95. Edmund clearly feels that his playing the role of a clergyman will be wrong, as does Fanny.

20. In *Fictional Truth*, Riffaterre argues the other side of this coin: that since the truth of fiction is not referential, it does not depend on the particular knowledge and experience of a particular reader.

21. Balzac, *Old Goriot*, tr. Marion Ayton Crawford (London, 1978), 28.

22. Walter Scott, unsigned review of Oct. 1815, in Southam, *Jane Austen*, 64.

23. Morgan discusses the conventionality of Mary's opinions from a different angle by showing their similarity to those of Charlotte Lucas in *Pride and Prejudice*. *In the Meantime*, 139–40.

24. See D. A. Miller's discussion of the reinterpretation of Mary at the end of the novel. *Narrative*, 83–89.

25. Critics have often described the "anomalous" status of *Mansfield Park* as its lack of irony or its castigation and banishing of irony. Though it is true that the kind of irony Mary practices is subject to criticism, it does not follow that the novel is

not ironic. Austen's irony in the novel is of the kind "as time is forever producing between the plans and decisions of mortals, for their own instructions, and their neighbours' entertainment" (359).

Chapter 6

1. See, for example, Moretti, *Way of the World*, 67.

2. Propp, *Morphology of the Folktale*, 20–21.

3. "Mixed company" in the preceding quote means "men and women together" but can be read also in the broader sense of comprising different, heterogeneous elements. The implicit double meaning shows the relation between marriage (the union of men with women) and the heterogeneity of society outside the home circle.

4. Thus, in trying to convince Harriet that the idea of a marriage between her and Mr. Elton is far from "strange," Emma says: "Your marrying [Elton] will be equal to the match at Randalls" (57). When Mrs. Weston suggests that Mr. Knightly may be considering a marriage with Jane Fairfax, Emma, for reasons yet unknown to herself, objects that this is an "imprudent" match, a "shameful and degrading connection" (173, 174). But Mrs. Weston, with herself as a model, can rightly respond: "Excepting inequality of fortune and perhaps a little disparity of age [there is] nothing unsuitable" (173). Since Emma herself approves of Mrs. Weston's marriage, she cannot object to such disparities, as she makes clear when she talks to Harriet about the latter's presumed love for Frank: "He is your superior, no doubt, and there do seem objections and obstacles of a very serious nature; but yet, Harriet, more wonderful things have taken place, and there have been matches of greater disparity" (267).

5. Arnold Kettle, in his analysis of the various critical responses to the question of class prejudice in *Emma*, concludes that though the novel's aristocratic bias limits its vision ("an essential side of the Hartfield world is being conveniently ignored"), this "inadequacy is not crippling." "*Emma*," in Watt, *Jane Austen*, 122. Duckworth agrees that Austen describes "social fragmentation," or what D. H. Lawrence termed "knowing in apartness," but argues against both Lawrence and Kettle that this is a social condition Austen deplores. *Improvement of the Estate*, 150–56. More recently, Parker has argued for both positions, claiming that "*Emma* can generate two readings of class: a progressive one, which emphasizes the insidious workings of class in Emma's disposal of Harriet; and a reactionary one, which sees and accepts this working as part of the price of social stability. Each reading turns on assumptions about the narrative voice: whether it is silently indignant or simply complicit." "End of *Emma*," 358–59.

6. Johnson comments on the contradiction that allows Emma to observe the rise of the Coles with some resentment and yet recommend Mr. Weston as the model gentleman. But she too quickly reduces this "confusion" or "fluidity" to a gender question and the instability of female power. *Jane Austen*, 136–37.

7. See, for example, Bush, *Jane Austen*, 163.

8. Rosmarin, in a very different context, notes that another character in the novel—Miss Bates—undergoes a "change" that similarly cannot be explained by an appeal to character development but rather through an analysis of that character's function in the narrative (not "realistically" but "strategically"): "After Box Hill, Miss Bates immediately becomes less present in the text and, when present, less

irritating. Immediate also is her acquisition of social status and emotional sensibility. A mimetic model can explain these changes only as occurring in Miss Bates—an explanation that musters little textual support—or as randomly occurring revelations of her character—an explanation that denies Austen's Jamesian control." " 'Misreading' *Emma*," 333.

9. Kurrik sees the epistemologically limited transformation of *Emma* as operating within "an unknown knowable" and emphasizes the fact that Emma's recognition does not change her. *Literature and Negation*, 82–96.

10. The discussion between Knightly and Emma of Harriet's acceptance of Robert Martin at the end of the novel (369–73) supports, rather than contests, this claim. When Knightly tells Emma, "You are materially changed since we talked on this subject before," she answers, "I hope so—for at that time I was a fool" (373). Her folly was precisely her "confusion of rank," her misguided idea that Harriet was as good as she, hence too good for Robert Martin. Her "change" of opinion about this marriage does not mean that her values have changed. It is merely that she has recognized them: Harriet's proper spouse is Martin, and her own is Knightly.

11. "In the gallery there were many family portraits, but they could have little to fix the attention of a stranger. Elizabeth walked on in quest of the only face whose features would be known to her. At last it arrested her—and she beheld a striking resemblance of Mr. Darcy, with such a smile over the face, as she remembered to have sometimes seen, when he looked at her. . . . There was certainly at this moment, in Elizabeth's mind, a more gentle sensation towards the original, than she had ever felt in the height of their acquaintance. . . . Every idea that had been brought forward by the housekeeper was favorable to his character, and as she stood before the canvas, on which he was represented, and fixed his eyes upon herself, she thought of his regard with a deeper sentiment of gratitude than it had ever raised before." *Pride and Prejudice*, ed. Mark Schorer (Boston, 1956), 185. It is the represented Darcy who has his eyes fixed on Elizabeth (contrary to what the syntax and the logic of the sentence would lead us to expect); hence it is possible to argue that Darcy's gazing at her is what makes Elizabeth see herself and him differently. For an analysis of this scene, see Brodsky Lacour, "Austen's *Pride and Prejudice*."

12. The difference between *Mansfield Park* and both other novels becomes clear when we take the visit to Sotherton as equivalent to the strawberry-gathering party and the visit to Pemberly I have been discussing. That visit is to *Maria's* future husband's estate, but Maria does not learn in this visit a truth that will bring her to accept the proper marriage (her marriage with Rushworth is not proper, and she does not accept it). Fanny, on the other hand, does not need any visit to teach her the appropriateness of her marriage to Edmund. And Edmund can see the appropriateness of his marriage to Fanny not in this visit, or in any present event, but only from the perspective of a re-turn.

13. Duckworth points out such doubling when he observes that "Mrs. Elton usurps Emma's social position, then Jane Fairfax pre-empts her intellectual prominence . . . and Frank Churchill takes over her powers of managing and directing." *Improvement of the Estate*, 162. Julia Prewitt Brown points out the way in which Mrs. Elton mirrors Emma. *Jane Austen's Novels*, 104. And Mark Schorer points out that Miss Bates is the specular opposite of the "handsome, clever, and rich" Emma,

and that Jane Fairfax is another contrasting double. "The Humiliation of Emma Woodhouse," in Watt, *Jane Austen*, 106–7.

14. My discussion of Girard's theories here is limited to his book *Desire, Deceit, and the Novel*.

15. The passage is in free indirect discourse: grammatically, it has the form of a third-person narrator's description of a character ("Her objections to Mr. Knightly's marrying did not in the least subside"), whereas other elements (such as the exclamation "No") suggest the character's inner thoughts. Together, they create a discourse whose source is equivocal. The use of free indirect discourse suggests both the narrator's complicity with the character and the irony that separates them.

16. The only example of "real" rivalry is that between Jane Fairfax and her friend Miss Campbell over Mr. Dixon. Of course, this erotic triangle has no basis in reality and is merely conjured up by Emma's imagination.

17. "Mrs. John Knightly was a pretty, elegant little woman, of gentle, quiet manners, and a disposition remarkably amiable and affectionate. . . . She was not a woman of strong understanding or any quickness; and with this resemblance of her father, she inherited also much of his constitution. . . . Mr. John Knightly was a tall, gentleman-like, and very clever man; . . . but with reserved manners which prevented his being generally pleasing; and capable of being sometimes out of humor. He was not an ill-tempered man . . . but his temper was not his great perfection" (71).

18. For example, Mansell speaks of the world of Emma as "a world made up largely by the private illusions of the heroine; and without much reference to any hypothetical 'objective' reality outside herself." *Novels of Jane Austen*, 149. See also the chapter on *Emma* in Tave, *Some Words*. My point is that the duplications and reflections are not the result of Emma's imagination, whether this imagination is judged positively—as artistic—or negatively—as self-centered—but part of the social "objective" reality.

19. Knightly's jealousy of Frank begins before Frank even arrives in Highbury, let alone starts flirting with Emma. It is the possibility of Emma's love for Frank that allows Knightly to start being aware of his love for her. Similarly, when Knightly is discouraged by Emma's attentions to Frank and goes to London to learn to be indifferent, it is Isabella's love and attention to his brother that keeps his love for Emma alive (339–40).

20. Kurrik, *Literature and negation*, 92, 91. The point of view of the "ruling class" is clearest in *Emma*, which does not have its Gardiners or Crofts, only its Eltons and Westons. For a short discussion of Austen's social sympathies, see Angus Wilson, "The Neighbourhood of Timbuctoo: Conflicts in Jane Austen's Novels," in Southam, *Critical Essays*, 189–90. See also Poovey, *Proper Lady*, 180–83.

21. It is of course possible to argue that such a view of change is finally ideologically determined by the interests of the "ruling class." Thus many critics have viewed the "de-centering of the subject" with its correlative, the claim that change is random or overdetermined, or at any rate, not under the control of a conscious agent, as a particular example of conservative ideology intended to delegitimize the agendas of marginal groups seeking to assert themselves. As I have suggested in the Introduction, the nonteleological view of narrative is neither inherently conservative nor inherently liberating; conversely, not all conservative narratives depend on a nonteleological view of history. I will discuss this point in more detail in the following chapter.

22. *Emma* thus does not subscribe to what Shaffer calls the "lover-mentor convention where the heroine's growth to maturity depends on learning from a male mentor whom she then marries." "Not Subordinate," 55.

23. Though Austen, unlike Dickens, sees manners as conventional—hence acquired—rather than as an inherent, or natural, part of one's character, she cannot do without some grounding of manners in "nature." Thus, though manners can be learned, since they are conventional marks, not everyone can serve as a teacher for anyone. Harriet, for example, does not profit from her association with Emma, as Miss Taylor did or as Jane profited from her associations with the Campbells. But Harriet can and does learn manners through her association with Mr. Martin and his family. The "natural" limit to learning is set not by the inherent qualities of the person who learns, but by the kind of interpersonal relations that allow imitation. It is in gender differences, rather than in rank differences, that the limits of imitation are set: women can learn manners, but invariably their model is a male (even Mr. Woodhouse). If Emma did not receive "a complete education" from Miss Taylor, she gave her governess a "good education" by playing the role of a husband (27).

24. For a discussion of how Mr. Woodhouse's abiding by every social convention is limited by his hypochondria, and how this hypochondria is, in turn, used to reassert the dominance of social prescriptions, see D. A. Miller, "Late Jane Austen," 66–67.

25. See White, "Ethnological 'Lie,'" especially 5–7.

26. See Veblen, *Theory of the Leisure Class*, 110, for example.

27. Ibid., 36.

28. This paragraph is drawn from ibid., 43–45.

29. See Veblen's related discussion, in his chapter "The Pecuniary Canons of Taste," of how the habit, perpetuated through imitation, of "approving the expensive and disapproving the inexpensive" reaches the stage where the maxim "cheap and nasty" seems totally natural to us. Ibid., 155.

30. Saussure makes this very same point in his discussion of another system of conventional signs—language. He quite explicitly states that the arbitrary nature of the sign means both that there is no reason for change (since one arbitrary sign is no better than another) and that for the same reason change will always occur. And just as in Saussure this change will be unsystematic (nonteleological), so in Veblen the course of history is the "blind drift" of Darwinian evolution.

Chapter 7

1. Moretti, *Way of the World*, for example, 7–8, 27–28, 59–60, 75, 200–201.

2. Ibid., 182. As we see, Goethe's *Wilhelm Meister* appears in Moretti's argument both on the side of the premodern and on the side of the modern. This is because, as Moretti himself argues, it includes both elements of transformation and elements of classification. But since Moretti also sees "transformation" as the modern element, he implicitly or explicitly argues that texts in the English, "conservative," tradition lack this tension. This is one of the points I am arguing against.

3. Ibid., 200. The subsequent three quotations are from 201, 200, and 205, respectively.

4. Ibid., 212.

5. I am arguing here against the position of most critics, who claim or imply that one kind of economy governs all relations of exchange in the novel, and that to some extent the novel is precisely about this deplorable fact. See, for example, James M. Brown, "Our Mutual Friend—The Dust-Mounds and the Principle of Speculation," in *Dickens*, especially 148, 153; and David, *Fictions of Resolution*, especially 90–91. J. Hillis Miller describes the economy of shares and paper money as "a closed circuit in which nothing is reflected by nothing"; the only thing that opposes this empty reflection is "the sheer, massive inertia of matter—heavy, impenetrable, meaningless, alien to man." *Victorian Subjects*, 72, 75. My point, however, is that the opposite to the shadowy economy or empty reflection of the Veneerings is not (or at least not only) the inert materiality of the Podsnaps; rather, the novel represents matter as (also) available for human transformation and production.

6. For another reading that sees Jenny as an emblem of the novel's plot, see Michie, "Who is this in Pain?"

7. What Dickens does not spell out is whether Esther's and Woodcourt's Bleak House will be subject to the same process of corruption and abuse as its ancestor, the Peaks, and as the legal system and other institutions. He does not, in other words, explain how a "non-plotted" or plotless existence is possible. One can perhaps say that this is not an ideological shortcoming on his part but something that a novelist cannot articulate: it is the old Bleak House and not the new one that can be a subject for a novel.

8. See, for example, Garett, *Victorian Multiplot*, 89–94; and Arac, *Commissioned Spirits*, 168.

9. By choosing *Our Mutual Friend* for my further analysis, I do not intend to imply that *Bleak House* is a "simple" text, which adheres dogmatically to one plot model, to one ideology. In principle, the same kind of analysis could be used for the earlier novel, though of course the actual choices and the way they are made to combine would differ.

10. It is, of course, possible that Eugene's wounds, just like Esther's pox marks, are healing, disappearing without leaving any scars. Thus even within Eugene's and Lizzie's plot there is considerable ambiguity.

11. Moretti, *Way of the World*, 211–12.

12. It is important to note that this "true account" nevertheless remains incomplete, and hence cannot have a fully authoritative status. See Hutter, "Dismemberment and Articulation," 160, 173 n. 40.

13. Lizzie's use of standard English despite her class and her illiteracy is often compared with Oliver Twist's. But the difference between the two is important: Oliver's pure language is a sign of his pre-plot belonging to the middle class, a sign of his status as his father's legitimate heir, which has been temporarily usurped by the villain Monk. Lizzie's language, on the other hand, points to her future transformation into a middle-class wife, a transformation that happens under certain circumstances, and as a result of certain actions.

14. For a different analysis of the tension in Headstone between hoarding and letting go, see Sedgwick, "Homophobia, Misogyny, and Capital."

15. Charles Dickens, *Great Expectations* (New York, 1972), 303.

16. Deirdre David is one of the few critics to insist that even though the scene of

Harmon's near drowning is presented as one of symbolic rebirth, "he is not reborn as anything other than John Harmon"—in other words, there is no radical transformation involved. *Fictions of Resolution*, 113.

17. Since the emphasis in *Our Mutual Friend* is on the distinction between recycling and its travesty, circulation, "conversion," which involves a genuine transformation, is contrasted to the pseudo-transformation of putting on and taking off a disguise. Thus "conversion" is allied with "recycling." In another context recycling, as a process without beginning or end, will be contrasted to "conversion," which, as an overcoming of error, of the world, of time, is emphatically teleological.

18. We can say that, in Bella's case, the economy of death and resurrection, the dialectical principle that allows one to think that losing, or giving up, something is the precondition for gaining a transformed, superior version of what was lost, is replaced by the wisdom of the reality principle, where one gives up something for now in order to win (the same thing, only with a dividend) a little later. As David astutely comments, Bella "by momentarily denying her desire for money, . . . is allowed to be rich." *Fictions of Resolution*, 117.

Chapter 8

1. J. A. Wards discusses James's intention in *The Princess Casamassima* "to do something on the order of the French naturalists and the English Victorians"; in both this novel and its rough contemporaries, *The Bostonians* and *The Tragic Muse*, "James most nearly matches Balzac, Zola, Dickens, and Thackeray in his representation of a dense, sprawling 'world.'" *Search for Form*, 115, 116. For Charles R. Anderson, the novel is "James's most sociological novel," the work where "more than anywhere else, he is concerned with social problems." *Person, Place, and Thing*, 124. Lionel Trilling comments that the charge leveled at the later novels, that they exist "in a social vacuum," cannot apply to *The Princess Casamassima* because here, as in *The Bostonians*, "James is at the point in his career at which society, in the largest and even the grossest sense, is offering itself to his mind with great force." *Liberal Imagination*, 56–57.

2. Trilling is probably the strongest advocate of James's success in representing—indeed in documenting—social reality: "there is not a political event of *The Princess Casamassima*, not a detail of oath or mystery or danger, which is not confirmed by multitudinous records"; the people who meet at the Sun and Moon "represent with complete accuracy the political development of a large part of the working class of England at the beginning of the eighties." *Liberal Imagination*, 64, 67. But many critics side with Irving Howe, who on the whole disagrees with Trilling: James "is skittish in his treatment [of the main issue in the novel, 'the nature and power of social radicalism'] because he is uncertain of his material; and he is uncertain of his material not merely because he does not know it intimately, but more important, because he vaguely senses that for a subject so explosive and untried something more is needed than the neatly symmetrical laying-out of his plot or the meticulous balancing of his characters." *Politics and the Novel* 146. In the last part of the sentence Howe suggests a basic incompatibility between the traditional novel and the representation of revolutionary movements.

3. See, for example, Dubler, "*Princess Casamassima*."

4. Sholto tells Hyacinth, "There was a time when I went in immensely for illuminated missals, and another when I collected horrible ghost-stories (she wanted to cultivate a belief in ghosts), all for her. The day I saw she was turning her attention to the rising democracy I began to collect little democrats" (346).

5. The only other character who, one may argue, can occupy, however precariously and problematically, the aesthetic position, is the Princess. Though her interest in art may be just a fad or a façade, her piano playing is repeatedly cast as truly artistic. And just like Hyacinth the Princess too occupies a double or ambiguous social situation—an illegitimate American adventuress and a Princess, married into one of the most ancient houses in Europe. The affinity between the two that we see all along accounts for Hyacinth's being the hero of a novel that has the Princess for the title character.

6. This predicament of looking at life through a glass window is not unique to Hyacinth. In *What Maisie Knew*, for example, we read, "It gave her often an odd air of being present at her history in as separate a manner as if she could only get at experience by flattening her nose against a pane of glass" (chap. 12), and "She was to feel henceforth as if she were flattening her nose upon the hard window-pane of the sweetshop of knowledge" (chap. 15). For Maisie, who shares with Hyacinth the fate of being torn between incompatible parents, the struggle not to succumb to the desire to possess what is beyond the glass is, as in his case, an attempt to resist the violence and betrayal of Oedipal relations.

7. The figure of the claimant is a common one in James (for example, *The Spoils of Poynton*). His claimants are always revolutionary, in the sense that they feel that the present structure of possession is unjust, that they have a better claim; but they are also conservative, since their aim is simply to adjust a particular, personal claim, not to change the structure. *The Princess Casamassima* emphasizes that changing the structure would result in the destruction of the objects of value: Hyacinth, seeing the choice as one between an exclusive possession of the objects of value and divided possession (as in the passage about the Veronese ceiling), rejects the latter because it would destroy the integrity of the object and hence its value. Though a third possibility—collective possession as institutionalized in the museum—is not explicitly discussed in the novel, it raises an analogous problem: giving up personal possession in favor of a collective one would destroy the uniqueness of the aesthetic experience and thus reduce its value. I thank Moshe Ron for his comments on this issue.

8. The scene in which Hyacinth, together with the Prince, spies on the Princess and Muniment, establishes most explicitly the equivalence between the political and the erotic. But the Prince, in suggesting that the political may be merely a euphemism for the erotic, trivializes the issue; hence the parodic tone of this scene (518–19).

9. Sigmund Freud, "Family Romances," Standard Edition, 9: 237–41. The child's view of the mother as a "prostitute" is normally understood as indicating his fantasy of her sexual availability, hence as revealing his unconscious desire for her. But it is also determined by the child's understanding of sexual difference. As I argue below, the discovery of the "certainty of maternity" means that the mother is seen as what is inescapably given; she is coded as material, bodily existence that no fantasy can transform. Such an understanding of the mother as irreducibly carnal is expressed by casting her as a prostitute. It is this aspect of the family romance (rather than the

unconscious desire for the mother) that is emphasized in Hyacinth's story. For a discussion of the family romance in its various aspects, see Robert, *Roman des origines*, 41–78.

10. As in the following conversation with the Princess, who, as an illegitimate child herself, knows what she is talking about: " 'You come out of the hole you have described to me, and yet you might have stayed in country-houses all your life. You are much better than if you had! . . . I have seen Italians with that sort of natural tact and taste, but I didn't know one ever found it in any Anglo Saxon in whom it hadn't been cultivated at a vast expense; unless, indeed, in certain little American women.' 'Do you mean I'm a gentleman?' asked Hyacinth, in a peculiar tone, looking out into the wet garden. She hesitated, and then she said, 'It's I who make the mistakes!' " (337).

11. Many critics take Hyacinth's paternity as given and assert—what he himself never does—that he is indeed Lord Frederick's son. This assertion then facilitates the argument that Hyacinth chooses the world of his father—as if this world were a given reality, to be chosen. But Hyacinth can only imagine and create his father, and this is not only the source of his social false position but, more important, the motive for his artistic creativity—what allows him to both create the world of the father and by the same stroke show his natural right to it.

12. For a discussion of the "primal scene" in James's fiction, see, among others, Silverman, "Too Early/Too Late."

13. On narcissistic creation, through the eye, as a substitute for sexual procreation (which would involve the mother), see Sarah Kofman's reading of Hoffman's "Sandman" and Freud's "Uncanny," in "Le Double e(s)t le diable," especially 159–72.

14. One can say that quite literally, at least if one believes James's Preface, *The Princess Casamassima* was produced "through the eye": "The simplest account of the origin of *The Princess Casamassima* is, I think, that this fiction proceeded quite directly . . . from the habit and the interest of walking the streets. . . . One walked of course with one's eyes greatly open, and I hasten to declare that such a practice . . . positively provokes, all around, a mystic solicitation, the urgent appeal, on the part of everything, to be interpreted and, so far as may be, reproduced" (33). But "walking the streets" (as well as "solicitation") can make one think of prostitution; such ambiguity will suggest the inevitable fall into sexuality of all artistic, aesthetic activity, even the "specular" or asexual one.

15. I here disagree with Mark Seltzer's reading of the novel in *Henry James and the Art of Power*. Clearly the novel, by showing vision to be creative, emphasizes the power of vision and of representations. In addition, imaginative creation does not occur in a power vacuum but takes place in conflict with the power of reality to impose itself (see, for example, the Preface to *The Portrait of a Lady*). But this is not the same as saying that the novel participates in a "fantasy of surveillance," demystifying and remystifying the "policing of the real."

16. That the "father" Hyacinth will have to kill to fulfill his vow is a duke is Oedipally overdetermined: not only was Hyacinth's father, according to Pinnie, a duke, not only is Hyacinth himself, according to Paul, "a duke in disguise," but the Princess's unavailability to Hyacinth, her "betrayal" of him, is twice attributed to dukes: when Hyacinth comes to the Princess's house with his gift of a bound book, he

learns from the butler that "she was on a visit to a 'juke,' in a distant part of the country" (254); when he comes back to London from Europe and does not find the Princess, "he saw her with other people, in splendid rooms, where 'the dukes' had possession of her" (401).

17. "He [Hyacinth] was thrilled by the frequency and familiarity of her [Rosy's] allusions to a kind of life he had often wondered about; this was the first time he heard it described with that degree of authority. By the nature of his mind he was perpetually, almost morbidly, conscious that the circle in which he lived was an infinitesimally small, shallow eddy in the roaring vortex of London, and his imagination plunged again and again into the waves that whirled past and around it, in the hope of being carried to some brighter, happier vision—the vision of societies in which, in splendid rooms, with smiles and soft voices, distinguished men, with women who were both proud and gentle, talked about art, literature and history" (145). Rosy is a "double" of Lady Aurora not only in the sense that she shows the appreciation for Inglefield that Lady Aurora lacks, but also in the sense that she plays (at least in her imagination) the role of the society lady that Lady Aurora declines to play. For example, apropos of the growing friendship between Lady Aurora and the Princess, Rosy "fancied them alluding, in the great world, to the occasion on which 'we first met, at Miss Muniment's, you know' " (438).

18. Even the fact that his freedom is clearly circumscribed ("mortgaged") makes Hyacinth resemble the privileged upper classes, who are repeatedly invited in the novel to enjoy their privileged position while they can, since its end is already in the offing (see, for example, 434).

19. This is the "logic" of narrative as elaborated by Claude Bremond: "When the function that opens the sequence is proposed, the narrator always has the choice of having it followed by the act or of maintaining it in a state of virtuality; when an act is presented as having to be realized, or if an event is foreseen, the actualization of the act or of the event can just as well take place as not. If the narrator chooses to actualize the act or the event, he still has the choice of allowing the process to continue on to its conclusion, or he can stop it on the way: the act can attain or fail to attain its goal; the event can follow or not follow its course up to the end which was foreseen." *Logic of Narrative Possibilities*, 387–88.

20. The Princess's plea for time also operates on another level. In his Preface to the novel, James presents Christina Light as a character who asks for an extension on her life. In granting Christina Light more time, in "resuscitating" her and allowing her to return to the novelistic world, James models himself, consciously, though only this once, on the one author who made this recurrence his productive strategy and trademark—Balzac. Is it pure coincidence that the one Balzac character who literally comes back from the dead, refusing to be put to rest, seeking more time, more life, is called *Hyacinth* Chabert?

21. That action is disjoined from feelings and beliefs (the inner self) was at first seen as the condition of possibility for a certain freedom: since the vow does not engage Hyacinth's sentiments, he is free to be whatever he wishes. But this disjunction also means that action is not in any sense organically or otherwise inextricably linked to a "character"; it thus can be filled with meanings, expropriated and appropriated by others. Action, in other words, can function as a "representation" but not

of the actor; freed from its relation to the actor, the action is free to represent any number of meanings. As Hyacinth fully understands, he has been chosen in order "to show that the revolution was not necessarily brutal and illiterate" (390). Not brutal or illiterate means beautiful, educated, cultivated. The culture to which the vow allows him entrance is appropriated and used politically.

22. "When at last the door opened and the servant, reappearing, threw it far back, as if to make a wide passage for a person of the importance of his mistress, Hyacinth's suspense became very acute; it was much the same feeling with which, at the theater, he had sometimes awaited the entrance of a celebrated actress. In this case, the actress was to perform for him alone" (244–45); "Hyacinth . . . perceived that . . . it was also her fancy to treat him as an old friend. . . . Her performance of the part she had undertaken to play was certainly complete, and everything lay before him but the reason she had for playing it" (310); "in Paris he [Hyacinth] saw, of course, a great many women, and he noticed almost all of them, especially the actresses; confronting, mentally, their movement, their speech, their manner of dressing, with that of his extraordinary friend. He judged that she was beyond them in every respect, though there were one or two actresses who had the air of trying to copy her" (384).

23. Millicent thinks Hyacinth should have been an actor rather than a bookbinder ("You would look very nice in a fancy costume"), and Hyacinth's thoughts, following her remark, are that "he was to go through life in a mask, in a borrowed mantle; he was to be, every day and every hour, an actor" (109). As we have seen, Muniment thinks of him as a "duke in disguise" and tells him, "That night I took you to Hoffendahl you had a little way with you that made me forget it; I mean that your disguise happened to be better than usual" (445). Thus at the moment of spontaneous enthusiasm, it is a matter not of authentic action but of a "better disguise." Hyacinth himself, long before he takes the vow, "plans" to play the role of a revolutionary martyr: "Hyacinth waited for the voice that should allot to him the particular part he was to play. His ambition was to play it with brilliancy, to offer an example—an example, even, that might survive him—of pure youthful, almost juvenile, consecration" (283).

24. The same problem of discrepancy between title character and hero exists in the other novel featuring Christina Light, *Roderick Hudson*. For a discussion of this confusion, see Cameron, *Thinking*, 47–65.

25. As de Man puts it, in another context, "the word does not function as a sign or a name . . . but as a vector, a directional motion that is manifest only as a turn, since the target toward which it turns remains unknown. In other words, the sign has become a trope, a substitutive relationship that has to posit a meaning whose existence cannot be verified, but that confers upon the sign an unavoidable signifying function." "Pascal's Allegory," 6–7.

26. Hyacinth's difference from Millicent on this score is not that he is "an artist" and she "a work of art," but that he knows what he is made to represent and why he is to represent it. And this knowledge makes him, as a representation of the revolution, a sham: "He already knew that his friend's view of him was that he was ornamental and adapted to the lighter kinds of socialistic utility—constituted to show that the revolution was not necessarily brutal and illiterate" (390).

Chapter 9

1. Henry James, *Art of the Novel*, 120.

2. For a discussion of James's works in relation to the commodity market and to professionalization, see Freedman, *Professions of Taste*.

3. See, for example, Auchincloss's discussion of the two novels under the heading "The Revulsion from Sex," in *Reading Henry James*. See also Peter Brooks's characterization of *The Awkward Age* as dealing with "the clash of untenable innocence with sophisticated corruption and evil." *Melodramatic Imagination*, 165. A third work one can add to these two on the grounds of theme and formal *tour de force* is *The Turn of the Screw*.

4. This similarity with difference is emphasized, for example, through the pictures on Nanda's mantelpiece in Book X, which remind one of the much-discussed pictures in Van's room in Book I.

5. Ruth Bernard Yeazell has convincingly argued that this notion of knowledge holds true for all the late novels: "The late style makes the Fall into knowledge not a dramatic reversal, but a gradual unfolding. . . . Knowledge does not come as a sudden violation of the self from an exterior and alien world." *Language and Knowledge*, 33. Manfred Mackenzie's notion of a character being "shocked into consciousness" (developed in his *Communities of Honor and Love*), though extremely helpful for the works he discusses, would not apply, as I will argue, to *The Awkward Age*.

6. Longdon tells Van that he "came up . . . to try [them] all" (31); and later, in a discussion between Longdon and Mitchy of "the really distinguished women of the past," Mitchy reports Van's opinion that Longdon has come to London "in pursuit of her," that is "the 'lady' " (105). The vagueness of these formulations underlines the imprecision of the motivation but also suggests that Longdon is primarily searching the past in the present, that he is in fact a ghost.

7. The best analysis of vicarious living and the logic of the "second go" in "The Middle Years," and in James in general, is Mackenzie, *Communities of Honor and Love*. On "The Middle Years," see 107–10.

8. Mrs. Brook implies that there is not much difference between marriage and adoption when she tells her husband that Nanda "has got what every woman, young or old, wants . . . a man of her own" (322–23).

9. In Book I, Van tells Longdon that Nanda is almost 19, and that her birthday is June 15th (37). Book X takes place on "a certain Friday afternoon in June" a year later (346).

10. However, if idealizing the past also entails the view that the past is fixed, unchanging, then Mrs. Brook participates in this idealization too when she says that "the past is the one thing past all spoiling" (150).

11. For a discussion of the relation between Nanda and Mitchy in terms of specular identification, see Shine, *Fictional Children*, 162–63.

12. We find a similar phantasmic projection in *La Peau de chagrin* where Rastignac is, for Raphaël, a person who lives totally at the expense of others, who lives on borrowed money, borrowed time, without having to pay for anything.

13. "Really, universally, relations stop nowhere, and the exquisite problem of the

artist is eternally but to draw, by a geometry of his own, the circle within which they shall happily *appear* to do so." James, *Art of the Novel*, 5.

14. Lorri Nandrea, in an unpublished essay entitled "Mimesis Imposed: Representation, Identification, and Imitation in *The Awkward Age*," discusses Nanda's status in terms of the logic of the simulacrum.

15. Thus, though it is right to insist, as Walter Isle does, on the characters' lack of development and growth in knowledge, it does not follow that the novel lacks "drama." *Experiments in Form*, 174–75.

16. According to Mrs. Brook, the purpose of the scene was to so impress upon Longdon the depravity of their circle that he will adopt Nanda in order to save her. Certainly the scene had this effect on Longdon, but this does not explain why *Van* felt "bruised and buried." He clearly had no fear of Longdon's finding out how immoral their circle is; in fact, the conversation between them in Book I shows Van seeking to shock Longdon, titillated by the old man's dismay and trying to increase it. "Were we absolutely odious?" he asks Longdon, and then again, "Just tell me as a kindness. *Do* we talk [too outrageously]? I want the truth"; he wants to know if Longdon was "really shocked" (49).

17. On this topic, see Tzvetan Todorov's excellent analysis of the novel in "The Verbal Age."

18. It seems as if Mitchy alone is "innocent." But since the book in question closely resembles a book Mitchy had lent Mrs. Brook earlier on (a French novel, identified by the color of its cover—blue here, pink there—and described as "abject, horrid, unredeemed vileness, from beginning to end"; 77–79), Mitchy too is a sharer in this community of knowledge.

19. Among the other books are the "folio" in Van's room, whose covers Nanda closes without "the smallest impression of what they enclosed" (118); the book she wishes she had brought along to the garden in Mitchy's rented country house, "the charm of which, precisely, would have been in feeling everything about her too beautiful to let her read" (158); and the "large book of facts" (243) Van has on his lap when she comes to him in Mr. Longdon's garden, which she leafs through and then closes (246).

20. On this issue, see especially James's discussion of *The Turn of the Screw* in the Preface to "The Aspern Papers," where he makes it clear that refraining from spelling out the "horrors" allows (or forces) the reader to project his/her own vision of horror on the (empty) text (rather than preventing the reader from "picking up" from the text a knowledge of evil). *Art of the Novel*, especially 176.

21. Could there be another name written on the cover of this book? We will never know whether James had a particular novel in mind, let alone which one. But the novel is French, and from the name of its author, Petherton concludes it must be "something very awful" (307); Mrs. Brook characterizes it as "too hideous" and speaks of the "awful subject" (309). The author who immediately comes to mind is Zola; and would it not make sense that the name everyone reads on the title page, besides Van's, would be a version of Nanda's name, as written by Zola—*Nana*? James's review of *Nana* addresses a similar issue to that raised in the Preface to *The Awkward Age*: in both places, he discusses the different ways the French, the English, and the Americans deal with "young unmarried ladies," but whereas the Preface has to do

with "talk," his concern in the review is with the writing of novels: "The novel, moreover, among ourselves [i.e., "in England or the United States"] is almost always addressed to young unmarried ladies, or at least always assumes them to be a large part of the novelist's public. This fact, to a French storyteller, appears, of course, a damnable restriction, and M. Zola would probably decline to take *au sérieux* any work produced under such unnatural conditions. . . . But under these unnatural conditions and insufferable restrictions a variety of admirable works have been produced: Thackeray, Dickens, George Eliot, have all had an eye to the innocent classes." "*Nana*," in *Future of the Novel*, 94–95. Whereas in the discussion of "talk" in the Preface, James's sympathies seem to be with the English system, as opposed to either the French or the American one (hence with Mrs. Brook), in the discussion of novelistic production, he aligns the English and the American approach against the French, and the novelistic parallel to Mrs. Brook is not James himself but Zola. James also discusses different attitudes toward a female reading public in his title essay to *The Future of the Novel*. There he explains the difference not by appealing to some static cultural typology (the French way as opposed to the English or American way) but rather by observing that the French, "having ridden their horse much harder than we, are at a different stage of the journey." The attitude toward a female reading public is different at different points in time, and hence the English novel is bound to change too: "The novel is older and so are the young." *Future of the Novel*, 36, 40.

22. At the same time, there are some indications that what Nanda picked up "in company" is not knowledge but certain habits, whose relation to knowledge remains quite ambiguous: "There was always in Nanda's face that odd preparedness of the young person who has unlearned surprise through the habit, in company, of studiously not compromising her innocence by blinking at things said" (177). If surprise would show that she understood, and hence that she is losing her innocence, a lack of surprise can be taken either as a sign of total innocence (complete lack of understanding) or a sign of absolute knowledge (knowledge, as Mitchy suggests, is manifested by the inability to be surprised by anything; 254). What Nanda in fact knows—how innocent, how knowledgeable she is—cannot be determined; all we are told is that she "unlearned surprise." The moment of surprise is the moment of learning (of passing from innocence to knowledge), and it is this surprise or learning she has "unlearned."

23. Todorov, "Verbal Age," 358, 369.

24. On the figure of the observer and his/her implication in the action, see Porter, *Seeing and Being*.

25. Ian Gregor, "Novel of Moral Consciousness," discusses the transformation of people into objects in *The Awkward Age* in somewhat different terms.

26. Mrs. Brook's lies involve substituting one person for another. For example, when Van visits her toward the end of the novel, she dissuades him from visiting Nanda by implying that Nanda has been receiving the attentions of Mr. Cashmore (which itself may be a lie); but when Mitchy arrives shortly after, she suggests that Van has been scared off his visit to Nanda out of jealousy, not of Mr. Cashmore, but of Mitchy himself (316, 334).

27. That Mrs. Brook has no interest in "watching" and "understanding" Nanda is made clear when we realize that, for all her intelligence, she failed to notice that her daughter is in love with Van and had to be told that by Mitchy (84).

28. Mizruchi, in "Reproducing Women," emphasizes the commodification of women in the novel. This is certainly part of the issue, but, as I have tried to show, this commodification is general rather than restricted to women, and Mitchy is as much a commodity in the marketplace as Aggie or Nanda. That Mitchy is a "nouveau riche" is certainly relevant here: the idealized image that Van attempts to project (and that is the source of the "sacred terror" he inspires), the image of being outside exchange, is related to the upper classes' attempt to differentiate themselves from people in trade.

29. Mrs. Brook is not unique in this desire—hence the struggle for power drama-tized in the novel. We can say that in the same way that Mrs. Brook wants Mitchy to marry Nanda so she can keep Van to herself, Nanda wants Mitchy to marry Aggie in the hope that this will enable her to keep Van for herself, and the Duchess wants Longdon to persuade Van to marry Nanda so she can get Mitchy for Aggie and thus keep Petherton for herself.

30. Thus, as Margaret Walters points out, when Van discovers the book with his name on it in Tishy's still empty drawing room, he immediately checks his appearance in the mirror in anticipation of the others, who, as his watch tells him, will soon be there. "Keeping the Place Tidy," 211.

Bibliography

Agnew, Jean-Christophe. "The Consuming Vision of Henry James." In Richard W. Fox and T. J. Jackson Lears, eds., *The Culture of Consumption: Critical Essays on American History, 1880–1980.* New York, 1983, 67–100.

Alleton, Viviane, Claude Premond, and Thomas Pavel, eds. *Du thème en littérature.* A special issue of *Poétique,* No. 64, 1985.

Anderson, Charles R. *Person, Place, and Thing in Henry James's Novels.* Durham, N.C., 1977.

Arac, Jonathan. *Commissioned Spirits: The Shaping of Social Motion in Dickens, Carlyle, Melville and Hawthorne.* New Brunswick, N.J., 1979.

Armstrong, Paul. *The Phenomenology of Henry James.* Chapel Hill, N.C., 1983.

Auchincloss, Louis. *Reading Henry James.* Minneapolis, 1975.

Banfield, Ann. "The Moral Landscape of *Mansfield Park.*" *Nineteenth-Century Fiction,* 26 (1971), 1–24.

Barthes, Roland. "Introduction to the Structural Analysis of Narrative." In *Image—Music—Text.* Tr. Stephen Heat. New York, 1977, 79–124.

———. *S/Z.* Tr. Richard Miller. New York, 1974.

———. " 'Vouloir nous brûle'." In *Essais Critiques.* Paris, 1964, 90–93.

Bernard, Claude E. "A propos de *La Peau de chagrin* d'Honoré de Balzac: Comment le sens vient au texte." *Nineteenth-Century French Studies,* 10 (1982), 244–67.

Bersani, Leo. *The Culture of Redemption.* Cambridge, Mass., 1990.

Berthier, Philippe, ed. *Stendhal: L'Ecrivain, la société, le pouvoir.* Grenoble, 1984.

Bilodeau, François. "Espace et temps romanesques dans *La Peau de chagrin.*" *L'Année balzacienne,* 1961, 47–70.

Bloom, Harold, ed. *Jane Austen's 'Mansfield Park.'* New York, 1987.

Bowie, Malcolm. *Lacan.* Cambridge, Mass., 1991.

Bremond, Claude. "The Logic of Narrative Possibilities." *New Literary History,* 11 (1980), 387–411.

Bremond, Claude, and Thomas Pavel, eds. *Variations sur le thème.* A special issue of *Communications,* 47, 1988.

Brodsky, Claudia. *The Imposition of Form: Studies in Narrative Representation and Knowledge*. Princeton, N.J., 1987.

Brodsky Lacour, Claudia. "Austen's *Pride and Prejudice* and Hegel's 'Truth in Art': Concept, Reference, and History." *ELH*, 59 (1992), 597–623.

Brombert, Victor. "Natalie ou le lecteur caché de Balzac." In *Mouvements premiers: Etudes critiques offerts à Georges Poulet*. Paris, 1972, 177–90.

———. *La Prison romantique*. Paris, 1975.

Brooks, Peter. *The Melodramatic Imagination*. New Haven, Conn., 1976.

———. *Reading for the Plot: Design and Intention in Narrative*. New York, 1984.

———. "Virtue-Tripping: Notes on *Le Lys dans la vallée*." *Yale French Studies*, 50 (1974), 150–62.

Brown, James M. *Dickens: Novelist in the Market Place*. Totowa, N.J., 1982.

Brown, Julia Prewitt. *Jane Austen's Novels: Social Change and Literary Form*. Cambridge, Mass., 1979.

Bush, Douglas. *Jane Austen*. London, 1975.

Cameron, Sharon. *Thinking in Henry James*. Chicago, 1989.

Chambers, Ross. *Room for Maneuver: Reading the Oppositional in Narrative*. Chicago, 1991.

Culler, Jonathan. *Structuralist Poetics: Structuralism, Linguistics, and the Study of Literature*. Ithaca, N.Y., 1975.

Culver, Stuart. "Censorship and Intimacy: Awkwardness in *The Awkward Age*." *ELH*, 48 (1981), 368–86.

David, Deirdre. *Fictions of Resolution in Three Victorian Novels*. New York, 1981.

Dédéyan, Charles. *Stendhal chroniqueur*. Paris, 1962.

de Lauretis, Teresa. *Alice Doesn't: Feminism, Semiotics, Cinema*. Bloomington, Ind., 1984.

de Man, Paul. "Pascal's Allegory of Persuasion." In Stephen J. Greenblatt, ed., *Allegory and Representation*. Baltimore, 1981, 1–25.

Didier, Béatrice. "Stendhal chroniqueur." *Littérature*, No. 5 (Feb. 1972), 11–25.

Dubler, Walter. "*The Princess Casamassima*: Its Place in the James Canon." *Modern Fiction Studies*, 12 (1966), 44–60.

Duchet, Claude, ed. *Balzac et 'La Peau de chagrin.'* Paris, 1979.

Duckworth, Alistair M. *The Improvement of the Estate: A Study of Jane Austen's Novels*. Baltimore, 1971.

Evans, Mary. *Jane Austen and the State*. London, 1987.

Ferguson, Moira. "*Mansfield Park*: Slavery, Colonialism, and Gender." *Oxford Literary Review*, 13 (1991), 118–39.

Frank, Joseph. "Spatial Form in Modern Literature." *Sewanee Review*, 53 (1945), 221–40.

———. "Spatial Form: Thirty Years After." In Jeffrey R. Smitten and Ann Daghistany, eds., *Spatial Form in Narrative*. Ithaca, N.Y., 1981, 202–43.

Freedman, Jonathan. *Professions of Taste: Henry James, British Aestheticism, and Commodity Culture*. Stanford, Calif., 1990.

Friedman, Alan. *The Turn of the Novel*. New York, 1966.

Gallagher, Catherine. "Bioeconomics of *Our Mutual Friend*." In David Simpson, ed., *Subject to History*. Ithaca, N.Y., 1991, 47–64.

———. "The Duplicity of Doubling in *A Tale of Two Cities*." *Dickens Studies Annual*, 12 (1983), 125–45.

Garett, Peter K. *The Victorian Multiplot Novel: Studies in Dialogical Form*. New Haven, Conn., 1980.

Gargano, James W., ed. *Critical Essays on Henry James: The Late Novels*. Boston, 1967.

Genette, Gerard. *Narrative Discourse: An Essay in Method*. Tr. Jane Lewin. Ithaca, N.Y., 1980. Originally published in *Figures III*. Paris, 1972.

Ginsburg, Michal Peled. "Stendhal's Exemplary Stories." *Nineteenth-Century French Studies*, 19 (1991), 394–403.

Girard, René. *Desire, Deceit, and the Novel*. Tr. Yvonne Freccero. Baltimore, 1965.

Goux, Jean-Joseph. *Symbolic Economies: After Marx and Freud*. Tr. Jennifer Curtiss Gage. Ithaca, N.Y., 1990.

Gregor, Ian. "The Novel of Moral Consciousness: *The Awkward Age* (1899)." In *The Moral and the Story*. London, 1962, 151–84.

Greimas, A. J. *Du sens: Essais sémiotiques*. Paris, 1970.

———. *Sémantique structurale*. Paris, 1966.

Guérin, Michel. *La Politique de Stendhal*. Paris, 1982.

Haig, Stirling. *The Madame Bovary Blues: The Pursuit of Illusion in 19th-Century French Fiction*. Baton Rouge, La., 1987.

Hardy, John. *Jane Austen's Heroines: Intimacy in Human Relationships*. London, 1984.

Howe, Irving. *Politics and the Novel*. New York, 1957.

Hutter, Albert D. "Dismemberment and Articulation in *Our Mutual Friend*." *Dickens Studies Annual*, 11 (1983), 135–75.

Isle, Walter. *Experiments in Form: Henry James's Novels, 1896–1901*. Cambridge, Mass., 1968.

James, Henry. *The Art of the Novel*. Ed. Richard P. Blackmur. New York, 1962.

———. *The Future of the Novel*. Ed. Leon Edel. New York, 1956.

Jefferson, Ann. *Reading Realism in Stendhal*. New York, 1988.

Johnson, Claudia L. *Jane Austen: Women, Politics, and the Novel*. Chicago, 1988.

Kaston, Carren. *Imagination and Desire in the Novels of Henry James*. New Brunswick, N.J., 1984.

Kermode, Frank. *The Sense of an Ending*. New York, 1966.

Kofman, Sarah. "Le Double e(s)t le diable." In *Quatre romans analytiques*. Paris, 1973, 135–81.

Kristeva, Julia. "Une poétique ruinée." In Mikhail Bakhtine, *La Poétique de Dostoievski*. Paris, 1970, 5–27.

Kurrik, Maire Jaanus. *Literature and Negation*. New York, 1979.

Lacan, Jacques. *Le Séminaire, livre XI: Les Quatres Concepts fondamentaux de la psychanalyse*. Paris, 1973.

Lachet, Claude. *Thématique et technique du 'Lys dans la vallée' de Balzac*. Paris, 1978.

Lastinger, Michaël. "Narration et 'point de vue' dans deux romans de Balzac: 'La Peau de chagrin' et 'Le Lys dans la vallée.'" *L'Année balzacienne*, 9 (1988), 272–90.

Le Huenen, Roland, ed. *Le Roman de Balzac: Recherches critiques, méthodes, lectures*. Ottawa, 1980.

Lévi-Strauss, Claude. "The Structural Study of Myth." In *Structural Anthropology*. Tr. Claire Jacobson and Brooke Grundfest Schoepf. New York, 1963, 206–31.

Litz, Walton A. *Jane Austen: A Study of Her Artistic Development*. Oxford, 1965.

Lukács, Georg. *Studies in European Realism*. New York, 1964.

Mackenzie, Manfred. *Communities of Honor and Love in Henry James*. Cambridge, Mass., 1976.

Mansell, Darrel. *The Novels of Jane Austen: An Interpretation*. London, 1973.

Marshall, Donald. "True Acting and the Language of Real Feeling: *Mansfield Park*." *Yale Journal of Criticism*, 3 (1989), 87–106.

Michie, Helena. " 'Who is this in Pain?': Scarring, Disfigurement, and Female Identity in *Bleak House* and *Our Mutual Friend*." *Novel: A Forum on Fiction*, 22 (1989), 199–212.

Miller, D. A. "Balzac's Illusions Lost and Found." *Yale French Studies*, 67 (1984), 164–81.

———. "The Late Jane Austen." *Raritan*, 10 (1990), 55–70.

———. *Narrative and Its Discontents*. Princeton, N.J., 1981.

———. *The Novel and the Police*. Berkeley, Calif., 1988.

Miller, J. Hillis. *Versions of Pygmalion*. Cambridge, Mass., 1990.

———. *Victorian Subjects*. Durham, N.C., 1991.

Miller, Nancy. " 'Tristes Triangles': *Le Lys dans la vallée* and Its Intertext." In Robert L. Mitchell, ed., *Pre-text, Text, Context: Essays on 19th-Century French Literature*. Columbus, Ohio, 1980, 67–77.

Mizruchi, Susan L. "Reproducing Women in *The Awkward Age*." *Representations*, 38 (1992), 101–30.

Moretti, Franco. *Signs Taken for Wonders: Essays in the Sociology of Literary Forms*. Tr. Susan Fischer, David Forgacs, and David Miller. London, 1988.

———. *The Way of the World: The Bildungsroman in European Culture*. London, 1987.

Morgan, Susan. *In the Meantime: Character and Perception in Jane Austen's Novels*. Chicago, 1980.

Mudrick, Marvin. *Jane Austen: Irony as Defense and Discovery*. Princeton, N.J., 1952.

Niess, Robert J. "Saint-Beuve and Balzac: *Volupté* and *Le Lys dans la vallée*." *Kentucky Romance Quarterly*, 20 (1973), 113–24.

Parker, Mark. "The End of *Emma*: Drawing the Boundaries of Class in Austen." *Journal of English and Germanic Philology*, 91 (1992), 344–59.

Perrone-Moisés, Leyla. "Balzac et les fleurs de l'écritoire." *Poétique*, 43 (1980), 303–23.

Poovey, Mary. *The Proper Lady and the Woman Writer: Ideology as Style in the Works of Mary Wollstonecraft, Mary Shelley, and Jane Austen*. Chicago, 1984.

Porter, Carolyn. *Seeing and Being: The Plight of the Participant Observer in Emerson, James, Adams, and Faulkner*. Middletown, Conn., 1981.

Propp, Vladimir. *The Morphology of the Folktale*. Tr. Laurence Scott. 2d ed. Austin, Tex., 1977.

Rabine, Leslie. "Ideology and Contradiction in *La Chartreuse de Parme*." *Substance*, No. 21 (1978), 117–39.

Richter, David. *Fable's End*. Chicago, 1974.

Riffaterre, Michael. *Fictional Truth*. Baltimore, 1990.

Robert, Marthe. *Roman des origines et origines du roman*. Paris, 1972.

Rosmarin, Adena. " 'Misreading' *Emma*: The Powers and Perfidies of Interpretive History." *ELH*, 51 (1984), 315–42.

Rowe, John Carlos. *The Theoretical Dimensions of Henry James*. Madison, Wis., 1984.

Said, Edward W. "Jane Austen and Empire." In Francis Mulhern, ed., *Contemporary Marxist Literary Criticism*. London, 1992, 97–113.

Saussure, Ferdinand de. *Course in General Linguistics*. Tr. Wade Baskin. New York, 1966.

Scott, P. J. M. *Jane Austen: A Reassessment*. Totowa, N.J., 1982.

Sedgwick, Eve Kosofsky. "Homophobia, Misogyny, and Capital: The Example of *Our Mutual Friend*." In *Between Men: English Literature and Male Homosocial Desire*. New York, 1985, 161–79.

Seltzer, Mark. *Henry James and the Art of Power*. Ithaca, N.Y., 1984.

Shaffer, Julie. "Not Subordinate: Empowering Women in the Marriage-Plot: The Novels of Frances Burney, Marie Edgeworth, and Jane Austen." *Criticism*, 34 (1992), 51–74.

Shine, Muriel. *The Fictional Children of Henry James*. Chapel Hill, N.C., 1968.

Silverman, Kaja. "Too Early/Too Late: Subjectivity and the Primal Scene in Henry James." *Novel: A Forum on Fiction*, 21 (1988), 147–73.

Smitten, Jeffrey R., and Ann Daghistany, eds. *Spatial Form in Narrative*. Ithaca, N.Y., 1981.

Sollors, Werner, ed. *The Return of Thematic Criticism*. Cambridge, Mass., 1993.

Southam, B. C., ed. *Critical Essays on Jane Austen*. London, 1968.

———. *Jane Austen: The Critical Heritage*. London, 1968.

Stowe, William. *Balzac, James, and the Realistic Novel*. Princeton, N.J., 1983.

Tave, Stuart. *Some Words of Jane Austen*. Chicago, 1973.

Todorov, Tzvetan. *Littérature et signification*. Paris, 1967.

———. "The Verbal Age." *Critical Inquiry*, 4 (1977), 351–71.

Trilling, Lionel. *The Liberal Imagination*. New York, 1957.

———. "*Mansfield Park*." In Ian Watt, ed., *Jane Austen: A Collection of Critical Essays*. Englewood Cliffs, N.J., 1963.

———. *Sincerity and Authenticity*. Cambridge, Mass., 1972.

Veblen, Thorstein. *The Theory of the Leisure Class: An Economic Study of Institutions*. New York, 1945.

Verrier, Jean. "Le Récit réfléchi." *Littérature*, No. 5 (1972), 58–68.

Walters, Margaret. "Keeping the Place Tidy for the Young Female Mind: *The Awkward Age*." In John Goode, ed., *The Air of Reality: New Essays on Henry James*. London, 1972, 190–218.

Wards, J. A. *The Search for Form: Studies in the Structure of James's Fiction*. Chapel Hill, N.C., 1967.

Watt, Ian, ed. *Jane Austen: A Collection of Critical Essays*. Englewood Cliffs, N.J., 1963.

Weber, Samuel. *Unwrapping Balzac: A Reading of 'La Peau de chagrin.'* Toronto, 1979.

Welsh, Alexander, ed. *Narrative Endings*. Special issue of *Nineteenth-Century Fiction*, 33 (June 1978).

White, Hayden. "Ethnological 'Lie' and Mythical 'Truth'." *Diacritics*, 8 (Spring 1978), 2–9.

Winnett, Susan. "Coming Unstrung: Women, Men, Narrative, and Principles of Pleasure." *PMLA*, 105 (1990), 505–18.

Yeazell, Ruth Bernard. "The Boundaries of *Mansfield Park*." *Representations*, 7 (1984), 138–52.

———. *Language and Knowledge in the Late Novels of Henry James*. Chicago, 1976.

Žižek, Slavoj. *Looking Awry: An Introduction to Jacques Lacan Through Popular Culture*. Cambridge, Mass., 1993.

———. *The Sublime Object of Ideology*. London, 1989.

Index

In this index "f" after a number indicates a separate reference on the next page, and "ff" indicates separate references on the next two pages. A continuous discussion over two or more pages is indicated by a span of page numbers. *Passim* is used for a cluster of references in close but not consecutive sequence.

Library of Congress Cataloging-in-Publication Data

Ginsburg, Michal Peled
Economies of change : form and transformation in the nineteenth-
century novel / Michal Peled Ginsburg.
    p.   cm.
Includes bibliographical references and index.
ISBN 0-8047-2611-6 (cloth : alk. paper)
1. English fiction—19th century—History and criticism.
2. Literature and society—Great Britain—History—19th century.
3. Literature and society—France—History—19th century.   4. French
fiction—19th century—History and criticism.   5. Form (Philosophy)
in literature.   6. Mimesis in literature.   7. Change in literature.
8. Narration (Rhetoric).   9. Literary form.   I. Title.
PR868.S615G56   1996
823'.80923—dc20
95-39789   CIP

Original printing 1996

Last figure below indicates year of this printing:

05 04 03 02 01 00 99 98 97 96